MW01153912

FARM ANATOMY
ACTIVITIES FOR KIDS
Fun, Hands-On Learning

DAWN ALEXANDER, MS

ILLUSTRATIONS BY TARA SUNIL THOMAS

ROCKRIDGE
PRESS

Copyright © 2021 by Rockridge Press, Emeryville, California

No part of this publication may be reproduced, stored in a retrieval system, or transmitted in any form or by any means, electronic, mechanical, photocopying, recording, scanning, or otherwise, except as permitted under Sections 107 or 108 of the 1976 United States Copyright Act, without the prior written permission of the Publisher. Requests to the Publisher for permission should be addressed to the Permissions Department, Rockridge Press, 6005 Shellmound Street, Suite 175, Emeryville, CA 94608.

Limit of Liability/Disclaimer of Warranty: The Publisher and the author make no representations or warranties with respect to the accuracy or completeness of the contents of this work and specifically disclaim all warranties, including without limitation warranties of fitness for a particular purpose. No warranty may be created or extended by sales or promotional materials. The advice and strategies contained herein may not be suitable for every situation. This work is sold with the understanding that the Publisher is not engaged in rendering medical, legal, or other professional advice or services. If professional assistance is required, the services of a competent professional person should be sought. Neither the Publisher nor the author shall be liable for damages arising herefrom. The fact that an individual, organization, or website is referred to in this work as a citation and/or potential source of further information does not mean that the author or the Publisher endorses the information the individual, organization, or website may provide or recommendations they/ it may make. Further, readers should be aware that websites listed in this work may have changed or disappeared between when this work was written and when it is read.

For general information on our other products and services or to obtain technical support, please contact our Customer Care Department within the United States at (866) 744-2665, or outside the United States at (510) 253-0500.

Rockridge Press publishes its books in a variety of electronic and print formats. Some content that appears in print may not be available in electronic books, and vice versa.

TRADEMARKS: Rockridge Press and the Rockridge Press logo are trademarks or registered trademarks of Callisto Media Inc. and/or its affiliates, in the United States and other countries, and may not be used without written permission. All other trademarks are the property of their respective owners. Rockridge Press is not associated with any product or vendor mentioned in this book.

Series Designers: Jane Archer and Karmen Lizzul
Interior and Cover Designer: Karmen Lizzul
Art Producer: Sara Feinstein
Editor: Elizabeth Baird
Production Editor: Ashley Polikoff

Illustrations © 2020 Tara Sunil Thomas. All other art used under license from © The Noun Project. Author photo courtesy of Arkansas Farm Bureau

ISBN: Print 978-1-64739-982-5 | eBook 978-1-64739-983-2
R0

CONTENTS

THIS WAS MADE ON A FARM

Have you ever thought about where the foods you eat or the clothes you are wearing come from? Your first thought might be, "Yes, they come from the store." And in a way, you are correct. But that's not where all of it begins. Have you heard of the word *agriculture*? Agriculture is the industry that grows plants and raises animals to bring us farming, food, fiber, fishing, forestry, and flowers. These are called the "six Fs of agriculture." Agriculture is everywhere, and it connects us all together. It's where almost everything we eat and use in our daily lives comes from.

Farming is the first step in making every kind of food you eat. Everything in your pizza, hamburger, or cookie starts as a seed or an animal that is grown, watered, fed, protected, and cared for by people. Then you have fish, which are farmed from oceans and rivers. Flowers are grown in nurseries. Timber is chopped from trees in forests and used to make paper and wood for our homes. Animal fiber, such as the wool or hair of sheep and goats, and plant fiber, such as cotton, are raised and grown on farms and used to make clothes, blankets, and carpet. All of this makes up agriculture.

This book teaches you about the plants and animals that are typically found on a farm. You'll learn where many of your favorite things come from. For example, did you know that crayons are made with soybeans and corn is used to make toothpaste? Even footballs, basketballs, baseballs, and tennis balls start on the farm. Their leather comes from cattle, and their rubber comes from trees!

You'll also learn about the people involved in agriculture, such as farmers and ranchers, who grow the plants and raise the animals that you'll learn about in this book. Today, one farmer or rancher can feed over 160 people! This makes them important for all of us. They not only make everything we need to live but also teach us important lessons about commitment, sustainability, hard work, innovation, and more.

The interactive lessons and activities in this book will help you think more like a farmer and understand how nature, farming, food, and animals shape the way you live. Let's go over different parts of the book so we can start your adventure in farming and ranching!

HOW TO USE THIS BOOK

There are 20 lessons in this book, each about a different part of agriculture. Each lesson is paired with an activity and journal exercise that will inspire you to ask questions, test your skills, and reflect on what you've learned. The lessons are all designed to help you use the skills that farmers and ranchers use every day as they work.

LESSONS

Each lesson teaches you about important ideas and elements in agriculture. You will learn interesting facts about popular plants and animals, where they live, how they grow, and how they are cared for. The lessons guide you step-by-step toward a learning goal and prepare you to test that goal in an activity.

ACTIVITIES

Activities are fun and exciting. They will challenge you to apply what you are learning in the lessons. Some activities are like science experiments. Others are arts and crafts projects. All have easy-to-follow instructions and tips to help you if you get stuck. Each activity also has a list of materials you'll need to get started. An adult can help you get the items in the list and swap them out for other things when needed. Be sure to pay close attention when you see the "Safety First" tips! These are important notes of caution and advice for completing the activity safely.

JOURNAL ENTRIES

After each lesson and activity, you will be prompted to write about what you are learning in a journal. You can use any type of notebook or paper—even a computer or tablet—to write down your observations. The journal sections will ask questions to guide your writing. You can copy these questions into your journal and write the answers beneath each one. You can also come up with your own questions about the activity. Write down these questions and answer them in the journal, too.

THE ANATOMY OF A FARM

Farms are homes to many plants and animals. And just like your home has rooms for eating and different rooms for sleeping, farms also have different areas that serve different purposes.

Think about the different things that you need to live—water, food, and shelter. Plants and animals need the same things, and farms are designed to provide for these different needs.

A dairy farm, for example, needs a place to milk cows every day. A cattle ranch needs space for cattle to graze. And a plant nursery (yet another type of farm) needs large greenhouses. This chapter guides you through different types of farms and helps you understand what farmers and ranchers need to take care of plants and animals.

WHERE DO FARM ANIMALS LIVE?

Apiculture

An animal farm is an area of land that is used to raise animals, and there are many different types, depending on the sort of animal being raised. Let's take a look at five types of animal farms.

Apiculture: This is another word for bee-keeping. Farmers who raise bees are called beekeepers. Many bees make honey and bees-wax. They also help crop farmers pollinate plants (pollination is the way that insects help plants make seeds). Beekeepers sometimes rent their bees to crop farmers for pollination.

Aquaculture

Aquaculture: Aquaculture farms raise things like fish, shellfish, and aquatic plants for food and products. Freshwater aquaculture includes cat-fish, trout, and other organisms found in bodies of water that do not have salt in them. Marine aquaculture farms oysters, mussels, clams, shrimp, seaweed, and other saltwater life from the ocean.

Dairy

Dairy: These farms raise animals that produce milk, which can be made into cheese, yogurt, butter, and other dairy products. Most dairy farms have cows, but some dairy farms raise sheep and goats for milk. All female dairy animals lactate, which means they produce milk, after giving birth.

Livestock: Livestock are farm animals that are raised for food or fiber. These include sheep, goats, rabbits, pigs, cattle, bison, llamas, and alpacas. They are usually kept in pens or large pastures, which are areas closed off by a fence. These animals are fed by farmers or ranchers.

Poultry: These farms raise chickens, turkeys, ducks, geese, and other birds (such as emus and ostriches) for meat, eggs, and feathers. Chickens are the most popular. Chickens raised for their eggs are called layers, and chickens raised for their meat are called broilers.

Now that you have learned about different types of farms, let's look at what these farms need in order to take care of animals. Animals, like humans, need comfortable places to live. These places on a farm are called shelters. Some animals, like cows, do well outside year-round in the right climate. They use trees for shade and protection from cold snow and rain. Other farm animals need to live in warm and dry places, like barns and sheds.

Barns: Barns are shelters that can be big like a house. In addition to protecting animals from the rain, wind, and cold, some barns also have space to store animal food, like hay.

Coops: Chickens live in special shelters called coops. These protect chickens from raccoons, skunks, owls, and other predators, and are comfortable homes in which they lay eggs and roost, or sleep.

Livestock

Poultry

Sheds: Other farms have shelters called sheds, which are usually smaller than a barn. These are usually open on all sides and have a roof to keep hay dry from rain and snow. Sheds are also used like garages to protect farm machines. Small farm animals such as pigs, sheep, and calves can use sheds as their home.

Animals, just like us, also need places to eat. These are called *feeding and grazing areas*. Cattle, sheep, and goats get their food from grass fields called pastures. In the winter, farmers and ranchers feed them hay. Pigs and chickens use smaller feeders to eat grain from. Farm animals also need special vitamins and minerals to help them grow stronger. These are kept in special containers that keep out the rain. Farmers also keep grains in tall, round metal towers called silos.

Fun Fact

Many farms, like the one in *The Wizard of Oz*, have windmills. Windmills have sails or vanes that are moved by the wind in circles. This movement produces energy. Windmills can use the energy from the wind to pump water for animals.

BUILD A BIRDHOUSE

TIME:
1 HOUR

CATEGORY:
CREATIVE, DESIGN AND BUILD

MATERIALS:
HALF-GALLON MILK CARTON, WASHED AND DRIED COMPLETELY

PEN OR PENCIL

BOX CUTTER OR SCISSORS

NEWSPAPER (OPTIONAL)

COLORED MARKERS OR ACRYLIC CRAFT PAINTS

NAIL

TWINE OR YARN

TIPS

➡ When drawing the door, make sure you leave some space around the edges. This will keep the house stable.

➡ If you want to turn your birdhouse into a birdfeeder, place some birdseed in the bottom of the carton.

You just learned that a barn can be a house where animals sleep and eat and also a place where farmers keep animal food, tools, and supplies. In this activity, you will build a birdhouse to provide a shelter to nearby birds with materials you can find in your home. A milk carton, for example, is already a great shape for a house—the top of the carton is like a pitched roof! Use your creativity to make your birdhouse unique.

Safety First: *Ask an adult to use a box cutter or scissors to cut the milk carton for you.*

INSTRUCTIONS

1. On one of the tall sides of the milk carton, use the pen to draw a rectangle or circle near the middle. This is the door the birds will use to get inside the house. Ask an adult to use the box cutter to cut out your shape.

2. If desired, lay down newspapers on a work surface to protect against spills. Use the colored markers or paints to decorate the birdhouse. If you're using paint, allow the paint to dry.

3. Use the nail to poke a hole on each side of the top of the milk carton.

4. Thread the twine through the two holes and make a knot at the top. This is how you will hang your birdhouse. Hang your birdhouse outside and watch the birds come and enjoy their new structure.

CONCLUSION:
Barns are one of the many structures on a farm. They are one of the places where animals live and can be protected from severe weather. In this activity, you built a shelter for birds, which protects them from the weather.

FARM JOURNAL ENTRY

Birdhouses are places for birds to build nests and have their young. They are also places for birds to keep dry and safe from severe weather. Use these questions to write about your birdhouse in your journal.

1. *What types of birds might live in your birdhouse?*

2. *Compare your birdhouse to your home. How are they similar? How are they different?*

3. *What are some ways you could improve the birdhouse to make it even more comfortable for the birds?*

WHERE DO CROPS GROW?

A crop is a plant or fruit that is grown to make food, clothes, and other products. Most crops are grown outside on large pieces of land, which are measured in units called **acres**. One acre is roughly the size of a football field. Like people, who live in different types of houses and in different places, crops grow in different environments.

Think about the things that grow around where you live. What is the weather like where you live? Does it get really hot in the summer? Does it snow in the winter? Farmers decide what crops to grow based on where they live, the type of soil, and the climate.

Let's look at a few vegetables and fruits that you probably like to eat. This table shows different types of crops, where they are grown in the United States, and what the climate is like there. What kind of crops grow best where you live?

Popular Crops and Where They Grow

CROP	TOP GROWING AREAS	CLIMATE AND SOIL
Bananas	Florida and Hawaii (but most are imported from Ecuador and Guatemala)	Tropical; 76°F to 86°F; rich, well-drained soil (but will grow in most soil types)
Corn	Heartland states, such as Illinois, Indiana, Iowa, Minnesota, and Nebraska	Warm, sunny weather; moderate rains; 130 frost-free days; rich, well-drained, sandy loam
Oranges	Arizona, California, Florida, and Texas	55°F to 100°F; light soil with good drainage
Potatoes	Colorado, Idaho, North Dakota, Washington, and Wisconsin	Cool to mild, not hot, weather; 70 to 90 cool days; soil that is well-drained and high in organic matter
Strawberries	California, Florida, North Carolina, Pennsylvania, and Wisconsin	Plenty of sunlight; 60°F to 80°F; soil rich in organic matter

Crops produce the most in regions where the growing conditions best suit their needs. As you can see in the table, banana trees grow well in tropical places, where the weather is warm and wet. Root plants like potatoes grow best in cool weather climates. If the climate is too hot, potatoes do not grow as well. The United States produces the most corn in the entire world, but corn is grown on every continent except Antarctica! However, not every country can produce every type of crop. Countries depend on being able to buy food they cannot grow from countries where it thrives. This is global trade.

Farmers can also change the natural growing conditions of the area around them. They might irrigate, or add water artificially, to soil when there is not enough rain. They add fertilizer to soil that does not have enough nutrients to produce healthy crops. Farmers also grow crops in greenhouses. The greenhouse traps the sun's heat to make growing conditions inside warmer than outside.

Fun Fact

Have you ever wondered why you can eat fresh blueberries with your yogurt in December? Your country likely buys blueberries from countries with warm Decembers, like those in South and Central America, so you can eat them in winter.

PLANTING CROPS WITHOUT SOIL

TIME:
30 TO 45 MINUTES ON DAY 1,
THEN 10 TO 15 MINUTES FOR
THE NEXT 8 TO 9 DAYS

CATEGORY:
EXPERIMENT,
OBSERVATION, PLANTS

MATERIALS:
WHEAT GRAINS

WATER

GLASS JAR OR RIMMED PLATE,
SUCH AS A PIE PLATE

SCISSORS

TIPS

➡ You can get wheat grain at garden centers or most health food stores. The amount you need depends on how big your glass jar or plate is. You need enough to cover the bottom of your container.

➡ Try planting wheatgrass seeds in soil and observe how they grow.

Most crops need sun, air, water, and soil in order for the plant to grow, but farmers and scientists have found new ways to grow plants without soil. One way is called hydroponics, which is growing plants so that they get food from water—without soil. Let's plant wheatgrass seeds and see what happens!

Safety First: *To harvest the wheatgrass, you will need a pair of scissors. Be careful when cutting and let an adult know you are using scissors.*

INSTRUCTIONS

1. Soak the wheat grains overnight in fresh, cold water.

2. The next day, pour off the water. Rinse the soaked grains well with water and drain them again.

3. Spread the grains out evenly in the glass jar or plate.

4. Continue to rinse and drain the grains well once or twice a day for several days. After about four to five days, your wheatgrass will begin to grow. The root hairs will look feathery; they are not mold. As long as you continue to rinse the grains, there should be no problem with mold.

5. After about six days of rinsing and draining, the leafy parts of the wheatgrass will appear.

6. After about eight days of rising and draining, your wheatgrass can be harvested! Just use scissors to cut close to the seeds. The wheatgrass will continue to grow like grass in someone's yard, so you can continue to harvest as you wish!

CONCLUSION:

In the lesson you learned about where some crops grow and what farmers need to think about when planting their crops. Plants can grow in different environments, and in the activity, you planted a crop that can grow in water without soil. However, soil gives crops nutrients to help them grow, so wheatgrass grown in water will have fewer nutrients than wheatgrass grown in soil.

FARM JOURNAL ENTRY

Planting seeds is a fun way to learn about plant growth. Use these questions to write about your experience with planting wheatgrass seeds in your journal.

1. *Describe the steps the plant takes to get food from the water. How does that compare with plants that are grown in soil?*

2. *What would you do differently if you were to do this activity again?*

3. *Draw a picture of your wheatgrass plant each day to record the changes in the plant.*

FARMING TOOLS AND MACHINES

Tools can improve a farmer's *efficiency*, or their ability to work without wasting time, energy, or money. When you have to write a paper using a pencil rather than a computer, the pencil requires more time and energy than the computer for you to complete your task. The principle of time-saving farm technologies is the same.

Agriculture has existed for a long time, as far back as ancient Egypt. Archeologists have found tools that the ancient Egyptians and other people throughout history have used to farm. Over time, people have invented ways to do the work easier, faster, and better. By observing the tools, you can see how farming technology has evolved throughout the years.

For example, ancient Egyptians used a type of plow that helped them plant seeds in the soil. It was pushed by hand and opened the earth. Later, when people were trying to farm in tougher soils, a different type of wooden plow was invented that could churn up the soil and loosen it enough for planting. Later still, the plow was redesigned so that animals, instead of people, could pull the plow; then farmers learned how to improve the plow's function by making it with different materials, and so on.

The History of THE PLOW

Ancient Egyptian plow

A plow pulled by a horse

Modern-day tractor

When farmers had to plow a field by hand, it took about 96 hours, or four days, for the farmer to plow one acre, which is about the size of a football field. When the wooden plow was redesigned to be pulled using oxen or horses, that cut the farmer's time down to just 24 hours, or one day, for that acre. In 1837, a man named John Deere improved the plow by making it with steel, so it could handle the black prairie soil of the American Midwest. Now a farmer could go out and plow that acre in five to eight hours! Why was it so much faster? In the past, sticky soil would cling to the cast-iron plow blade, so the farmer would have to stop and clean it every few feet. Steel, on the other hand, is a slick metal, and the soil would not stick to the blades.

Today, plows with multiple moldboards—the main part that turns over the soil to loosen it—can plow several rows at once, which means a farmer can plow 50 acres (69 football fields) in one day. The plows are also pulled by tractors, which is another technology that has developed over the years. Recall that, before tractors were invented in the 1890s, oxen and horses were used to help the farmer in the field. It's tough work, and expending all that energy meant the farmers and animals had to rest. The work took so long that it limited how much food farmers could grow. Most people could only grow enough food to feed their families, and growing and harvesting that food took up all of their time.

Fun Fact

A tractor that a farmer uses today can help grow enough food to feed not just the farmer's own family but also 160 other people every year.

By the early 1900s, gas-powered tractors were becoming more popular among farmers. These tractors were mechanical and didn't need to rest like the farmers and horses did, and the tractors were faster all around. This helped farmers grow more food more efficiently. The tractor has continued to evolve to this day. For example, modern tractors are built to help reduce the impact of machinery in the fields so they are better for the environment, they cover more ground with each trip up and down the field, and they are equipped with computer technology to help the farmer apply just the right amount of seed and chemicals. It is predicted that in the future, there will be driverless tractors!

DESIGN AND BUILD A TRACTOR

TIME:
1 HOUR

CATEGORY:
CREATIVE, DESIGN AND BUILD

MATERIALS:
HALF-GALLON MILK CARTON, WASHED AND DRIED WELL

HALF-PINT MILK CARTON, WASHED AND DRIED WELL

TAPE OR GLUE

ACRYLIC PAINT OR MARKERS

PLASTIC LIDS OR BOTTLE CAPS (4)

EMPTY PAPER TOWEL OR TOILET PAPER ROLL

ALUMINUM FOIL

SCISSORS

TIP

➡ Draw your design in your journal before you start building. To test the functionality of your tractor, design something for it to pull and a hitch to pull it with. What will the hitch be made of?

In this activity, you will use your innovation skills to design and build a tractor, just like early farmers designed and built tools to help them farm. Use materials you find around your house, such as those listed here, to build your model. However, these are just suggestions; use your creativity to find what works. Try to design your tractor so that it is able to pull things behind it, just like tractors on a farm. It may take more than one try to get it right!

Safety First: *You may want to use hot glue to attach the milk cartons. An adult will need to help you with this part.*

INSTRUCTIONS

1. Look at pictures of tractors and use your imagination and engineering skills to decide what materials you want to use for your tractor. Tractors have a body, a cab where the farmer sits, wheels, an air stack, and

headlights so they can be used at night. What could you use to make each of these elements?

2. If desired, use the half-gallon milk carton as the body of the tractor and the half-pint carton as the cab, or use your own materials. Next, you'll need to attach the cab to the body of the tractor. Think about whether glue, tape, or another method would work best, and then try it out.

3. After the cab has been attached to the body, color your tractor. You may use paint, markers, or a different method. Be sure to let your decorations dry before moving on to the next step.

4. If desired, use plastic lids and bottle caps for the wheels of your tractor, or use your own materials. Keep in mind that most tractors have smaller tires in the front and bigger tires in the back. Next, you'll need to attach the wheels to the body of the tractor. If you want the tractor to be able to move, how will you attach the wheels so that they can spin?

5. Once the wheels are attached, create the air stack. Trim a paper towel roll to size, or use your own materials. Paint the air stack and let it dry, then figure out the best method to attach it.

6. If desired, the aluminum foil can be cut into circles and attached to the front of the tractor for headlights.

FARM JOURNAL ENTRY

Designing and creating new things can lead to better ways to do something. Write about your experience of making a tractor.

1. *Was there a problem with your initial design that had to be changed? If so, how did you improve on your design?*

2. *Draw a picture of your tractor. Then draw a picture of a tractor in the future.*

CONCLUSION:

You just designed and built a tractor that could be used to pull equipment behind it. You had to use what you had available to make your tractor, just like early farmers had to work with what they had to create tools. Remember, it took hundreds of years for farm tools to develop into what we use today. Throughout history, different people improved the tools. Likewise, it may have taken you more than one try to make the tractor functional. You may have gone through a period of trial and error to figure out what worked and how you could improve your tractor.

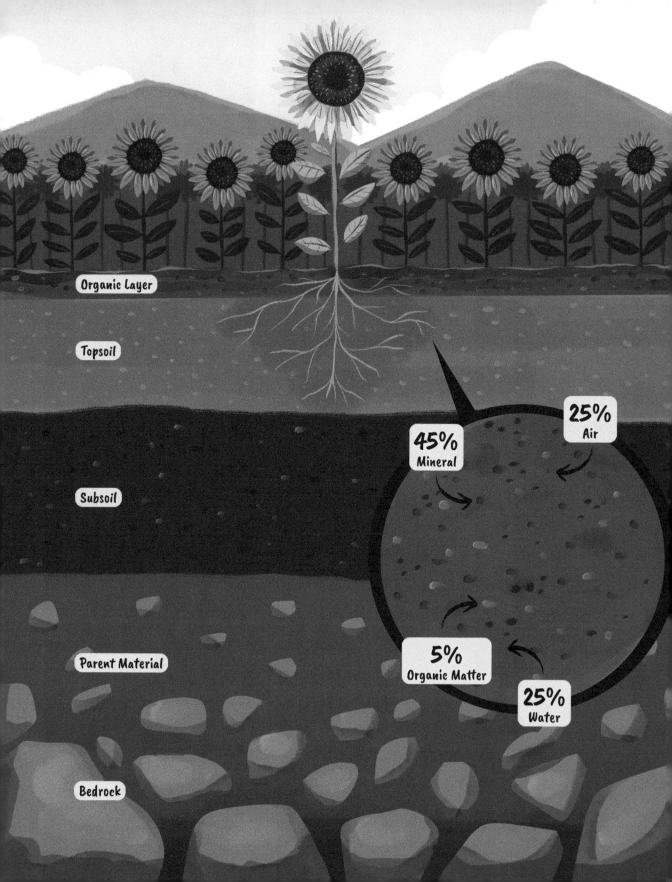

BENEATH THE GROUND

oil is the top layer of Earth. You can kind of think of it as the "skin of the planet," and it's where plants grow. Have you ever wondered why soil helps plants grow? It all comes down to what it's made of.

In this chapter, you'll learn what soil is and why it helps plants grow. You'll also learn about different types of soil, and that different crops are suited to certain soils. Soil also has a life cycle, just like humans, and we'll learn about that, too.

Soil covers much of Earth's land surface and is an important natural resource because plants are rooted in it and get their food, or nutrients, from it. Animals, by comparison, get their nutrients from plants or from other animals that eat plants. In other words, all the energy that plants and animals need to live starts in the soil.

DIFFERENT TYPES OF SOIL

You've just learned that soil is made up of many different things. When all of these elements work together, they provide nutrients for plants, which then provide food for us and other animals. Let's take a closer look at the different materials that make up soil.

Air: Pockets of air are trapped within soil. These pockets provide a place to store water and also provide oxygen to animals that dwell in the soil, such as earthworms, moles, and mites.

Rocks: Rock particles are inorganic material. The word inorganic means that something is not made from anything that was once alive. Rock particles make up approximately half of soil. The particles come from larger rocks, called parent rocks. Just like genes from your parents give you certain characteristics, parent rocks determine what the soil will look like and feel like, as well as what kind of plant life it will support. This is because different rocks contain different minerals, and different plants need different minerals to live.

Soil nutrients: Organic matter provides nutrients in soil. The word organic refers to things or substances that are or once were alive. Organic matter derives from plants and animals. When plants and animals die, they decay, or break down, and their nutrients become available to other organisms living in the soil. For example, leaves fall from trees and break down on the ground over time. As the leaves break down, nutrients that were once stored in them are transferred to the soil. Now the plants and animals that live in the soil take in those nutrients.

Water: Water is needed for soil to sustain plant life. When it rains or when plants are watered by irrigation, water leaches, or seeps, underground. It moves through air pockets in the soil, and plants absorb the water through their roots.

There are many kinds of soil. Different soils form depending on the climate, vegetation, geology, and landscape of an area. Different types of soil help some plants grow better than others. This table provides an overview of a few different types of soil and the plants that grow well in them.

Common Types of Soil

TYPE OF SOIL	DESCRIPTION	CROPS THAT GROW WELL IN IT
Clay	Smallest of the three soil particles; can be seen only with a high-powered microscope; sticky when wet and hard like a brick when dry	Beans, broccoli, cabbages, cauliflower, kale, potatoes, and radishes
Loam	A balanced mixture of sand, silt, and clay; usually made up of 40 percent sand, 40 percent silt, and 20 percent clay; if you increase the sand, it becomes "sandy loam"	Cotton, cucumbers, lettuce, onions, pulse crops (edible seeds from legumes, such as chickpeas, edible beans, lentils, and peas), sugarcane, tomatoes, and wheat
Sand	Biggest soil particle; you can see the individual grains of sand with your eye; feels gritty, weighs the most, and water and air can move easily through it	Vegetable and root crops such as carrots, corn, lettuce, parsnips, potatoes, squash, strawberries, and zucchini
Silt	Medium soil particle, in between sand and clay; individual grains are too small to see with your eye; can feel like flour and is very smooth when you rub it in your hands	Berry bushes, grasses, most flowering plants, and most vegetables and fruit trees

WHICH SOIL DO PLANTS PREFER?

TIME:
30 MINUTES THE FIRST DAY, A FEW MINUTES EACH DAY AFTER THAT FOR OBSERVATION

CATEGORY:
EXPERIMENT, OBSERVATION, PLANTS

MATERIALS:
DIFFERENT TYPES OF SOIL, SUCH AS SAND, POTTING SOIL, AND LOCAL SOIL (3)

CLEAR PLASTIC CUPS (3)

MARKER

RADISH SEEDS

WATER

JOURNAL

TIP

➡ Be sure to keep careful records of what happened to each cup. Date and label each observation in your journal.

Soil types influence the kinds of plants that will grow. This activity encourages you to experiment with several types of soil to see which type will have the fastest-growing radishes. After you gather your materials, predict which soil will produce radishes the quickest.

INSTRUCTIONS

1. First, find three different kinds of soil. Try collecting samples from local areas around your home, like a park or your backyard.

2. Place about 1 cup of each type of soil in three separate cups. Using the marker, carefully label each cup with the type of soil inside.

3. Place three or four radish seeds in the soil of each cup. Be sure to place the seeds in the middle of the cup about ¼ inch deep. Cover the seeds with soil.

4. Place a little bit of water in the cup. If you have a little water mister, that will work great!

5. Record in your journal the date you planted the seeds, the type of soil in each of the cups, and what you observe. Scientists also draw pictures and label them to help with their experiments, so you can, too.

6. Every day, observe your cups and make notes in your journal. Which type of soil sprouted the radish seed the fastest? Add a little water when the soil is dry.

7. You can continue to observe and make notes for as long as you want.

FARM JOURNAL ENTRY

Planting and growing seeds in different types of soil can be a fun way to learn about soil. Respond in your journal to the following questions:

1. *Describe the steps in planting the radish seeds.*

2. *What happened to the radish seeds that grew in the sand?*

3. *What happened to the radish seeds that grew in the potting soil?*

4. *What happened to the radish seeds that grew in soil you used from someplace close to your home?*

5. *What do you think is different about each type of soil you used?*

CONCLUSION:

Planting seeds in different types of soil allows you to see which type of soil grows the best radishes. Not all types of soil grow all types of food. It is a farmer's job to know what type of soil they have and what types of food will grow best in that soil. For example, corn grows best in loamy soil, which is a combination of clay, silt, and sand. Soybeans grow best in loose, well-drained soil.

MINERALS AND NUTRIENTS

Your parents probably tell you to eat your fruits and vegetables. That's because fruits and vegetables have lots of nutrients that help our bodies grow strong and give us lots of energy. Those fruits and vegetables get their nutrients from our soil.

The three main nutrients in our soil are nitrogen, phosphorus, and potassium. Scientists use the chemical symbols N, P, and K to identify each of them, respectively. These nutrients are primary macronutrients because plants eat large (macro) amounts of them. Secondary macronutrients are calcium, magnesium, and sulfur. Plants also need micronutrients, which means they only eat small (micro) amounts to help them grow. These include boron, carbon, chlorine, copper, hydrogen, iron, manganese, molybdenum, nickel, oxygen, and zinc.

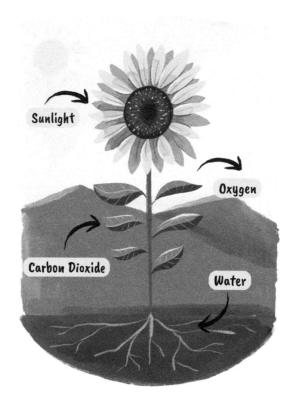

Let's take a closer look at the six primary and secondary macronutrients.

Calcium: It makes your bones and teeth strong and helps plants build new cells. You can get calcium from milk. When a dairy cow eats grass and other grains, she turns that energy from plants into milk, which provides calcium for your body.

Magnesium: This nutrient helps you fight disease and keeps your nerves and muscles working. Plants need it to make food with photosynthesis.

Nitrogen: You need this nutrient to grow strong, healthy muscles. Plants use it to make proteins, fruits, seeds, and chlorophyll for photosynthesis.

Phosphorus: This nutrient makes your bones and teeth strong, and it gives plants energy to grow strong roots and flowers.

Potassium: This nutrient helps your nerves and muscles work, and it helps plants grow strong stems and fight disease.

Sulfur: Sulfur helps plants make proteins and chlorophyll for photosynthesis. Sulfur also helps you have healthy skin, muscles, and bones.

Photosynthesis is the process that plants use to make food. First, they get energy from the sun. "Photo" means "light," and "synthesis" means "put together." Plants have a pigment inside their leaves called chlorophyll. Chlorophyll gives plants their green color and helps them absorb energy from the sun to make food. Plants also get water and nutrients from the soil. They absorb water and nutrients through their roots and move them up the stem to the leaves, where photosynthesis takes place. This food gives plants energy to grow, and when animals or people eat plants, this stored energy is what helps our bodies work.

Farmers test their soil to make sure that it has the proper amount of nutrients so their crops will grow and be productive. If needed, they add nutrients to the soil in the form of fertilizer to provide the exact amount of nutrients needed for that soil and crop.

Fun Fact

Plants need a total of 17 nutrients to help them grow and develop.

SOIL NUTRIENT TESTING EXPERIMENT

Water —
Clay —
Silt —
Sand —

Soil testing helps farmers know which type of soil they have and whether their soil has the best nutrients to grow crops. If the soil is missing nutrients, farmers adjust it by adding fertilizer. This activity will show you how to test a sample of soil for nitrogen, phosphorus, and potassium levels.

Safety First: *This activity has chemicals in the testing kit that are nontoxic, but you will still need to remember to wash your hands after using them.*

TIME:
1 HOUR, PLUS 2 HOURS TO 1 DAY
OF DOWNTIME

CATEGORY:
EXPERIMENT

MATERIALS:
SOIL (½ CUP)

WATER (2½ CUPS)

1-QUART MASON JAR, OR OTHER
CLEAR LIDDED CONTAINER

SOIL TESTING KIT

INSTRUCTIONS

1. Gather soil from your yard or someplace nearby. Be sure to get your sample from 4 to 6 inches below the surface of the ground.

2. Place the soil and water in the mason jar. Seal the jar and shake it for about 1 minute. This creates a solution of soil and water.

3. Let the soil solution sit for at least 2 hours or overnight. You want the soil to settle to the bottom of the jar with just a small portion of it floating in the water. If the solution is too dark or cloudy, the test won't be as accurate.

4. Test your soil for nitrogen, phosphorus, and potassium with the testing kit according to its directions. Usually, you take three samples of your soil solution (one for each nutrient) with a pipette or an eye dropper, placing one sample in each of three testing cups from the kit. When gathering your sample, be careful not to shake up the jar, and be sure to take a sample from the top where the water is, not near the bottom, which is full of soil. Most kits have colored capsules of testing ingredients, each one a different color for the different nutrients. Carefully open the capsule and pour the powder into the corresponding testing cup. Give each cup a good shake and then let them settle for 5 to 10 minutes.

5. Use the scale from the kit to pick which colors match your soil samples. This tells you if there is none, some, or a lot of the nutrient in your sample.

TIPS

➡ Soil testing kits can be purchased from most garden centers, or online, and cost around $10. Make sure you get a kit that tests for nitrogen (N), phosphorus (P), and potassium (K).

FARM JOURNAL ENTRY

Finding out which nutrients are in your soil and the amount of each nutrient is important so your plants can stay healthy. Use your journal to respond to the following questions:

1. *Which nutrient showed up the most in your soil sample?*

2. *What is soil made of?*

3. *Why is soil important to farmers?*

CONCLUSION:

In this activity, you learned to measure how many nutrients are in soil, which you can't see with your naked eye. However, there are some minerals you can see. When you add water to the soil, shake the jar, and then let the soil settle, you can see the different types of minerals in it. This happens because the heaviest particles (sand) settle first on the bottom of the jar. The next layer is silt because it's made up of medium-size particles. And the last layer to settle on the top is clay, which has the lightest particles of all.

TIPS

➡ Try testing soil from different places and comparing the results. For example, you may get samples from a field near your house, from your garden, or from a nearby wooded area.

THE LIFE CYCLE OF SOIL

Soil starts as rock

Elements cause rock to break down

Lichen forms on rock

Rock breaks down into soil

Just like you and me, plants and other animals go through a life cycle, a series of changes that occur from the beginning of life to the end. Some life cycles are short. The mayfly, for example, only lives for one day. Other life cycles are longer. Our pet dogs and cats live for 13 to 16 years on average, and a person's average life span is 68 to 73 years. Soil has a life cycle, too, and it's much longer than ours. It can take 500 years for one inch of soil to form!

The study of soil is called pedology. The more scientists know about our soil, the better they can help farmers anticipate problems, manage resources, and create solutions for some of their farming practices. Today, farmers strive to give soil what it needs to stay healthy, which is important because it takes so long to develop. Soil holds the key to our future.

Let's look at the life cycle of soil. Soil begins as rock. Wind and water cause rock to break down over time, and changes in temperature cause rock to expand (make larger) and contract (make smaller), which creates cracks in the rock. Next, plants enter the scene by attaching on bare rock and creeping into the cracks. Lichen is often the first plant that forms on rock. As a lichen's roots expand and grow, it causes the rock to break down. This mixing of organic plants with inorganic rock is the birth of new soil.

The more plant life grows on the rock, the more the plant roots work at breaking it down.

The plants eventually die and become organic matter full of nutrients, which are needed to make the soil healthy. Now, the soil has nutrients, which are broken down further by animals such as earthworms, making the nutrients accessible to new plant life and animals in the soil.

The soil grows deeper as the cycle keeps going. Remember, this process takes many, many years. As soil ages, it becomes more balanced. Nutrients that are taken out by animals and plant life are returned to the soil as other plants and animals die.

Sometimes soil's life cycle can come to a quick end. Soil that has taken hundreds of years to form can be washed away suddenly by floods, events like the Dust Bowl, or volcanic eruptions that cover the soil in lava and ash. Sometimes, soil is lost because people don't protect it from erosion or because they build houses and other buildings on top of it. Farmers and ranchers work hard to maintain healthy soil by using appropriate soil and water conservation practices. They work with scientists to find ways to conserve soil so that it's protected.

Fun Fact

If you like history, research the Dust Bowl of the 1930s. During this period, drought and poor farming practices created destructive dust storms across the Great Plains that damaged agriculture. Farmers did not know then what they know now about taking care of soil. The Dust Bowl led to widespread hunger and poverty.

MOVERS AND SHAKERS UNDERGROUND

TIME:
1 HOUR, THEN 10 MINUTES
FOR OBSERVATION EACH DAY
FOR 2 WEEKS

CATEGORY:
DESIGN AND BUILD, OBSERVATION

MATERIALS:
2-LITER PLASTIC BOTTLE

SCISSORS

TAPE

16-OUNCE PLASTIC WATER
BOTTLE WITH LID, FILLED WITH
ROOM-TEMPERATURE WATER

SAND (1 CUP)

SOIL (2 CUPS)

SPRAY BOTTLE FILLED
WITH WATER

BROWN PAPER BAG, SUCH AS A
GROCERY BAG

EARTHWORMS (2) (YOU CAN
PURCHASE EARTHWORMS FROM
A BAIT SHOP, A GARDEN STORE,
OR ONLINE)

WORM FOOD, SUCH AS
RAW VEGETABLE SCRAPS,
APPLES, MELON RINDS, LAWN
CLIPPINGS, COFFEE GROUNDS,
AND LEAVES THAT ARE CUT UP
INTO SMALL PIECES

PIECE OF CHEESECLOTH

RUBBER BAND

Earthworms live underground in holes or tunnels called burrows. These burrows help get air and water into the soil. Farmers see earthworms as small, living plows that are important for their crops. In this activity, you'll make a habitat, or home, for worms, then observe how they behave to learn more about the ways they break down things and help plants grow.

Safety First: *You will need an adult to carefully cut the top off the 2-liter plastic bottle.*

INSTRUCTIONS

1. Ask an adult to cut the top off the 2-liter plastic bottle with the scissors. Use tape to cover the sharp edge. Put the 16-ounce plastic bottle inside the 2-liter bottle, in its center. (Don't skip this step! It encourages the worms to tunnel in the outer part of the large bottle so you can see them).

2. Place some of the sand in the bottom of the 2-liter bottle, around the small bottle. Place a little of the soil on top of the sand, then add some more sand, then more soil. Continue this process until the bottle is about two-thirds full. Do not pack the soil down, which would make it difficult for the worms to make tunnels. Keep the soil loose.

3. Use the spray bottle to squirt in enough water to make the layers of soil damp but not soggy.

4. Earthworms like a dark environment. Cut a strip of the paper bag the size of the bottle, then tape it around the bottle to keep the light out.

5. Gently place your earthworms on top of the soil.

6. Place some worm food (see Materials) on top of the soil and earthworms. Cover the habitat with the piece of cheesecloth, then secure it with a rubber band.

7. Place the habitat in a cool, dark place before removing the paper. Now you can observe earthworm behavior. Make sure you replenish the habitat with more worm food as it disappears, and don't forget to dampen the soil every few days. Observe the worms for two weeks, then place them in a garden or another suitable area so they can help improve the soil!

FARM JOURNAL ENTRY

Observe what is happening in your habitat, and record it in your journal.

1. *What did the earthworms eat? Which foods did not get eaten?*

2. *Can you see the worms? If so, describe where they are located in the habitat.*

3. *What evidence can you find of worm activity?*

CONCLUSION:

Just like all plants and animals have a life cycle, our soil does, too. Earthworms help in that cycle by breaking down organic matter, like leaves and grasses, into nutrients that plants can use. Their droppings, or "castings," fertilize the soil. You can see them in the soil—they look like churned-up bits of soil. This activity helps you see the role earthworms have in soil's life cycle.

TIPS

➡ Do not feed citrus, cooked foods, dairy, garlic, onions, meat, oil/grease, or tomatoes to your worms. Food that is too salty or acidic can kill worms.

Prep the soil

1

Plant the seeds

2

Chile

Water the seeds

3

Sun and water help plants grow

5

Seeds sprout

4

ABOVE THE GROUND

Farmers have learned different techniques to help prepare the land for growing crops. These steps and methods have changed over time as the technology and science of agriculture has improved.

Think about the ways weather affects you every day. What happens when you want to play outside but rain pours down? Most of the time, you have to stay indoors or make other plans. Just as weather can impact your plans, weather can impact farmers' plans, too. That's why farmers have to always think about the weather and how nature affects everything that grows and lives on the farm.

Let's take a look at how crops grow and how weather affects everything we eat.

HOW CROPS GROW

Think about how you have changed since you were a baby. For example, what are some changes you have gone through since you started school? Plants go through different changes and stages, too. Let's take a look at the chile (sometimes called chile pepper) as an example to explain how crops grow.

Chiles start out as seeds planted in soil. Farmers generally plant chile plants between March 1 and April 1. Before farmers plant, they must prepare the soil by plowing (which loosens and turns the soil), disking (breaking up the soil clods), and smoothing before making raised beds for the plants. Chiles grow best in sandy loam soil that is well-drained. Farmers need to irrigate the soil to keep it moist for when seeds are planted. This provides the seeds with the best chance for good growth.

After the seeds are planted, they sprout, or germinate, in 10 to 12 days, depending on the type of chile. During this time, the seeds need a lot of sunlight and water. The plants continue to grow and eventually produce flowers, the flowers are pollinated by insects, and then chiles grow from the pollinated flowers, just like an apple grows from an apple blossom. As they mature, chiles grow edible flesh on the outside and seeds inside, just like other fruits. Chiles start out as green fruits that turn red as they ripen.

Most farmers pick their fields twice, once for green chiles and then again for red chiles. The first green chiles are ready for harvest about 120 days, or four months, after planting.

This usually happens in early August. The red chiles take about 165 days, or five to six months, to grow. These are usually harvested in mid-October.

Most crops planted in the spring, like chiles, mature and are harvested during the fall months. However, annual crops like winter wheat are planted early in the fall and begin growing before going dormant during the winter months. During the winter, the soil stores water from precipitation. Once temperatures start warming up, the water is available to plants as they resume growing.

Once chiles are picked, their life cycle continues as they are used in various foods and products. For example, chiles are used to make natural food colorings. They also contain capsaicin, the stuff in chiles that makes your mouth feel hot, which is a key ingredient in creams and patches that are used for pain relief. Jalapeños are a type of chile that you might eat in various dishes. Dried spices, such as cayenne and paprika, are also made from chiles.

Fun Fact

Even though people call chiles vegetables, they are technically classified as fruits because they contain seeds and originate from the flowering part of the plant.

PLANTING AN EGGSHELL HERB GARDEN

By using eggshells to start your plants, you are using something that is biodegradable, meaning that it will break down naturally over time, and you won't have to remove the shells when you plant the seedlings outside. The eggshells will slowly degrade, putting calcium from the shell into the soil. The shells also serve as pest control, keeping slugs, cutworms, or other insects away from your plants. Herbs are a great way to get started with an eggshell garden, so let's go!

Safety First: *Ask an adult to prepare the eggshells for you by using a sharp knife to carefully remove the upper third (the pointed end) of the eggshell. Empty the contents and save the yolks and whites for eating! Then ask the adult to use a sharp needle to prick the ends of the eggshells, creating a small hole in each one for drainage. Now you are ready to very carefully wash and dry your eggshell bottoms.*

TIME:
1 HOUR

CATEGORY:
DESIGN AND BUILD,
OBSERVATION, PLANTS

MATERIALS:
NEWSPAPERS (OPTIONAL)

SPOON (OPTIONAL)

SEED-STARTING POTTING MIX
(SEE TIPS)

PREPARED EMPTY EGGSHELL
BOTTOMS (SEE SAFETY FIRST),
WASHED AND DRIED WELL (12+)

EGG CARTON (1+)

HERB SEED PACKETS OF CHOICE
(SEE TIPS)

PERMANENT MARKER

SPRAY BOTTLE FILLED
WITH WATER

INSTRUCTIONS

1. If you are planting the seeds indoors, lay out some newspaper to avoid getting soil all over your work area. Use the spoon or your hands to place the potting mix into each eggshell, filling them almost (but not all the way) to the top.

2. Place the seeds into the soil, making sure to follow the directions on the seed packets. Usually four to five seeds will work.

3. Add a little more potting mix to cover the seeds.

4. Use the permanent marker to write the name of the herb on the outside of each shell so that later you will know what you planted.

5. Using the spray bottle, spritz the seeds until they are wet, and place the egg carton in a warm place. Now you are ready to watch your seeds grow!

6. Spritz the seeds every day with the spray bottle. When you see the seeds sprouting (germinating), move the egg carton to a sunny spot. When the sprouts are strong enough to be planted outside, gently crack the eggshells a little before planting them, so that the roots can easily grow out of the shell and spread out in the ground.

FARM JOURNAL ENTRY

Use your journal throughout this activity to record what herbs you planted, the date, and general observations while they are growing.

1. *Draw a sketch of each of the herbs you planted. As your herbs grow, draw a new sketch to show each new stage of growth.*

2. *Which herb sprouted first? Second? Were there some herbs that did not sprout? What do you think caused them not to sprout?*

3. *How will you use your herbs when you have harvested them?*

CONCLUSION:

Farmers follow steps in growing their crops: preparing the soil, planting seeds, watering the seeds, and making sure they grow healthy and can be harvested when they are ready. In this activity you planted seeds in soil, watered the seeds, and took care of them so you would have herbs to eat and use.

TIPS

➡ Make sure you select herbs that work for your area. For example, oregano requires lots of sun. Thyme also loves the sun and can take a little dryness in the soil. Rosemary doesn't mind cold climates. It likes plenty of sun and moist soil.

➡ Try to find soil specifically for growing herbs. It is lighter and drains water well.

UNDERSTANDING YOUR ECOSYSTEM

An ecosystem is a home for different organisms that live together in the same environment. The organisms that live in an ecosystem are well-suited to living there. While some plants and animals can adapt to different or changing ecosystems, many can only live in the specific conditions of one ecosystem.

People, for example, can live in all types of ecosystems. Think about where you live. Do you live near the forest, on the plains, or in the desert? What types of plants are around you, and why do you think they grow well there? What kind of animals live where you do, and how do they interact with the plants? Even if you live in a city, you are part of what's called an urban ecosystem, one shared by plants, animals, humans, and built structures.

Ecosystems can be different sizes and can be marine (ocean or sea), aquatic (all kinds of bodies of water, especially freshwater), or terrestrial (land). Ocean ecosystems are the most common as they cover 75 percent of Earth's surface. Freshwater ecosystems are the rarest, covering only about 2 percent of Earth's surface. Terrestrial ecosystems cover the remainder of Earth, and you may be more familiar with them because they are where people usually live.

There are five main types of terrestrial ecosystems: deserts, forests, grasslands, rain forests, and tundra. Let's take a closer look at each type.

Deserts: Deserts are hot and dry, and the plants that live there have adaptations to survive the harsh environment. For example, desert plants are good at storing water, since water is scarce there. Cacti have a wax coating so water can't escape, and their spines protect them from being someone else's dinner. Coastal deserts have a variety of plants, such as salt bush, rice grass, and black sage. These plants have thick leaves that can absorb and store water whenever it is available.

Deserts

Forests: Forests are characterized by the trees that grow in them. Deciduous forests have trees that lose their leaves seasonally and then grow them back. In the summer, their broad leaves absorb sunlight to make food through photosynthesis. And when the temperature cools, the green pigment (chlorophyll) in the leaves breaks down, and they change color and drop to the ground. Coniferous forests are made up of cone-bearing, needle-leaved evergreen trees. Typically, these trees do not lose their leaves.

Forests

Grasslands: There are many types of grasslands: savannah, prairie, steppe, and more. They are all characterized as being dominated by different types of grasses. In general, these environments allow shorter plants to thrive, but it's hard for taller plants, such as trees, to grow there.

Grasslands

Rain Forests

Tundra

Some plants that might live in these ecosystems include grasses such as wild oats, foxtail, and ryegrass and flowers such as goldenrods, sunflowers, clover, and asters.

Rain forests: Rain forests are forests that get quite a lot of rainfall, which means the plants that live there are adapted to all the rain. For example, most rain forest trees have thin, smooth bark. Unlike other trees, they don't need thick bark to keep them from drying out because rain forests are so wet. Many plants in rain forests have leaf shapes that help water drip off the plant to avoid bacterial and fungus growth. Some of the plants in the rain forest are called epiphytes. These plants live on the surface of other plants.

Tundra: Tundra exists in cold environments with short growing seasons. These conditions make it very hard for large plants to live there. Instead, plants like mosses, lichens, and small shrubs thrive on tundra. The plants that live here adapt to the weather by being short and grouping together for protection and to resist winds.

Fun Fact

Tropical rain forests cover less than 3 percent of Earth's area, yet they are home to more than 50 percent of animal species on the planet.

DESIGN AND BUILD A TABLETOP GREENHOUSE

Greenhouses are used to shield crops from excess cold or heat and unwanted pests. They make it possible to grow certain types of crops year-round in different environments, even if they don't normally grow in that environment. In this activity, you will design and build your own greenhouse with the materials suggested. You will then plant lima bean seeds to grow in your greenhouse.

TIME:
1 HOUR

CATEGORY:
DESIGN AND BUILD,
OBSERVATION, PLANTS

MATERIALS:
JOURNAL

PLASTIC STRAWS (8 TO 12)

8-OUNCE OR HALF-GALLON EMPTY
CARDBOARD MILK CARTON, TOP
CUT OFF (SEE SAFETY FIRST)

MASKING TAPE

SCISSORS

SOIL

LIMA BEAN SEEDS

WATER

PLASTIC WRAP OR A LARGE
ZIP-TOP PLASTIC BAG

Safety First: *Ask an adult to cut the milk carton for you. If you are using the 8-ounce size, cut just the top off so you have a box container. If you are using a half-gallon size, cut the box almost in half so you have a good size container.*

INSTRUCTIONS

1. Sketch your greenhouse design in your journal. Think about how you will use the materials you have for the different parts of the greenhouse: straws for the frame, plastic wrap for the walls and roof, and tape to connect things together. How can you use the straws to support the plastic wrap and create clear walls and a clear roof? How will you attach the straws to your milk carton planter? You may need to sketch more than one design before you find one that works.

2. Use the straws to build the frame of the greenhouse, based on your design. If you are using the smaller milk carton, you may want to cut the straws in half. Use the tape to attach the straws to each corner of the milk carton, which is the base of your greenhouse and where you will put the plants. You want them to stick up like poles so you can use the plastic wrap for your frame.

3. Add soil to the milk carton and plant the seeds according to the packet directions.

4. Water the seeds so the soil is damp.

5. Use plastic wrap, which you can cut into pieces and tape to the frame structure, or a large zip-top plastic bag to cover the frame. Make sure to completely seal the milk carton.

FARM JOURNAL ENTRY

Once you have planted the seeds, use your journal to record your observations over the next several weeks of what is happening to your seeds. Note the date your seeds germinated.

1. *Sketch what the plants look like as they grow.*

2. *How long was it from the time you planted the seeds until they germinated?*

3. *What is the purpose of the plastic covering?*

4. *Do you think your seeds would germinate faster if they weren't planted in a greenhouse?*

CONCLUSION:

Your greenhouse is like an ecosystem because it provides light and heat (warmth) to your plants. The soil provides the nutrients the plants will need to grow. The water will condense on the plastic wrap so the seeds will sprout. This lets you grow lima beans at any time of year, even when it would be too cold outside to grow lima beans. Greenhouse nurseries help farmers grow flowers and vegetables year-round.

TIPS

➡ You will want to check your greenhouse to make sure the soil is always damp so the seeds will sprout and continue to grow.

PREDICTING THE WEATHER

ecause weather affects crops in many ways, farmers are always preparing for different conditions. They live by the weather and use signs like the color of the sky and animal behavior to predict it.

Some ways of predicting the weather are so common, they've become proverbs, like "red sky at night, shepherds delight." In this example, the sky becomes red when dust and small particles are trapped by high pressure in the atmosphere. This will make the next day dry and pleasant. But if a farmer says, "red sky in the morning, shepherds take warning," this means that the sky is red because a high-pressure system is moving in. And most likely, this will bring wet and windy weather.

Farmers also learn how to predict the weather by reading different cloud types:

Cirrus clouds: These clouds can be seen high in the sky. They are thin and wispy, made out of ice crystals. A blue sky and a few cirrus clouds usually means that it will be a nice day.

Cumulus clouds: These clouds are puffy and look like giant cotton balls. Think of the word "accumulate," which means things pile up, when thinking of cumulus clouds. White fluffy clouds mean no rain, but dark gray clouds mean it will probably rain.

Nimbus clouds: These are the really dark clouds that you see during a thunderstorm with thunder and lightning. They already have rain or snow falling from them.

Stratus clouds: These clouds cover the sky like an enormous blanket. Farmers say that they are a sure sign of rain or snow. Stratus clouds near the ground are called fog.

Animals are also great weather predictors. Sheep and cows will huddle together when a storm is approaching. Birds fly lower to the ground when a storm is coming because the air pressure hurts their ears.

The amount of rain that falls in a year is probably the most important weather-related factor when it comes to farming. If rainfall is low or hail damages the crops, the farmer's yield, or the amount the farmer produces, will be low, creating a shortage of that product. Shortages on farms increase the prices of animal feed and also the food that you and I pay for in the store. This is an example of supply and demand, and it all starts with weather.

Fun Fact

In addition to reading signs from nature, farmers also get weather information from other sources, such as weather balloons, local news stations, satellites, and drones. Now, they can also get information with an app on their phones! This helps them plan ahead.

WIND POWER FARM

TIME:
1 HOUR

CATEGORY:
DESIGN AND BUILD, OBSERVATION

MATERIALS:
RULER

SHEETS OF PAPER (6 TO 8)

SCISSORS

THUMBTACK

STRAWS (6 TO 8)

BRADS (6 TO 8)

PLASTIC BASKET WITH HOLES ON
THE BOTTOM OR A COLANDER

BLOW-DRYER

TIPS

➡ If you don't have access to a blow-dryer, take your wind turbine farm outside to see what happens.

Many farmers grow trees on the edges of their fields to slow down the wind and stir up air. This tactic benefits crops in the field, and wind turbines have a similar effect. Like trees, they mix up the air and slow down wind speeds, delivering more carbon dioxide to crops. Wind turbines can also change the temperature, making nights warmer and days cooler. They reduce dew on leaves, which helps crops avoid diseases that are caused by fungi. In this activity, you use paper and straws to simulate a wind turbine.

Safety First: *You may want an adult to assist you while using the thumbtack.*

INSTRUCTIONS

1. Use the ruler to measure a 6-inch square on each sheet of paper. Use the scissors to cut out the squares. You will have six to eight squares depending on how many wind turbines you want.

2. From each corner of each square, cut toward the center about 3 inches. Do not cut all the way to the center.

3. Using the thumbtack, carefully poke a hole in each corner so that each corner has a hole in it. These will be bent into the middle.

4. Poke a hole in the center of each square. For each square of paper you have, take a straw and poke a hole through one end of it, making sure it goes all the way through.

5. Put one brad through each hole you made in the straws. Take one straw and push the brad through the center of the square of paper. One at a time, take each of the four corners, bend them toward the brad, and put the brad through the corner hole. Now that you have each of the arms of the turbine through the brad, bend the arms of the brad to secure it in place. Repeat this process with the remaining straws and squares of paper.

6. Turn the basket or colander upside down, and place each of the turbines through the holes.

7. Plug in the blow dryer, aim it at the turbines, and turn it on. Use the lowest setting at first to observe how the turbines react. Then try each setting to see what happens. This simulates blasts of air, or wind gusts.

CONCLUSION:

Wind is one type of weather that farmers have to deal with. In this activity, you made wind turbines, which help farmers. As the "wind" from the blow dryer moved the turning blades, you could see how the "turbines" were mixing up the air. This mixing action gets more carbon dioxide to crops, which they need, and helps reduce the amount of dew on leaves, which can lead to crop diseases.

FARM JOURNAL ENTRY

In your journal, respond to the following questions:

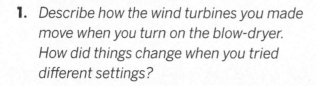

1. *Describe how the wind turbines you made move when you turn on the blow-dryer. How did things change when you tried different settings?*

2. *What do you think would happen if you made your wind turbines with larger blades?*

Flower

Leaf

Seed

Stem

Root

KNOW YOUR CROPS

Just like animals are alive, plants are living things, too. The purpose of every plant is to produce its own food so that it can grow, mature, and reproduce. Plants grow from tiny seeds into mature plants that farmers then harvest. We use these plants for food, fiber, fuel, building materials, and more. Plants are kind of like the building blocks of our world. They are an important part of the food web that moves energy to other living organisms when they are eaten. But they also sustain life by producing oxygen that many organisms, including people, need to breathe. In this chapter, we'll take a look at the anatomy—the different parts—of plants and how to take care of them.

4

THE ANATOMY OF A CROP

J ust like the different parts that make up your body, plants have different parts, too, and each has a special function. Let's take a closer look at the anatomy of a crop.

Seeds: Most plants reproduce by making seeds, and since a seed can only produce one plant, plants make a lot of seeds to ensure the survival of their species. A seed contains a young plant, called an embryo, and it usually comes with a food supply and an outer protective coat. The food supply helps the embryo grow before it can get nutrients from the soil, and the outer coat protects it until it can be planted. After a seed eventually sprouts, the parts of the plant, including the roots and stem, develop. Seeds come in many shapes and sizes. People sometimes eat seeds, including peas, nuts, and beans.

Roots: Roots absorb water and nutrients from the soil and help anchor the plant in the soil. They also store nutrients for future use by the plant. People sometimes eat the roots of plants, including radishes, carrots, and potatoes.

Stem: Stems hold the leaves and flowers of the plant and help carry water and nutrients from the roots and leaves. The stem also provides support for the plant. Edible stems include asparagus and kohlrabi.

Leaf: Leaves utilize photosynthesis to make food for the plant, absorb carbon dioxide, and catch sunlight. An opening on the leaf, called a stoma, allows water and air into and out of the plant. Leaves we eat include lettuce, cabbage, and spinach.

Flower: The flower is the reproductive part of a plant that contains pollen and eggs called ovules. Seeds form after pollination. Flowers we eat include cauliflower and broccoli.

Fruit: Fruit is the ripened ovary of a plant that contains the seed. Fruits protect their seeds in either a hard shell or a fleshy pulp. Fruits that we eat include apples, citrus, and bananas.

Most plants develop in similar ways, but there can be some differences. Let's compare the way corn grows to the way potatoes grow.

A corn seed is called a kernel, and when it sprouts, the leaves look like grass. Corn kernels grow into what are called stalks, with a main stem and fat leaves growing up all around it. Corn stalks can reach as high as 15 feet, about the height of two grown men and a toddler standing on top of one another. Once the corn plant is almost fully grown, the male flower appears at the top. This is called a tassel, and it is full of pollen. A little farther down the stalk, one or two ears of corn develop from the female flower with silks sticking out the top of the ear of corn. There is one silk for each kernel of corn, and each ear of corn has about 800 kernels. The silks wait for the pollen to blow in the wind and pollinate them.

Fun Fact

The average American eats about 124 pounds of potatoes per year.

On the other hand, potatoes usually grow from other potatoes, not individual seeds. A "seed potato" is a piece that was cut from a larger potato and has several buds, called eyes, on its surface. After the seed potato is planted, these buds will sprout and develop into independent plants that have their own roots and stems. It usually takes several weeks for the main stem and first leaves to grow aboveground. But underground, the root system grows fast by absorbing nutrients in the seed potato until the food supply is used up. The leafy part at the top grows a lot during the first month after planting, and the main stem of the plant stops growing when it produces a flower bud. The leaves will eventually make more food than what the plant needs, and all that extra energy will go down into the thick underground stems, called tubers, where it is stored. We know these tubers as potatoes.

GROWING RADISHES FROM SEEDS

TIME:
30 MINUTES FOR THE
PLANTING PART

CATEGORY:
OBSERVATION, PLANTS

MATERIALS:
SPOON (OPTIONAL)

10- TO 15-OUNCE CLEAR PLASTIC
CUP, WITH 2 OR 3 DRAINAGE
HOLES IN THE BOTTOM (1+)

POTTING SOIL

RADISH SEEDS

TRAY WITH SIDES

SPRAY BOTTLE FILLED
WITH WATER

TIPS

➡ You may cover the cup(s) with plastic wrap after planting. This creates a green-house effect to speed up the germination process. Once the leaves sprout, remove the plastic wrap.

Planting vegetables from seeds can be a fun way to grow your own food and to observe the different stages a plant goes through as it grows.

Safety First: *Ask an adult to poke two or three drainage holes in the bottom of each plastic cup for you.*

INSTRUCTIONS

1. Use the spoon or your hands to fill the cup(s) half-way with potting soil. Feel free to plant in as many cups as you'd like.

2. Plant the radish seeds ½ inch deep into the soil and about 1 inch apart from one another.

3. Place the cups in the tray. Use the spray bottle to moisten the soil and the seeds. The tray will catch any water that drains through the cups.

4. Place the container in a sunny spot. Now you are ready to observe the seeds as they grow!

TIPS

➡ Radishes need plenty of water to make root bulbs plump. The soil should stay moist but not overwatered. Watering every other day should be fine.

CONCLUSION:

All seeds go through stages of growth. In this activity, you started with a radish seed. After about three to four days, the seed grew into a seedling, or sprout. A seedling is a young plant that grows out of a seed. It is much smaller than the adult plant but looks about the same, with a stem and green leaves. As the plant grew, you noticed little red bulbs, which are the root of the radish and the part you eat.

FARM JOURNAL ENTRY

In your journal, respond to the following:

1. *Draw and label the parts of your radish and its stages of growth, including the seed, leaves, stem, and root.*

2. *Are radishes fruits or vegetables? Why?*

THE MOST POPULAR CROPS

If you take a drive across the United States, you will see crops growing in every state. Did you ever wonder what the most popular crops that farmers grow are? The following five crops account for 90 percent of the harvested land in the United States.

Corn

Corn: Corn is considered a type of grain. It is used to feed livestock and to make foods like cereal, corn chips, and corn bread. It's also used to make ethanol, which is a blend of gasoline and alcohol that can be used in motor vehicles. There are over 4,200 uses for corn and more being discovered all the time! Corn is the number one crop grown in the United States and the second largest crop in the whole world. There are almost 92 million acres of corn planted in the United States alone. That's about 69 million football fields!

Cotton

Cotton: Cotton is mainly used as a fiber for clothing. One bale of cotton weighs about 480 pounds and can make 680,000 cotton balls, 215 pairs of jeans, or 6.5 million cotton swabs. China, the United States, India, and Pakistan are the leading producers of the world's cotton. Cotton seed is also used in livestock feed.

Hay: Hay is a forage crop that is dried and then collected and compacted into bales that are more manageable for transporting. Hay is mainly used to feed livestock during the winter months, when the pasture grass is not growing. Alfalfa and grass hay are the most common types in the United States.

Hay

Soybeans: Soybeans are an oilseed like sunflowers, peanuts, cotton, and flax. Soybeans are used to make animal feed, biodiesel for vehicles, and hundreds of items at the grocery store, like milk alternatives, tofu, salad dressings, chewing gum, candles, and even crayons! Soybeans were first cultivated in northern China and brought to the United States in the early 1800s.

Wheat: Wheat is grain that is mostly used to make food for people, like bread, pasta, and cereal. Your favorite pizza is made with dough made from wheat flour. Last year, the United States made 3 billion pizzas—that's about 40 pizzas for each person!

Soybeans

Fun Fact

One acre of soybeans can produce 82,368 crayons.

Wheat

MAKING BIODEGRADABLE BIOPLASTIC

TIME:
30 MINUTES

CATEGORY:
EXPERIMENT

MATERIALS:
CORNSTARCH (1 TABLESPOON)

WATER (1 TABLESPOON)

CORN OIL (2 DROPS)

FOOD COLORING OF CHOICE
(2 TO 3 DROPS)

ZIP-TOP PLASTIC BAG

MICROWAVE

TIPS

➡ Try this activity again, mixing two different primary colors (blue, red, and yellow are the primary colors) of food coloring into the mixture. What happens when you do this?

Plastic is made from petroleum, a fossil fuel that is a nonrenewable resource. In this activity you will make a bioplastic from cornstarch and corn oil, products made from corn, which is a renewable resource. When bioplastics are exposed to the environment, they break down into nontoxic compounds so they are biodegradable, meaning they will decompose into natural elements over time. This activity just makes a small amount so you can see what bioplastic is.

INSTRUCTIONS

1. Place the cornstarch, water, corn oil, and food coloring into the plastic bag. Seal the bag and gently squish it to mix everything together.

2. Open the bag a little bit so steam can escape. Carefully place the bag into the microwave, propping it upright, and microwave the mixture for 20 seconds. Be careful when removing the bag: It will be hot!

3. Let the mixture cool for several minutes, then take it out of the bag and knead it with your hands. Form it into a ball. What does it feel like?

Corn is one of the most widely used crops. In this activity you used corn products to make a type of plastic. The most popular crops a farmer grows are not just food that you and I eat every day but also raw materials for the products we use.

FARM JOURNAL ENTRY

Use your journal to reflect on the following questions:

1. *Describe the mixture in your bag after adding the four ingredients. How does it feel when you slowly squish the bag?*

2. *What does your new mixture look like after you microwave it?*

3. *What does it feel like after the mixture cools?*

4. *What could you use your bioplastic for?*

TAKING CARE OF CROPS

What are some essential things that you need in order to survive? You probably named food, shelter, water, and the sun. Plants need these same things, and it's the farmer's job to take care of them. The better a farmer takes care of their crops, the higher the yield, or output, the farmer gets and the better quality of food for people to eat. Let's take a close look at what plants need to thrive.

Potatoes

Air and sunlight: These are essential to plant growth and part of the elements that mother nature provides for all of us. Plants need carbon dioxide from the air and sunlight to produce food through photosynthesis.

Insects: Some insects are beneficial to plants. Most of the crops that are used to make food for humans depend, at least in part, on pollinators. Pollination ensures the production of seeds and is necessary for many plants to reproduce.

Nutrients: Very much like the vitamins and minerals that we eat, nutrients from the soil give plants the energy that they need to grow. Early farmers planted the same crops, year after year, without changing fields. But this would use up the nutrients. Modern farmers discovered that they can add nutrients back to depleted soil. To do this, they add animal waste (manure), decayed plants, and fertilizer to the soil so it contains the nutrients they need to grow more crops. They also practice crop rotation, where one year they may plant a field with oats and the next year they'll plant that field with a different crop that uses different nutrients from the soil.

Soil: Soil is vital to a farmer producing quality food. Farmers do many things to help protect the soil. Erosion is a big problem with our soil, so farmers use terracing, where they create levels in the field to prevent erosion. Terracing reduces the steepness of the hill, making it harder for topsoil to wash away. No-tillage plowing is when a farmer only takes the fruits or vegetables from the crop and leaves the stalks and roots to rot in place, putting nutrients back into the soil and providing ground cover, which helps prevent erosion.

Water: Water is essential for all life, and farmers use a variety of irrigation systems to get water to plants. Surface irrigation relies on gravity to flow water over the soil, while sprinkler irrigation sprays water onto plants through pipes.

FARMER'S SOIL BABY

TIME:
30 MINUTES

CATEGORY:
CREATIVE, OBSERVATION, PLANTS

MATERIALS:
GRASS SEED (1 TO 2 TEASPOONS)

KNEE-HIGH NYLON STOCKING

POTTING SOIL (2 CUPS)

MARKER OR CRAFT SUPPLIES,
SUCH AS POM-POMS,
GOOGLY EYES, AND PIPE
CLEANERS (OPTIONAL)

10- TO 12-OUNCE PLASTIC CUP

WATER

SCISSORS (OPTIONAL)

TIPS

➡ Instead of making a face on your soil baby, take a picture of just your face, print it, and glue it onto the side of the cup. This makes a fun soil kid!

Just like parents take care of children, farmers care for the crops they are growing. When you take care of plants, you need to make sure they have nutrients from soil, water, sunlight, and air. This activity will allow you to make a soil baby using grass seed and to care for it while it grows. Your soil baby will grow "hair" from its head in the form of grass.

INSTRUCTIONS

1. Place the grass seed in the toe of the nylon stocking—this is where the grass will sprout and grow. The toe of the stocking will become the top of the soil baby's head.

2. Pour the potting soil into the nylon stocking, covering the grass seed. Pack the soil down and form it into a ball shape, making it the head of the baby. Tie a knot in the stocking right under the ball of soil to secure it.

3. If desired, make a face on the soil baby with the marker or other craft supplies.

4. Fill the cup about two-thirds full with water.

5. Place the soil baby in the cup, with the grass seed on top. The stocking will hang in the water and wick it up to saturate the head of the soil baby.

6. In 10 to 15 days, the grass seed will germinate from the top to look like hair.

7. Add water when you see that the tail of the stocking is no longer soaking up water. As the grass grows, you can cut the grass "hair" and style it as desired.

TIPS

➡ If the tail of the nylon is really long, use scissors to cut part of it off, but be sure to leave it long enough to soak up water.

FARM JOURNAL ENTRY

Use your journal to reflect on the following questions:

1. *How does taking care of your soil baby compare to a farmer taking care of their crops?*

2. *What are some basic things a plant needs to live?*

3. *How are your needs similar to and different from a plant's needs?*

CONCLUSION:

This activity allowed you to plant and take care of grass seed. Just as you need air, sunlight, food, and water, so do the crops that a farmer grows. Without ways to meet these essential needs, plants and animals would not survive.

GOOD AND BAD BUGS FOR CROPS

H ave you ever thought about what our world would be like without insects? Perhaps we wouldn't have the pesky fly that seems to bother us when we want to rest. Or maybe we wouldn't live in fear of being stung by a bee anymore. But we need insects!

Insects are essential for many ecosystems and perform many important functions. They help build the soil, play a key role in pollination, and some even help farmers by eating other insects that might be destroying their crops. They also help loosen the soil so that air, water, and nutrients can penetrate the roots of plants. Insects turn dead plants and animals into decomposed organic matter by eating them, which helps recycle nutrients back into the soil. Let's take a close look at some of the insects that help out around the farm.

Ants, bees, butterflies, and wasps pollinate flowering crops. Many farmers have their own hives of bees to help pollinate their crops. Other beneficial insects eat pests that harm crops. Dragonflies, ladybugs, praying mantises, and spiders help control aphids and caterpillars, for example.

Then there are some insects that destroy crops. Grasshoppers and corn earworms can do major damage to crops. Cutworms are a type of caterpillar that strips leaves from plants and eats holes in fruit. The tiny flea beetle and the Japanese beetle feed on the leaves and roots of plants. Aphids and spider mites emerge in large numbers that can cover nearly the entire stem and all the leaves of plants. They can also transmit diseases to plants and take important nutrients from them.

Harmful insects can literally consume a whole crop in a day or two if they are not controlled. Farmers help control harmful pests by enlisting the help of the pest's natural enemies, such as the good bugs; rotating crops; applying pesticides to repel harmful bugs and keep their numbers down; and maintaining healthy soil, which discourages some bad insects.

Fun Fact

A mason bee lives an average of four weeks. During that time, she will fill as many nesting tunnels as she can and pollinate flowers while she forages for food to supply her nest.

MAKE A MASON BEE HOUSE

The objective of this activity is to build a mason bee house that will attract mason bees to your yard or garden. Mason bees are beneficial (which means "good") bugs for agriculture, as they pollinate many crops that farmers grow. Mason bees are harmless and don't sting people like honeybees do.

Safety First: *You will need an adult to cut the neck of the bottle off if you are using a plastic soda bottle or to help take off both ends of the can and make sure the edges are not sharp.*

TIME:
30 MINUTES

CATEGORY:
CREATIVE, DESIGN AND
BUILD, OBSERVATION

MATERIALS:
SMALL WATERPROOF CONTAINER,
SUCH AS A SODA BOTTLE
OR A CAN, ENDS REMOVED
(SEE SAFETY FIRST)

ACRYLIC PAINTS (OPTIONAL)

PAPER STRAWS OR PAPER BAGS

SCISSORS (OPTIONAL)

PENCIL (OPTIONAL)

TAPE (OPTIONAL)

STRING

INSTRUCTIONS

1. The soda bottle or can is the frame of your bee house. If desired, decorate the frame with the acrylic paints.

2. Fill the frame with paper straws. (You can also make your own paper straws by cutting paper bags into strips that are as tall as your container and four to five inches wide. Use a pencil to roll up the pieces of paper, then use a piece of tape to secure the edge. Put the finished tubes into the container.) Pack the straws tightly enough so that they do not fall out.

3. To make a hanger so you can hang your bee home outside, wrap the string around the center of the bottle, then tie the two loose ends together in a knot. If using a can, have an adult poke two holes in the top, thread the string through, and tie the loose ends together in a knot.

4. Choose a location for your mason bee home. Place it four to seven feet off the ground in a place where it can get the warm sun in the morning and also be protected from wind and rain. Bees need the warm sunlight to fly and also need dry nesting tunnels. Ideally, the house should be firmly fixed to a tree or post. The bees use mud to help seal the bee house, so it's a good idea to have some soil and a little water available to the bees, within about 50 feet.

5. Observe how the bees fly in and out of the house, where they lay their eggs, and how they gather pollen and nectar for their young.

TIPS

➡ Make sure you place your frame within 200 to 300 feet of blossoming plants and trees that are pollen-rich.

FARM JOURNAL ENTRY

Use your journal to reflect on the following questions:

1. *What do you observe the mason bees doing in their home?*

2. *Can you see the sections being created in the tubes? Pollen is placed in the tube, then the female lays the egg, and then she sections the tube off with mud. The female will do this several times in each tube.*

3. *Why are mason bees and other pollinators important?*

CONCLUSION:

You just made a bee house that will attract mason bees, pollinators that help flowers grow. We owe much of our food to bees and other pollinators. Some seeds can only be produced when pollen is transferred from the male plant to the female plant. By making bee houses, you are not only helping bees but also our environment, and you're helping ensure that our food supply continues to grow.

TIPS

➡ Keep your mason bee house in a dry, cool place in winter and bring it out again in spring.

MEET THE FARM ANIMALS

In this chapter, you'll meet some of the animals we typically see on farms. Just like people and plants, animals live in communities and have basic needs. You'll learn about the animals that live on farms, how they grow, and what their purpose or job is on the farm. Did you know, for instance, that pigs are one of the smartest animals on the planet? They learn faster than dogs! Or that it takes only 48 hours for the milk that you drink to go from the farm to the store? It's true! We'll start off with exploring the life cycle of a typical farm animal, then move on to learning about common farm animals and how to take care of them.

5

THE LIFE CYCLE OF A FARM ANIMAL

Just as crops have a life cycle on the farm, so do farm animals. Many farm animals are mammals, just like people, which means their life cycle is similar to our own. Mammals are a group of animals that feed their young with milk from their mothers, have hair or fur, are warm-blooded, and are typically born alive (as opposed to inside eggs). To better understand, let's take a closer look at the life cycle of mammals on the farm.

Cows, sheep, goats, pigs, horses, rabbits, llamas, and alpacas are all mammals. Chickens, turkeys, and ducks also live on farms, but they are aves (birds)—not mammals—because they lay eggs, which means their life cycle starts a little differently.

Baby mammals, such as calves, start out as embryos inside the pregnant mother. The babies grow inside the mother, and this is called the female animal's gestation period. Each farm animal has a different gestation period: Female sheep (called ewes) and goats (called does or nannies) are pregnant for five months, female pigs (called gilts and sows) are pregnant for about four months, and female cattle (called heifers and cows) are pregnant for nine months. People are also pregnant for nine months.

After the gestation period, the baby animal is born alive. It nurses from its mom for different periods of time, depending on the type of animal. When the baby no longer needs milk from its mother, it will be weaned—or separated from the mother—and put into a pasture or pen with other weaned animals. At this point, it starts a different feeding plan. The mother is then able to prepare to become pregnant with another baby.

The type of farm animal and the type of farm it is being raised on determine what happens next. Some of the males and females are kept for breeding and continuing the farmer's herd, while others are grown to what is called market size. When they reach market size, they are harvested for the meat you and I eat and the many by-products we get from animals. For example, dairy cows, after they have had a calf, are put into the herd and give us delicious milk, which can also be made into cheese, butter, and other products.

Fun Fact

During her lifetime, a cow will produce about 200,000 glasses of milk. Studies show that cows produce more milk when they listen to music!

POETRY OF AGRICULTURE

TIME:
45 MINUTES

CATEGORY:
CREATIVE

MATERIALS:
FARM ANIMAL BOOKS OR
COMPUTER, FOR RESEARCH

PENCIL

JOURNAL

Georgic is a Greek word that means "relating to agriculture or rural life." The subject of georgic poems is agriculture. In this activity, you will write a poem about a farm animal and its stages of growth and importance on the farm.

INSTRUCTIONS

1. Choose a farm animal that you would like to write a georgic poem about. You may want to look at some farm animal books or do a little research about your favorite farm animal on the computer.

2. In your journal, brainstorm a list of words that pertain to your animal of choice. Use your senses to think of words related to how the animal looks when it is a baby and when it is full-grown. What would the animal smell, see, hear, and do on the farm? The more words you can brainstorm, the better.

3. Choose a format for your poem (see Tips), then write a poem related to the life cycle of your farm animal and its important place on the farm.

4. When you have finished writing your poem, draw a picture of the farm animal.

➡ There are lots of types of poetic forms out there. Here are a few to try out. <u>Haiku</u> have three lines: The first line has five syllables, the second has seven syllables, and the third has five syllables. <u>Acrostic poems</u> use a word that is written down the paper, vertically (instead of across the paper from left to right). Using the single letter on each line to begin that line of poetry, you write words or phrases that begin with those letters. A <u>cinquain</u> is simply a five-lined poem, and some cinquains follow rules similar to those of haiku.

CONCLUSION:

All farm animals have life cycles that take them from babies to adults. Most of the farm animals are similar to you and me because we are mammals. In this activity you used poetry to write about farm animals, their life cycles, and the food and other important products that you and I use every day.

FARM JOURNAL ENTRY

Use your journal to reflect on the following questions:

1. *What images did you create with your poem? Draw them in your journal.*

2. *What message about the farm animal were you trying to express?*

3. *How did you show the animal's stages of growth in your poem?*

THE MOST POPULAR FARM ANIMALS

Cattle

Dogs and Cats

Horses

Farmers will tell you that all farm animals have a purpose. For example, many farm animals, such as pigs, are raised for their meat. Others, such as cows and goats, are raised to provide milk and other products. Animals that are raised for their meat are called livestock. Not all animals on farms are livestock. Some, such as horses and dogs, serve other purposes, such as helping farmers with their work. Let's meet the most popular farm animals.

Cattle: Cattle are raised on farms for several different reasons. Males are called bulls, and females that have had calves are called cows. Beef cattle are raised mainly for meat and other products, such as leather, some medicines, and their manure, which is used for growing crops and fuel. Dairy cattle are raised for their milk, which is a popular beverage and can also be used to make other products like ice cream and butter.

Dogs and cats: Dogs and cats are not only good companions to farmers but also work on the farm. They protect livestock from predators and chase away mice and rats. Some dogs are even specially trained to herd sheep and cattle. Border collies and Australian shepherds are two of the most popular breeds of dogs for farmers and ranchers.

Horses: Horses can help farmers move large numbers of sheep and cattle from one place to another. The rancher rides a horse and uses a rope to catch the cattle so they can be branded or given medical treatment. This is especially important if the rancher is far away from the barn and corrals. The quarter horse is the most popular ranch horse.

Pigs: These animals are a lot like us! Their hearts and organs work in the same ways as ours. Doctors have used pig heart valves to fix human hearts, and pigskin can be used to treat people with bad burns. We also get meat from pigs, such as ham and bacon. Males are called boars, and a female who has given birth is called a sow.

Pigs

Poultry: These domesticated birds are raised for their eggs, meat, and other products. The most popular poultry includes chickens, ducks, and turkeys. Roosters are male chickens, and hens are the females.

Poultry

Sheep: Sheep are mainly raised for their meat and wool. Wool is used for clothing, such as sweaters and hats. Lanolin, which is the natural oil found in sheep's wool, is used in the pharmaceutical (medicine) and cosmetic (makeup) industries. Lanolin can be found in hand lotions, too. Rams are the males of the species, and ewes are the females that have had a lamb.

Sheep

Fun Fact

Scientists believe that the closest living relative to the *Tyrannosaurus rex* is the chicken.

NO-MACHINE ICE CREAM

Dairy cows are raised on farms and usually milked twice a day. Their milk is then processed and ends up as different products in our grocery stores like butter, cheese, and yummy ice cream. In this activity, you can make your own ice cream at home using cow's milk. As you make the ice cream, think about how the milk started on the farm and made it into your refrigerator.

TIME:
30 MINUTES

CATEGORY:
FOOD

MATERIALS:
WHOLE OR 2 PERCENT MILK (1 CUP)

HALF-AND-HALF (1 CUP)

SUGAR (½ CUP)

VANILLA EXTRACT (½ TEASPOON)

1-QUART ZIP-TOP FREEZER BAG

DUCT TAPE

1-GALLON ZIP-TOP FREEZER BAG

CRUSHED ICE

ROCK SALT (¾ CUP)

SMALL TOWEL

CUP AND SPOON

INSTRUCTIONS

1. Put the milk, half-and-half, sugar, and vanilla into the quart bag. Seal the bag and place tape over the opening, making sure the opening is completely covered to avoid any leaks.

2. Put the quart bag inside the gallon bag, and then pack crushed ice around it. Pour rock salt evenly over the ice, and then close the gallon bag, while removing as much air as you can.

3. Wrap the towel around the bag, and shake the bag for 5 to 10 minutes.

4. Open the outer bag and take the inner bag with the ingredients out. The temperature may not be cold enough if the inner bag is still soupy after 10 minutes. Drain the excess water from the outer bag, then add more ice and rock salt. Shake for about 5 more minutes, then check again.

5. Scoop out the ice cream into the cup and enjoy!

TIP

➡ You can substitute flavored milk, such as chocolate or strawberry, to make flavored ice cream. If using this option, reduce the sugar to ⅓ cup. If desired, when ready to eat, add your favorite ice-cream toppings!

FARM JOURNAL ENTRY

Use your journal to reflect on the following questions:

1. *What happened to the liquid when you started shaking the bag?*

2. *What other animals have you seen on farms? What foods or services do they provide for us?*

3. *Draw a picture of your favorite farm animal, and then draw pictures of foods and goods we get from that animal.*

CONCLUSION:
Farm animals provide much of our food supply, as well as other products we use every day. The foods you eat that are not plants come from animals and provide us with essential nutrients that we need. Think about the foods you eat during the day and the farm animals that those foods came from. They all serve a purpose.

TAKING CARE OF FARM ANIMALS

Animals need many of the same things we need: food, water, shelter, cleanliness, and love. It's true that farmers who raise animals are not keeping them for the same reasons you keep your pets. They are raising them to provide people with food and other products. However, that doesn't mean they don't care for the animals; they still need to keep them healthy. Let's take a closer look at how a farmer takes care of farm animals.

Health: Farmers need to keep their animals healthy. This includes making sure they are free from disease and insects. Just like you and me, farm animals sometimes need a visit from a doctor, called a veterinarian. A farmer is always checking for signs of illness: bad eyes, feet, or teeth or even a runny nose! And sometimes the females need help birthing their young.

Food: Feed provides the nutrients animals need and gives them energy. Farm animals are herbivores, meaning they eat plants. Grass is the main plant they eat. In the summer months, many farmers grow forage grasses and forage legumes, which are harvested as silage and hay to feed the animals in the winter months. Farm animals also eat grains, which are high in protein. Plenty of fresh water, air, and sunlight keep animals healthy.

Love: Social needs are important to farm animals. Because they have a herding instinct, they like to hang out in groups. Unlike animals in the wild, farm animals are domesticated animals. They are less stressed living with other members of their species. And, because they are domesticated, they need the farmer to help protect and take care of them.

Shelter: This doesn't mean that all animals need to live in a barn. Most farm animals live outside in big open spaces, on pastures, or out on the range. Sometimes, trees for shade and shelter from severe weather are sufficient. Some farms have three-sided structures for their animals to protect them from the elements. Pigs and poultry need the most protection from the weather and predators. Pigs do not have sweat glands, so on some farms that is why you see pigs in mud, so they can stay cool.

Fun Fact

Pigs are one of the only animals besides humans that can get sunburned!

MAKING DOG BISCUITS

TIME:
1 HOUR

CATEGORY:
FOOD

MATERIALS:
MEDIUM BOWL

MIXING SPOON

BEEF OR CHICKEN BOUILLON
(1 TEASPOON)

HOT WATER (½ CUP)

WHOLE-WHEAT OR ALL-PURPOSE
FLOUR (2½ CUPS)

SALT (1 TEASPOON)

EGG

ROLLING PIN

KNIFE OR BONE-SHAPED
COOKIE CUTTER

BAKING SHEET

WAX PAPER OR COOLING RACK

TIPS

➡ Try adding a banana or ¾ cup of pumpkin puree to the recipe for a differently flavored dog biscuit.

The best way to take care of an animal or person is to feed them. Just like farmers take care of their animals by providing food for them, you can take care of your pet dog by making this yummy treat for them. If you don't own a dog, make this for a friend's or neighbor's pet.

Safety First: *This project involves using hot water and the oven. An adult should help with those parts.*

INSTRUCTIONS

1. Preheat the oven to 350°F.

2. In a medium bowl, dissolve the bouillon in the hot water. Add the flour, salt, and egg, stirring to combine.

3. Knead the dough until it forms a ball, about 3 minutes.

4. Roll out the dough with the rolling pin until it is ½ inch thick.

5. Cut the dough into pieces. You can cut smaller pieces for small dogs and larger pieces for large dogs. Try using a cookie cutter to make fun shapes, like a bone. Place the pieces on a lightly greased baking sheet.

6. Bake for 30 minutes, or until the biscuits are golden brown.

7. Transfer the dog biscuits to a sheet of wax paper or cooling rack to cool until they are hardened.

CONCLUSION:

You just finished making dog biscuits at home to help care for your dog or a friend's dog. Just like pets, all farm animals need special care. The way we take care of our pets is very similar to how a farmer takes care of their livestock. Our animals depend on us to keep them safe and healthy.

FARM JOURNAL ENTRY

Use your journal to reflect on the following questions:

1. *How will the dog biscuit keep a dog healthy?*

2. *Can you name foods that farm animals need?*

3. *Pick a farm animal. Draw a picture and label all of the things they need to stay healthy.*

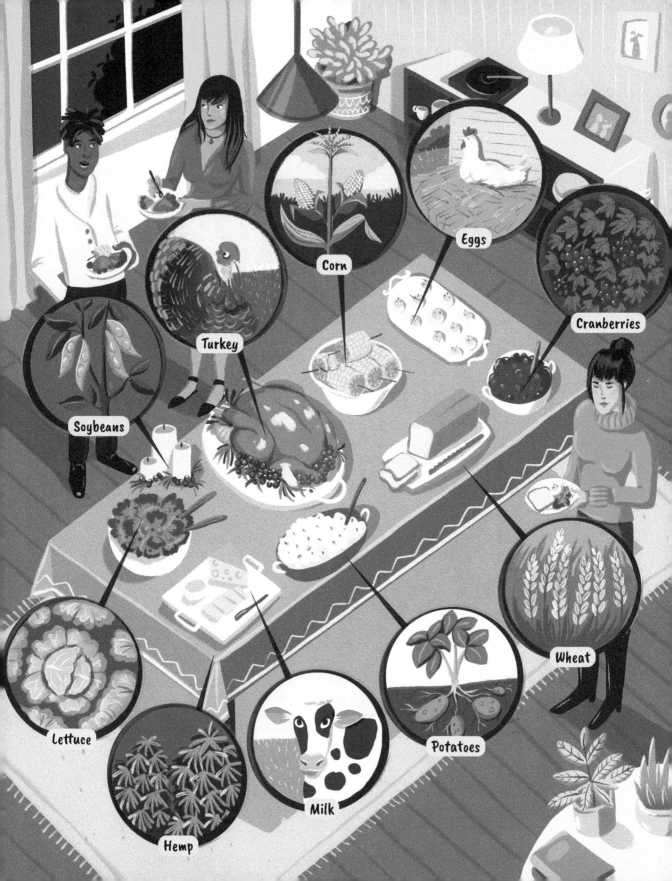

Corn

Eggs

Cranberries

Turkey

Soybeans

Lettuce

Hemp

Milk

Potatoes

Wheat

FROM THE FARM TO YOUR HOME

Agriculture affects every part of our lives, from the foods we eat to the clothes we wear to the objects in our homes. Understanding where the things you enjoy come from helps you create meaningful connections between farming, food, animals, nature, and your home. This chapter teaches you how to break down different parts of the farming ecosystem and reconnect them with the place that you live.

6

IDENTIFYING FARM FOODS IN YOUR HOME

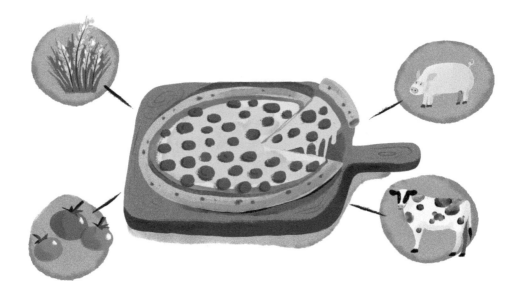

The food that you consume every day comes from either plants or animals. The next time you open your refrigerator, make a list of the foods inside and look up the ingredients to see if you can trace them back to the farm. Let's take a closer look at one of the most popular foods: pizza! Every ingredient in that slice of pizza started on a farm:

Pizza crust: Pizza crust is made from wheat. The seeds of this grain are planted and then harvested, cleaned, and ground into flour. It takes about six months for wheat to go from seed to harvest. Bakeries combine this ingredient with yeast, water, and oil to make the dough for the pizza crust.

Sauce: The sauce on a pizza is made from tomatoes. Tomato seeds are planted and then take about 85 days to ripen into mature plants. After tomatoes are picked, they are carefully packed into boxes and loaded into semitrucks to be transported to grocery stores. Some of the tomatoes are sent to a cannery, where they are processed to make sauces or ketchup.

Cheese: This dairy product is made with milk from cows, goats, sheep, and other animals. After farmers milk the animal, they heat the milk and then quickly cool it off in a process called pasteurizing. This kills bacteria in the milk and makes it safe to store and drink. The milk is then formed into a soft creamy substance called curd, and it is cut into small cubes that are later shaped into blocks or wheels. When we buy cheese in stores, the cheese is already wrapped in plastic and has been aged in cool storing rooms for months.

Pepperoni and sausage: These meats come from pigs. After the pig is butchered, the meat is ground up and mixed with different seasonings to make sausage, pepperoni, salami, and hot dogs. Beef is processed in much the same way, in case you prefer hamburger on your pizza.

Fun Fact

Pepperoni is the most popular pizza topping in the United States. About 36 percent of all pizzas contain pepperoni.

MAKE AN EASY PUMPKIN PIE

TIME:
30 MINUTES

CATEGORY:
FOOD

MATERIALS:
COLD MILK (2 CUPS)

1-GALLON ZIP-TOP FREEZER BAG

4-OUNCE PACKAGE OF INSTANT
VANILLA PUDDING MIX (2)

15-OUNCE CAN
SOLID-PACK PUMPKIN

PUMPKIN PIE SPICE (1 TEASPOON)

GRAHAM CRACKER SQUARES
(20 TO 25)

PLATE OR NAPKIN

SCISSORS

WHIPPED CREAM TOPPING

TIPS

➡ Try this recipe using other spices, such as cinnamon or ground ginger. This is a great afternoon snack to enjoy with friends.

The food you have in your home likely came from the store, but all of that food started on a farm. As you make this pumpkin pie, think about the ingredients in this recipe and trace them back to the farm where they started. Pumpkins are usually harvested in the fall, but this quick and nutritious pie can be made any time of the year.

INSTRUCTIONS

1. Pour the milk into the freezer bag. Add the pudding mix, then seal the bag. Knead the bag with your hands until the mixture is well-blended.

2. Add the canned pumpkin and pumpkin pie spice to the bag. Seal the bag again, while removing as much air as you can. Squeeze and knead the bag until the mixture is well-blended.

3. Arrange the graham cracker squares on a plate or napkin.

4. Cut off one bottom corner of the freezer bag. Squeeze about 2 tablespoons of pie filling carefully onto each cracker square.

5. Top each "pie" with whipped cream topping, and enjoy!

FARM JOURNAL ENTRY

Use your journal to reflect on the following questions:

1. *List the ingredients in your easy pumpkin pie. What is the source of each of those ingredients?*

2. *Name your top three foods at home. Now, break down each food into its ingredients. Name which farm animal or plant each ingredient came from.*

CONCLUSION:

You just made an easy pumpkin pie snack from several ingredients. Every recipe brings farm foods together into one dish. Farmers grow pumpkins in big fields, and then the pumpkins are used in pies, breads, and soups. The milk and whipped topping came from a farmer's dairy cows. Graham crackers are made from graham flour, which is a coarse wheat flour, made from a farmer's field of wheat. The pudding mix is made from sugar, cornstarch, and vanilla, which all came from plants that started on farms.

IDENTIFY FARM PRODUCTS IN YOUR HOME

Just as all of the food you eat comes from farmers, you can't go a day without coming in contact with products from plants and animals that were grown and raised on farms. When a farm animal or crop is used to make something else, the end result is called a by-product. For example, peanut oil is a by-product of peanuts.

Plants have many by-products that we use every day, as do livestock. There's a saying that everything in livestock but the "moo" and the "oink" can be used for by-products. Let's take a look at the by-products that come from popular crops and livestock.

Beef hide is used to make baseball gloves

Beef: Beef hide and hair are used to make shoes, luggage, purses, baseball gloves, footballs, violin strings, wallets, and car upholstery. Bones and horns are used to make piano keys, knife handles, vitamin capsules, lipstick, and combs. The glands and organs can be made into asphalt, cosmetics, fertilizer, insulation, medicines, insulin for diabetes patients, paint, soap, and tires. Collagen is an ingredient in gelatin that comes from cattle and is also used to make candies, gums, and marshmallows.

Cotton is used in printing money

Cotton: Cotton is much more than just a fiber source. Besides jeans, bed sheets, bath towels, and socks, cotton is made into the paper used in printing money as well as other apparel and home textiles. The seeds are also pressed and turned into cottonseed oil for cooking, cosmetics, and soap. **Linters**, the fuzz left after processing cotton, are often used for medical supplies and cotton balls and swabs. You can also find cotton by-products in ice cream, wallpaper, hot dog casings, and baseballs!

Corn: We eat ripe sweet corn, but the **kernels** of some corn make the snack popcorn, and **dent corn** is used for animal feed and processed into cornstarch. **Cornstarch** is used to make baby food, glue, deodorant, batteries, rubber tires, and spark plugs. **Corn syrup** is used in sodas, fireworks, and adhesives. **Dextrose** is used not only in bakery goods and fruit juices but also in antibiotics and oil. **Ethanol** is used for fuel and hand sanitizer and also in the corn-based plastics used to make bags, containers, and cups. Some other products that are made from corn include toothpaste, gum, shampoo, cosmetics, envelopes, and glass cleaner, which has at least five different ingredients derived from corn.

Toothpaste has ingredients derived from corn

Soybeans: Soybeans are used in biodiesel fuel for diesel engines, many brands of home carpet and car upholstery, some of the plastic in cars, many cleaners, paints, candles, soy ink, and crayons. **Soy foam** can be used in coolers, refrigerators, and shoes.

Soybeans are used in candles

Swine or pigs: A pig's **heart valves** are used to replace damaged or sick human heart valves, and the **skin** from hogs can be used to help treat burn victims. Pig by-products are also in insulin, other medicines, buttons, glue, anti-freeze, crayons, chalk, and water filters.

Pig by-products are used to make crayons

BY-PRODUCTS FARM CHARM

TIME:
30 MINUTES

CATEGORY:
CREATIVE

MATERIALS:
PIPE CLEANER (ANY COLOR)

WHITE BEAD

YELLOW BEADS (2)

GREEN BEAD

BROWN BEAD

PINK BEAD

REDDISH BROWN OR BLACK BEAD

BLACK BEAD

TIPS

➡ The pipe cleaner and beads can be purchased at any craft store.

➡ Design a different bracelet with other colored beads to represent other plants and animals of your choice.

The farm is the source of the food that we eat and other products we use every day. The farm charm is a beaded bracelet that you can wear to help remind you of the importance of farms in our lives and how many products started there.

INSTRUCTIONS

1. Take the pipe cleaner and place each of the colored beads onto the pipe cleaner. You can place the beads in the order of your choice.

2. Each bead represents a farm plant or animal. White represents cotton, yellow represents corn and wheat, green represents soybeans, brown represents forests, pink represents pigs, reddish brown or black represents beef cattle, and black represents sheep.

3. As you place each bead onto the pipe cleaner, think about the products in your home that come from that plant or animal.

4. Close the pipe cleaner into a circle, then twist the two ends together. Place the bracelet on your wrist.

FARM JOURNAL ENTRY

Use your journal to reflect on the following question:

1. *Draw six columns on a sheet of paper in your journal. Label the columns with these names of plants and animals that are grown on farms (which are also called* agricultural commodities*): Corn, Cotton, Cows, Pigs, Soybeans, and Timber. Write the names of items in your bedroom under the agricultural commodity from which they could have been made.*

CONCLUSION:
We use many products every day that come from the farm. Each one of the beads on your bracelet represents a plant or animal that was raised on a farm and all of the many products that are made from that plant or animal. Think about this as you go through your day and ask yourself, "Is this something that came from a plant or animal that a farmer raised?" It might only be one ingredient in the product, such as the cornstarch used in batteries, but that one ingredient started on a farm, and batteries couldn't be made without it.

AGRICULTURE BRINGS THE WORLD TOGETHER

Think about the foods that are your favorites to eat. Did you think of burgers and French fries, chocolate ice cream, or pineapple on pizza? Many of these foods are popular in America today, but 500 years ago, depending on where you lived, many people did not have pineapples, chocolate, potatoes, or beef! Back then, food supply chains were different. For example, in North America, people had potatoes, but they did not have cows for beef.

Many of the foods we eat today originally came from different parts of the world. People from different cultures brought many types of delicious foods to the United States. Today, US farmers grow many of these foods because of the different climates and soil, and with the aid of farm machines that help them make more food than ever before. Let's take a look at these tables to see where some of your favorite farm animals and crops came from.

Livestock from Around the World		
ANIMAL	PLACE OF ORIGIN	BIGGEST PRODUCERS TODAY
Cattle	Southwest Asia	India, Brazil, United States
Chicken	China, India	United States, China
Eggs	Southeast Asia	China, United States
Hogs	Southwest Asia	China, Germany, United States
Horses	Ukraine	United States, Mexico, China
Sheep	Middle East, Central Asia	China, Australia, India

Crops from Around the World

CROP	PLACE OF ORIGIN	BIGGEST PRODUCERS TODAY
Bananas	Malaysia (Asia)	Asia, South America
Carrots	Afghanistan (South Asia)	China, United States
Coffee beans	Ethiopia (Africa)	Africa, Asia, South and Central America
Cotton seeds	South Asia	Brazil, India, United States
Grapes	Turkey	France, Italy, United States
Olives	Mediterranean region	Mediterranean region, North Africa, South America
Oranges	Pakistan	Brazil, China, United States
Rice	India	Asia
Soybeans	Northeast China	Argentina, Brazil, United States
Sugarcane	India	Brazil, China, India
Watermelon	Africa	China, Turkey
Wheat	Turkey	China, India, Russia

REGROW FOOD FROM SCRAPS

TIME:
30 MINUTES, THEN A FEW MINUTES
FOR OBSERVATION EACH DAY

CATEGORY:
OBSERVATION, PLANTS

MATERIALS:
AVOCADO, PINEAPPLE, OR POTATO

TOOTHPICKS

TOWEL

WIDEMOUTHED JAR,
GLASS, OR BOWL

WATER

KNIFE

PLANTER AND SOIL

Farmers are great at recycling our food. They have learned that some crops, originally grown in other countries, can be regrown from scraps of that crop. Choose one or more of the foods listed here that originally grew outside the United States and regrow them from scraps.

INSTRUCTIONS

1. **To regrow an avocado:** Clean off the avocado's pit and rinse it under cold water. Towel-dry the pit, then, with the point-side up, push four evenly spaced toothpicks into the middle of the pit. Fill a jar or glass (even a cut-off 2-liter plastic bottle will work) with enough water so that, when balanced by the toothpicks on the opening, the pit will be halfway submerged. With the point-side up, place the pit into the container using the toothpicks to balance it on top. Put the container in a sunny area and change the water every 1 to 2 days. After 3 to 6 weeks, the top of the pit should begin to split open. It will take about 3 months for your tree to be around 7 to 8 inches tall, and then you can replant it in a 10-inch pot.

2. **To regrow a pineapple:** Have an adult help you slice off the top of the pineapple (the part with the crown, or leaves, on it). Hold the sliced-off top by the leaves and, holding the fruit part with your other hand, twist off the leafy part of the pineapple and eat or discard the fruit part. Then peel back the leaves around the base of the leaf crown and strip off any leaves around the bottom so some of the stem is exposed. Without damaging the stem, remove any excess fruit to keep it from rotting or

possibly killing the plant. Poke 3 to 4 toothpicks into the pineapple base, right above the area where the leaves were peeled back. Use the toothpicks to hold up the pineapple top over your jar. Add enough water to cover the base of the pineapple top in the container. Place it in a sunny spot and change the water every 2 days. Roots should form after a week, and the green leaves will also be longer. Plant the pineapple in a pot as soon as the roots are fully formed. Keep it in a sunny spot and water it regularly. A pineapple tree can take up to 2 years to bear fruit.

3. To regrow potatoes: Cut the potato into two pieces, and make sure each half has at least one or two eyes. Let the pieces sit overnight at room temperature until the cut parts are dry. Place the pieces 1 foot apart in a planter with about 8 inches of soil, with the cut-side facing down. Keep the soil wet, and if the potato is exposed, cover it with more soil. After a few days, green sprouts will appear. Eventually the potato plant will die, sometimes after flowering. Check to see if the potatoes are big enough to eat. If they are still small, leave them for a few days. You can harvest potatoes for several months.

CONCLUSION:
Some plants regrow from the root system, while others need to grow from a seed. Some crops will only grow with the right soil mixture, lighting, temperatures, and climate. Farmers need to know the best conditions for the crops they grow.

TIPS

➡ There are many more foods that can be regrown. Experiment with some of your other favorite plants and see what happens.

FARM JOURNAL ENTRY

Use your journal to reflect on the following questions:

1. *Why is regrowing food important?*

2. *What did you observe about your plant as it was regrowing?*

TAKE CARE OF YOURSELF AND THE PLANET

J ust like we need to do things to take care of our bodies—such as eating healthy food, practicing good hygiene, and getting plenty of exercise—farmers need to do certain things to take care of their plants and animals. This ensures that the quality of their products will be good, and it also ensures that they will be able to grow our food for generations to come. Today's farmers and scientists are also working on ways to use farming to help protect the environment. Agriculture is the key to keeping both ourselves and the planet alive.

Successfully growing crops depends on three things: the seeds, the soil, and what goes into the soil, such as water and nutrients. Crops flourish in soil that is full of nutrients. Farmers use manure, which is animal waste, and compost, which is rotted plant matter, to help enrich their soil. By planting certain crops, such as soybeans, farmers can put essential nitrogen back into the soil. Man-made fertilizers contain all the mineral nutrients needed in different types of soil.

Farmers also rotate their crops, meaning that the soil is not planted with the same crop year after year. Different plants take different nutrients out of the soil, so if you plant the same thing over and over, some nutrients will be depleted, leaving the soil unhealthy. Rotating crops helps prevent this. No-till, a type of conservation tillage, is another way that farmers are protecting the soil by not working the ground as much.

Some fruits and vegetables can be grown successfully by just using water with key nutrients added. This is called hydroponics, and it is a system that is becoming more widely used. With this system, food can be grown vertically in "hydroponic towers," which means you can grow more food in less space.

Fun Fact

Every year, hundreds of thousands of trees are planted on farmland. Farmers plant trees to provide habitat for wildlife while also protecting the soil from wind and their crops from severe weather damage.

Precision agriculture, which uses GPS-based mapping and drone technology for applying pesticides and fertilizer, is used by farmers today to increase their outputs, lower their production costs, and reduce chemical use, which helps the environment.

Today's livestock are more efficient thanks to technology and scientific advancements. Cows now eat 40 percent less feed than 30 years ago to produce 100 pounds of milk! That may seem like a long time to you, but in the history of our food system, that is a drop in the bucket.

CREATE EASY COMPOST

TIME:
30 MINUTES , THEN A FEW
MINUTES EACH DAY FOR 30 DAYS

CATEGORY:
DESIGN AND BUILD, OBSERVATION

MATERIALS:
SOIL

2-LITER PLASTIC BOTTLE,
TOP AND LABEL REMOVED
(SEE SAFETY FIRST)

COMPOSTABLE MATERIAL, SUCH
AS LEAVES, NEWSPAPER, AND
SPOILED/LEFTOVER PRODUCE

SPRAY BOTTLE FILLED
WITH WATER

TAPE

TIPS

➡ Not all organic material can be composted. Some good materials for compost are fruit and vegetable scraps, eggshells, coffee grounds, leaves, newspaper, and coffee filters. Never compost meat, fat, bones, cheese, milk, and oils.

Experts say that Americans throw away enough food to fill a 90,000-seat football stadium every day! Composting is one way that you and I can help the environment. Compost is decomposed organic matter, and this activity will teach you how to make it.

Safety First: *Have an adult cut the top off the 2-liter bottle and help remove its label.*

INSTRUCTIONS

1. Place 2 to 3 centimeters of soil in the bottom of the plastic bottle. Next, place a layer of compostable material. Alternate layers of soil and compost, until the layers almost reach the top of the bottle.

2. Moisten the mixture with water from a spray bottle.

3. Tape the top of the bottle back on and place the bottle in a sunny place.

4. If moisture condenses on the inside of the bottle, remove the top and let it dry out. If the contents are dry, add a little water.

5. Roll the bottle around every day to mix its contents. The compost is ready when it is brown and crumbly, which should take about 30 days.

6. Spread the compost in your garden, or use it like soil to start a container garden.

CONCLUSION:

You just recycled food scraps into compost, which is a nutrient-rich material that you can use to help plants grow. Just as farmers have become more efficient in farming practices and continue to find new and improved ways to ensure that we have food now and in the future, this activity shows how much food waste is created and how much of your food can be saved and reused to reduce your impact on the environment.

FARM JOURNAL ENTRY

Use your journal to reflect on the following questions:

1. *What do you notice happening in your compost as the days and weeks go by?*

2. *How would you describe the compost after a month?*

3. *What can you plant in your finished compost?*

RESOURCES

This book is by no means the complete story of agriculture, and I encourage you to continue to learn more about our food and fiber systems.

BOOKS

Anderson, Susan. 2013. *Soybeans in the Story of Agriculture.* Bedford, Nova Scotia: Northwest Arm Press.

Andrews, Andy. 2014. *The Kid Who Changed the World.* Nashville, TN: Thomas Nelson.

Brisson, Pat. 2018. *Before We Eat: From Farm to Table.* 2nd ed. Thomaston, ME: Tilbury House Publishers.

Butler, Viola. 2020. *Tales of the Dairy Godmother: Chuck's Ice Cream Wish.* Washington, DC: Feeding Minds Press.

Butterworth, Chris. 2011. *How Did That Get in My Lunchbox? The Story of Food.* Somerville, MA: Candlewick Press.

Butterworth, Chris. 2015. *Where Did My Clothes Come From?* Somerville, MA: Candlewick Press.

Cheng, Andrea. 2002. *When the Bees Fly Home.* Thomaston, ME: Tilbury House Publishers.

Darbyshire, Tom. 2009. *Who Grew My Soup?* Morton Grove, IL: Publications International, Ltd.

Detlefsen, Lisl H. 2019. *Right This Very Minute: A Table-to-Farm Book about Food and Farming.* Washington, DC: Feeding Minds Press.

Dufek, Holly. 2015. *A Year on the Farm: With Casey & Friends.* Austin, TX: Octane Press.

Icenoggle, Jodi. 2010. *'Til the Cows Come Home.* Honesdale, PA: Boyds Mills Press.

Mason, Helen. 2013. *Agricultural Inventions: At the Top of the Field.* New York: Crabtree Publishing.

Maurer, Tracy. 2017. *John Deere, That's Who!* New York: Henry Holt and Company.

Mosca, Julia. 2017. *The Girl Who Thought in Pictures: The Story of Dr. Temple Grandin.* Seattle, WA: The Innovation Press.

Peterson, Cris. 1999. *Century Farm: One Hundred Years on a Family Farm.* Honesdale, PA: Boyds Mills Press.

Peterson, Cris. 2019. *Popcorn Country: The Story of America's Favorite Snack*. Honesdale, PA: Boyds Mills Press.

Shores, Erika. 2016. *How Food Gets from Farms to Store Shelves.* North Mankato, MN: Capstone Press.

Siddals, Mary McKenna. 2014. *Compost Stew: An A to Z Recipe for the Earth.* Decorah, IA: Dragonfly Books.

Thomas, Peggy. 2019. *Full of Beans: Henry Ford Grows a Car.* Honesdale, PA: Calkins Creek.

WEBSITES

BestFoodFacts.org
This is a great resource for fact-based information about food from food experts.

AgClassroom.org
Check out National Agriculture in the Classroom's "Student Center" section for virtual farm tours, links for your state's agricultural website, and more.

USDA.gov
This is the website of the United States Department of Agriculture.

AgFoundation.org/projects /my-american-farm
This page of the American Farm Bureau Foundation for Agriculture website is an educational platform with agriculturally themed games. Check out their page "Common Questions About Agriculture" (under "Resources") to find accurate, well-sourced answers to questions you might have about plants and animals on the farm.

Soils4Kids.org
Explore games, experiments, career paths, and more on this website of the Soil Science Society of America.

NutrientsForLife.org/for-students
This is a great website that includes online soil challenges and videos of mining for potassium and phosphorus.

4-H.org
4-H is America's largest youth development organization.

FFA.org
Future Farmers of America is a student organization for older students interested in agriculture and leadership.

ACKNOWLEDGMENTS

I would like to thank my parents, Don and Mary Albert, who inspired me to love agriculture; my husband, Ron, and son, Cooper; and the rest of my family who support me no matter what.

I'd also like to thank my "village" in the ag community—Sue Hoffman, Jessica Jansen, and the rest of the people in the Agriculture in the Classroom organization—for their guidance and wealth of ideas. Thanks to the Deschutes County Farm Bureau, who support my ag literacy endeavors, and to all of my coworkers and students I've had the privilege of working with during my teaching career.

Finally, to all the farmers and ranchers who grow our food and fiber: You are my heroes.

ABOUT THE AUTHOR

Dawn Alexander, MS, lives in Central Oregon and has been an elementary educator for 35 years. She spent most of her youth on a ranch outside of Reno, Nevada, participating in 4-H and the Nevada junior Hereford program. She has actively promoted agriculture literacy and was honored to receive the 2019 Excellence in Teaching about Agriculture Award from the National Agriculture in the Classroom organization. She has also received the Presidential Award for Excellence in Mathematics and Science Teaching. She's been married to her husband, Ron, for 28 years, and they have one son, Cooper.

CPSIA information can be obtained
at www.ICGtesting.com
Printed in the USA
JSHW040930170821
17843JS00002B/6

NATURE ANATOMY
ACTIVITIES FOR KIDS
Fun, Hands-On Learning

KRISTINE BROWN, RH (AHG)

ILLUSTRATIONS BY KIM MALEK

ROCKRIDGE
PRESS

Copyright © 2020 by Rockridge Press, Emeryville, California

No part of this publication may be reproduced, stored in a retrieval system, or transmitted in any form or by any means, electronic, mechanical, photocopying, recording, scanning, or otherwise, except as permitted under Sections 107 or 108 of the 1976 United States Copyright Act, without the prior written permission of the Publisher. Requests to the Publisher for permission should be addressed to the Permissions Department, Rockridge Press, 6005 Shellmound Street, Suite 175, Emeryville, CA 94608.

Limit of Liability/Disclaimer of Warranty: The Publisher and the author make no representations or warranties with respect to the accuracy or completeness of the contents of this work and specifically disclaim all warranties, including without limitation warranties of fitness for a particular purpose. No warranty may be created or extended by sales or promotional materials. The advice and strategies contained herein may not be suitable for every situation. This work is sold with the understanding that the Publisher is not engaged in rendering medical, legal, or other professional advice or services. If professional assistance is required, the services of a competent professional person should be sought. Neither the Publisher nor the author shall be liable for damages arising herefrom. The fact that an individual, organization, or website is referred to in this work as a citation and/or potential source of further information does not mean that the author or the Publisher endorses the information the individual, organization, or website may provide or recommendations they/it may make. Further, readers should be aware that websites listed in this work may have changed or disappeared between when this work was written and when it is read.

For general information on our other products and services or to obtain technical support, please contact our Customer Care Department within the United States at (866) 744-2665, or outside the United States at (510) 253-0500.

Rockridge Press publishes its books in a variety of electronic and print formats. Some content that appears in print may not be available in electronic books, and vice versa.

TRADEMARKS: Rockridge Press and the Rockridge Press logo are trademarks or registered trademarks of Callisto Media Inc. and/or its affiliates, in the United States and other countries, and may not be used without written permission. All other trademarks are the property of their respective owners. Rockridge Press is not associated with any product or vendor mentioned in this book.

Series Designers: Jane Archer and Karmen Lizzul
Interior and Cover Designer: Jane Archer
Art Producer: Sue Bischofberger
Editor: Laura Apperson
Production Manager: Jose Olivera
Production Editor: Melissa Edeburn

Author Photo by Andrew Dobson
Illustrations © 2020 Kim Malek

ISBN: Print 978-1-64739-834-7 | eBook 978-1-64739-531-5
R2

CONTENTS

ACT LIKE AN EXPLORER. THINK LIKE A SCIENTIST.

Calling all young nature lovers! As you enjoy the great outdoors with this book, I want you to act like an explorer and think like a scientist. Why? Because both scientists and explorers use key observational skills in their work to establish accurate and reliable information for the rest of the world. Scientists and explorers follow five basic steps whenever they conduct an experiment, study nature, or come up with new ways to do things.

The first step is to observe. Scientists and explorers observe the situation or object they are studying. For example, American agricultural scientist George Washington Carver (1860–1943) observed that some cotton crops were not thriving. He noticed that crops that were rotated with peanuts and sweet potatoes grew much better. The peanuts and sweet potatoes improved the soil for the cotton, resulting in larger cotton harvests.

The second step is to ask many questions. Galileo di Vincenzo Bonaulti de Galilei (1564–1642) was an Italian astronomer, physicist, and engineer who studied the night sky. His many questions about the night sky led him to create a version of the telescope that let him view the stars up close. With his new telescope, he was able to better observe the night sky and answer his own questions.

The third step is to imagine. Scientists and explorers use their imagination to answer their questions, which arise from their observations of their environment. English botanist and photographer Anna Atkins (1799–1871) used her imagination to figure out how to make images of seaweed. Her imagination led her to place specimens directly onto paper coated with chemicals that turn the paper blue when exposed to the sun, thereby creating a silhouette effect. Using the process, she published a series of cyanotype books.

The fourth step is to test. Percy Lavon Julian (1899–1975) was an American chemist who observed that plants contained medicinal properties. He asked many questions, which led him to imagine that scientists could create synthetic (or human-made) versions of the medicinal properties of plants. He decided to test his theory by creating synthetic versions of the plants he studied.

The fifth step is to reflect on the work that's been done. English naturalist, geologist, and biologist Charles Robert Darwin (1809–1882) observed many plant and animal species and asked many questions, which led him to conclude that species arise and change over time through natural selection. Before publicizing his theory of evolution, which contradicted the prevailing view of creation, he had to reflect on everything he had studied and tested to make sure he was correct.

As you complete the lessons and activities in this book, you will follow in the footsteps of explorers and scientists by observing, asking, imagining, testing, and reflecting. My hope is that you will become a lifelong steward of Earth and continue to apply these five skills throughout your life.

HOW TO USE THIS BOOK

You will find this book easy to navigate. There are five chapters, each of which contains a theme related to our natural world: the sky, the earth, water, plants, and animals. Each chapter contains several lessons that are paired with an activity to get you thinking about nature as you observe, ask questions, imagine outcomes, test ideas, and reflect on your findings. Everything in this book is designed to help you better understand the natural world around you. Feel free to skip around and do the lessons and activities that you find most interesting or those that correspond with the time of year. Let's take a closer look at how each chapter is set up.

THE LESSON

This book contains 20 lessons divided into five chapters. Each lesson focuses on a basic element of nature and gives you an objective, or goal. For example, in chapter 1, the goal of The Phases of the Moon lesson on page 16 is to understand why the moon changes appearance throughout the month.

Each lesson teaches you to think like a scientist and act like an explorer with thought-provoking questions to inspire you to explore the topic.

After reading each lesson, you'll test and prove your ideas by using your observation skills. Later, you'll reflect by journaling your thoughts about the experience.

THE ACTIVITY

An activity accompanies each of the 20 lessons. Step-by-step instructions help you apply scientific principles from each lesson just as a scientist would perform an experiment. These instructions are preceded by a list of materials you'll need and prep work you'll need to complete beforehand.

Some activities require you to be cautious or to ask an adult for help. These activities include a Safety First warning. You'll also find tips on how to adapt an experiment, if necessary, and to troubleshoot any issues that might arise.

THE NATURE JOURNAL ENTRY

In addition to this activity book, you'll need a journal to keep track of your experiments and write your answers to questions. You'll describe what you see and what you're doing, and you'll note any questions that come up and how you tested ideas. Your journal is also the place to reflect on the activities and their outcomes and answer the journal prompts that are listed at the end of each section. You may also want to sketch pictures as visual reminders of each activity.

You can use any type of journal you'd like. If you think you'll be doing a lot of drawings, you may prefer a blank journal. If you think you'll be doing more writing than drawing, choose a lined journal. You can also choose a dot grid journal, which gives you guidelines for writing but still provides plenty of blank space for drawing if you think you'll be doing a lot of both. Some of my favorite journals are listed in the Resources section on page 95.

Setting up your nature journal is easy! Once you have chosen a style of journal, write your name on the first inside page (there's often a space for this) and the date you start the journal. Once your journal's filled, you can write the date you complete it on the same page.

To begin using your nature journal, you may choose to start a new section for each activity. Make a heading with the lesson and activity you're working on, and

add the date you begin that lesson. Then write down any questions you have, as well as answers to the questions in the activities and journaling exercises.

You may also choose to divide the book into 20 sections by taking the number of pages (many journals are numbered) and dividing it by 20. An adult can help you with this step! For example, if your journal has 140 pages, dividing 140 by 20 gives you seven pages for each activity. Every seven pages, write the name of the activity in sequential order (the order they are listed in the book), then dedicate those seven pages to that activity.

From there, you can either fill in the pages as you do each activity or you can further divide the pages to create categories for each activity. For example, you can include headings such as "Observations," "Questions," "Imagined Outcome," "Testing the Idea," "Journal Prompts," and "Sketches." Choose the way that you like best.

Now that you've got an idea of how this book works, dive in and start exploring!

THE BIG BLUE SKY

This chapter invites you to look up! What do you see in the sky? The sun? The moon? Stars? Clouds? A storm? Lightning? What about the things you don't think you see, such as the atmosphere? Or things you hear, such as thunder? What about the things you may not necessarily see in the air but are all around you, such as the changing of the seasons?

In this chapter, we'll go over many aspects of that big blue space above us and answer many common questions about the natural elements of the sky.

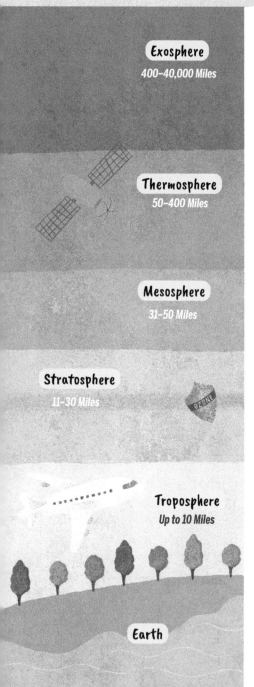

Exosphere
400–40,000 Miles

Thermosphere
50–400 Miles

Mesosphere
31–50 Miles

Stratosphere
11–30 Miles

OZONE

Troposphere
Up to 10 Miles

Earth

LAYERS OF THE ATMOSPHERE

We call the sky, which is layers of various gases, the atmosphere. The atmosphere protects us from radiation from the sun and other sources, keeps our temperature from becoming too extreme, gives us the air we breathe, and recirculates water back to Earth.

The atmosphere is made up of five layers of gases, including the troposphere, stratosphere, mesosphere, thermosphere, and exosphere. The air is very dense close to Earth but thins out farther away from Earth. Let's take a look at these layers a bit more closely.

Troposphere. Closest to Earth and extending 10 miles into the sky, the troposphere circulates our water through evaporation and transpiration, condensing the water into clouds that get heavy then release the water, in the form of rain, back to Earth. The troposphere also contains three-fourths of the mass of the entire atmosphere. This layer is where commercial airplanes fly.

Stratosphere. Extending 20 miles from the troposphere is the stratosphere, where the ozone layer is found. The ozone layer is the protective layer of the atmosphere that shields us from harmful ultraviolet radiation emitted by the sun.

Mesosphere. The middle layer is the mesosphere, reaching 31 to 50 miles above Earth.

The mesosphere is the coldest layer, and space debris generally burns up when it hits this layer.

Thermosphere. The fourth layer, the thermosphere, is broken into the ionosphere and the magnetosphere and extends 50 to 400 miles out from our planet. This layer is where satellites orbit Earth. The beautiful and colorful northern lights are created in the magnetosphere layer from magnetically charged particles, and the ionosphere allows long-distance radio wave communication.

Exosphere. The final, extremely thin layer of our atmosphere is the exosphere, found 400 to 40,000 miles out from Earth.

Fun Fact

DO YOU KNOW WHY THE SKY IS BLUE?

Most sunlight, which contains all the colors of the rainbow, shines through our atmosphere. Blue light, however, has a shorter wavelength than other colors of light. The blue light is absorbed by gases and particles in the atmosphere, giving the appearance of a blue sky.

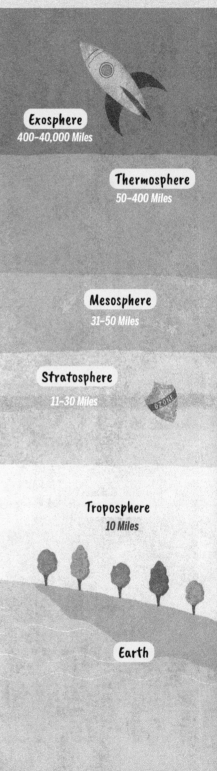

Exosphere
400–40,000 Miles

Thermosphere
50–400 Miles

Mesosphere
31–50 Miles

Stratosphere
11–30 Miles

OZONE

Troposphere
10 Miles

Earth

WEIGHING AIR

TIME:
15 TO 20 MINUTES

CATEGORY:
INDOOR, EXPERIMENT

MATERIALS
PIECES OF STRING, ABOUT
12 INCHES EACH (4)

BALLOONS, ALL THE SAME SIZE
AND NOT FILLED WITH AIR (4)

MASKING OR PAINTER'S TAPE

DOWEL ROD OR YARDSTICK

TIP

➡ If you have trouble trying to balance the rod on your finger, cut a fifth piece of string to tie to the center of the rod. Now, you can balance the rod by holding the string.

We can't see the air that surrounds us, so does that mean it has no weight? How do you even weigh air to find out? In this experiment, you'll determine whether air—even though you can't see it—has weight.

PREP WORK

1. Loosely tie each piece of string to a balloon.

2. Use the masking tape to secure two of the strings (with the balloons attached) to one end of the dowel rod. Tie the remaining two strings to the other end of the rod.

3. Balance the rod horizontally on your finger.

4. Make a mark over your finger where the rod is evenly balanced with two balloons on either side.

INSTRUCTIONS

1. Look at the rod as it balances on your finger. Notice how the balloons on either side pull down to help the rod remain balanced. Why do you think it's currently balanced?

2. Make an illustration in your journal of how the rod and balloons look now.

3. What do you think will happen if the balloons on one side of the rod are filled with air? Can you imagine what that would look like? Write down what you imagine will happen and draw a quick sketch in your journal of how you think it will look if two of the balloons on one side are filled with air.

4. Set the rod down and carefully untie two of the balloons from one side.

5. Blow up both of the balloons and tie them off so the air stays in them. Carefully tie them back onto the rod.

6. Balance the rod back on your finger. What happens? Does the rod stay balanced? If not, which side tilts up and which side tilts down? Why do you think that happened? Sketch in your journal how the rod looks now.

7. Can you get the rod to rebalance by moving the filled balloons closer to the middle or farther away from the middle? Why do you think this helps to rebalance the rod?

CONCLUSION:

In this lesson, you learned that the troposphere was the densest layer in the atmosphere, holding three-quarters of the mass in the entire atmosphere. Even though we can't see air, it does have weight! We can move the filled balloons closer to the center to help redistribute the weight and bring balance back to the rod.

NATURE JOURNAL ENTRY

Now that you've learned about the layers of the atmosphere and seen a demonstration that proves air has weight, answer these questions to reflect on what you've learned.

1. *Why do you think air has weight?*

2. *What do you think would happen if you added air to one of the empty balloons on the other side of the rod?*

WEATHER, SEASONS, AND STORMS

D id you know that where you're located geographically determines the type of weather and seasons you'll experience? What does the climate look like where you live? What does it feel like? If you live near a beach, you may experience lots of warmth and sunshine. Sometimes hurricanes may appear in the ocean near you, causing lots of wind and rain. If you live up in the mountains, winters are probably colder and filled with lots of snow. If you live in the plains, summer lightning storms and tornadoes are often a possibility for your area.

We describe weather as a natural event that brings about sunshine and rain, clouds and lightning, thunderstorms, tornadoes, hurricanes, and more. Weather can be broken into four seasons: spring, summer, fall, and winter. Depending on where you live, the seasons mark changes in weather, temperature, and the amount of daylight. Two equinoxes and two solstices mark the amount of daylight every year. Some places experience four distinct seasons, whereas others have similar weather for two seasons or more. Let's take a closer look.

Spring. This is the time of year that you'll see equal amounts of day and night if you live away from the equator (people living near the equator see equal days and nights year-round). The *spring equinox* marks the time in spring when both day and night are equal in length. After the spring equinox, days gradually lengthen while nights shorten. During the spring, Earth starts to warm up and plants start to emerge from the ground after disappearing over the winter. Cold winter temperatures give way to milder spring temperatures.

Summer. During the summer, days are longer and nights are shorter. The longest day of the year is called the *summer solstice.* After the summer solstice, each day starts to gradually shorten while the night gradually lengthens. During summer, plants are lush, flowering, and often start fruiting. This time of the year can be hot, humid, and muggy, depending on where you live.

Fall. Also referred to as autumn, fall is another time of year that provides equal amounts of day and night, but during this time of year, the days start to shorten and the nights begin to lengthen. The *fall equinox* marks the time when both day and night are equal in length. Nights get longer from here. In fall, leaves begin falling from deciduous trees and plants begin dying back. Temperatures start to drop as the season heads into winter.

Winter. Nights are longest and days shortest in winter. The longest night of the year is called the *winter solstice*. After the winter solstice, the nights get shorter again. In winter, most plants have died back, and in colder locations, snow often falls instead of rain. The temperature turns cold, requiring many animals (such as bears, snakes, and bats) to hibernate, so they can avoid the cold and lack of food.

Clouds are closely related to weather. They are formed when water evaporates from Earth. The water vapor clings to dust particles in the air and forms into clouds. If the clouds accumulate too much water, they become too heavy and form rain.

Ten different cloud types can be found anywhere from 1.24 to 3.73 miles into the atmosphere. (That distance is equivalent to 4.5 to 13.5 Empire State Buildings stacked end to end!) Recall that this part of the atmosphere is called the troposphere (see page 2). The troposphere has three layers. The *lower layer* is about 1.24 miles away from Earth, the *middle layer* is about 2.49 miles away, and the *top layer* starts about 3.73 miles away. Different types of clouds form in these layers. Let's take a closer look.

Stratus. These clouds form in the lower layer. They appear on overcast days and hang low. They are gray, flat, and typically fill the entire sky.

Nimbostratus. These clouds form in the lower layer. They are dark gray but may appear a bit fluffy. When you see these clouds on the horizon, you know rain is coming soon.

Stratocumulus. These clouds form in the lower layer. They can be gray or white, or a combination of the two, and are fluffy in appearance. They appear in patches.

Cumulus. These clouds form in the lower layer. They are the big, white, fluffy clouds that you watch on a warm summer day as you lie back on the ground and gaze up at the sky. Though their tops are white, the bottoms are gray.

Cumulonimbus. These clouds form in the lower layer. However, they are found in all three layers, starting at the lowest layer and developing vertically into what we call an "anvil head" that ranges all the way up to the top layer. These clouds indicate rain and can bring about severe weather, including heavy rainfall, hail, and tornadoes.

Altocumulus. These clouds form in the middle layer. Smaller than stratocumulus clouds, altocumulus clouds are small puffy clouds that are white to gray and are the most commonly seen clouds in the sky. These clouds are most often seen in the summer and can indicate that storms are on their way or that a cold front is moving in.

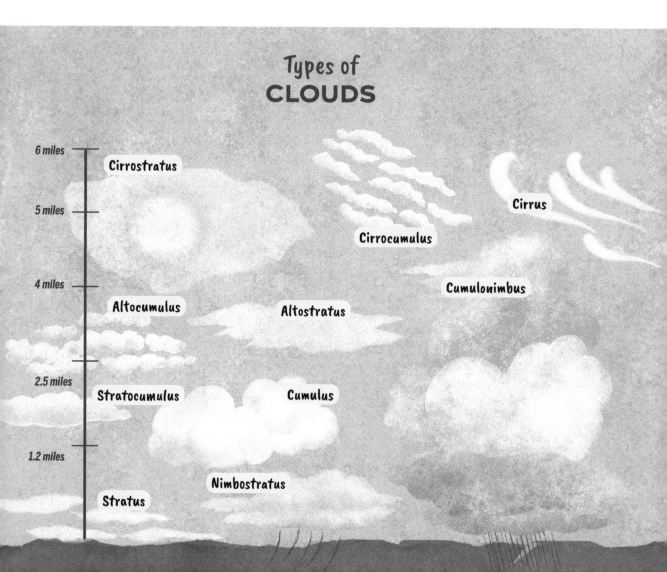

Types of
CLOUDS

6 miles
Cirrostratus

5 miles
Cirrus
Cirrocumulus

4 miles
Cumulonimbus
Altocumulus
Altostratus

2.5 miles
Stratocumulus
Cumulus

1.2 miles
Nimbostratus
Stratus

Altostratus. These clouds form in the middle layer. They are gray and hang in sheets across the sky, allowing the sun to dimly shine through them. They generally indicate a warm front is on the way, though if they are combined with cumulus clouds, they can indicate a cold front instead.

Cirrocumulus. These small, white clouds, made of ice crystals, form in the top layer. They are less commonly seen and generally appear in the winter or when it's cold outside. Some people call them cloudlets because they are so small.

Cirrostratus. These transparent, whitish clouds form in the top layer and cover the entire sky. When they are present, you will see a halo around the sun or moon. These clouds generally indicate a warm front is moving in.

Cirrus. These clouds form in the top layer. These wispy clouds streak across the sky, curling upward on one end. They are white and, like cirrocumulus clouds, are made up of ice crystals instead of water.

Fun Fact

DID YOU KNOW THAT THE SEASONS ARE REVERSED IN THE SOUTHERN AND NORTHERN HEMISPHERES?

When it is summer in the Northern Hemisphere, it is winter in the Southern. Spring and fall are also reversed.

MAKE A CLOUD

TIME:
15 MINUTES

CATEGORY:
EXPERIMENT, INDOOR

MATERIALS
⅓ CUP HOT WATER

JAR WITH A LID, SUCH AS A CLEAN EMPTY PICKLE JAR

ICE CUBES

SMALL CAN OF AEROSOL HAIR SPRAY

Have you ever wondered how a cloud is formed? Have you ever gone into the mountains, hoping to touch a cloud, only to find that the clouds disappear when you are among them? This activity will help you see how clouds are formed from a combination of water and warm and cool air, which creates vapor.

Safety First: *Use caution with the hot water, so you don't burn yourself.*

PREP WORK
1. Gather your items together, so they are ready to go.

INSTRUCTIONS
1. Pour the hot water into the jar, and swirl it around to warm up the glass.

2. Place the lid upside down on the jar, so it forms a small tray. Fill the lid with ice cubes.

3. Let the ice sit in the lid for 20 to 30 seconds.

4. Set the can of hair spray right next to the jar. Position the nozzle where the lid meets the top of the jar. Quickly lift the lid a little, spray a good squirt of hair spray into the jar, then set the lid back down, leaving the ice on top.

TIP

➡ If you're having trouble getting the hair spray into the jar quickly, have a parent, sibling, or friend help you with this step.

5. Watch the jar and see what happens. Based on your observations, can you guess what is creating the cloud? What is the hair spray mimicking? What will happen if you open the lid?

6. Lift the lid and watch the cloud disappear into the air.

NATURE JOURNAL ENTRY

This lesson covered a lot! From the seasons, equinoxes, and solstices to the 10 different types of clouds that fill the sky, you learned many things that happen in the troposphere. Reflect on everything you learned, and answer the following questions in your journal.

1. *Why do you think the cloud formed when the hair spray was introduced into the jar? Do you think the "cloud" was there before you added the hair spray?*

2. *Have you ever seen fog rise from the ground? What do you think creates the fog? Do you think fog is the same thing as a cloud? What makes it different from a cloud?*

CONCLUSION:

In this lesson, you learned that clouds are formed from evaporated water that rises from Earth into the sky. This activity demonstrates this action as warm water and air turn to vapor in the jar and rise to meet the cold air near the lid, which pushes back down on the water vapor. When the hair spray is sprayed into the jar, it mimics dust particles in the air, giving the vapor something to cling to and forming a cloud.

SUNRISE AND SUNSET

Have you ever woken up early in the morning to see the sunrise? Or watched the sunset? What brings about the reds, oranges, purples, and yellows? In the Layers of the Atmosphere lesson (see page 2), you learned why the sky is blue. The colors of sunrises and sunsets are on the opposite end of the color spectrum from blue.

When the sun rises and sets, it "sits" at a longer angle away from Earth. As the short blue light waves bounce, they get deflected away from our eyes, becoming too small to see. The longer red and yellow light waves can still reach our eyes, causing the beautiful range of colors in the morning and evening.

The sun rises in the east every morning and sets in the west every evening. Although the sun seems to move from east to west throughout the day, it is

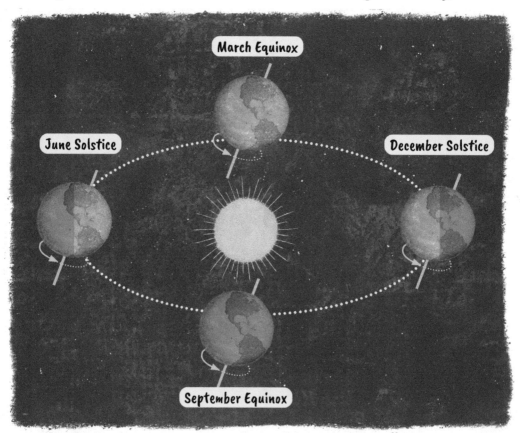

actually stationary. Rather, Earth rotates, or orbits, around the sun, all while rotating toward the east. It takes Earth 24 hours to complete one full rotation, which is why one day is 24 hours.

Before clocks, people told time by the sun. When the sun is directly overhead, it is roughly noon. When you know when the sun rises and sets, the horizons can be broken up between the rise/set time and when the sun is directly overhead. You can then split that space evenly into the hours between rise/set and noon, and the time can be counted off. Adults can hold their hands below the sun in the evening and gauge how long until sunset by counting the number of fingers from the horizon—four fingers represent one hour. Since your hands are smaller, each hand will count for about 30 minutes.

In addition to Earth orbiting around the sun—which takes one full year—and spinning on a rotation, Earth also tilts closer and farther away from the sun, which creates our longer and shorter days. The June and December solstices mark the longest or shortest day of the year, depending on your hemisphere, and the March and September equinoxes mark dates in which day and night are exactly the same length.

That's a lot of movement! We'll talk more about all this movement in the next chapter.

Fun Fact

DID YOU KNOW THAT WHEN THE EARTH'S ORBIT IS CLOSER TO THE SUN, IT'S WINTER? AND WHEN EARTH'S ORBIT IS FARTHER AWAY FROM THE SUN, IT'S SUMMER?

You'd think that being closer to the sun would make us warmer. However, as Earth's orbit nears the sun, we get less daylight and our days shorten, and as it moves away from the sun, we get more sunlight and our days lengthen.

TELLING TIME WITH THE SUN

TIME:
30 MINUTES TO MAKE
THE SUNDIAL, PLUS A FEW
MINUTES TO OBSERVE

CATEGORY:
CRAFTS, OBSERVATION, OUTDOOR

MATERIALS
WHITE PAINT

PAINT BRUSH

PLYWOOD BOARD, ABOUT
12 × 12 INCHES

RULER

PENCIL

NAIL, 6 INCHES OR LONGER

HAMMER

TIP

➡ If you don't have a piece of plywood and large nail, you can use a piece of cardboard painted white and a pencil or dowel rod. The sundial won't be as permanent, but it will last quite a while.

Have you ever used a sundial to tell time? As the sun travels across the sky, its shadows mark time throughout the day. Many ancient civilizations, including the Mayans in Central America, used sundials to keep track of the hours of the day. The accuracy of a simple sundial depends greatly on your latitude, so keep that in mind!

Safety First: *Be careful when hammering the nail.*

PREP WORK

1. Use the white paint and paint brush to paint your board on one side, then let the paint dry.

2. Using the ruler, diagonally line up two corners and lightly draw a line with the pencil in the center of the board.

3. Repeat this step with the other two diagonal corners to create an "X" in the center of the board.

4. Use the hammer to carefully tap the nail into the center of the board, just deep enough so it won't fall out. Now you have a sundial!

INSTRUCTIONS

1. Begin setting up your sundial early on a sunny day. Observe your yard for a day to find an ideal spot. Set your sundial on level ground in full sun, in a location where it will not be disturbed.

2. Once you set your sundial down, mark where the sun's shadow falls at the top of an hour, such as at

6 a.m. Use the ruler to draw a line from the nail to the edge of the board and label it with the time.

3. Draw a line along the shadow and mark the hour every hour until sunset. Can you guess where each hour's shadow will land before sunset? After watching the pattern emerge, sketch the sundial in your journal and mark where you think the shadows will land. When you've finished marking the true sundial, go back to your journal and compare your results to your guesses.

4. Use your sundial to tell time.

CONCLUSION:
Even though your regional location may need some adjusting for the time to be completely accurate, it's easy to see how ancient people harnessed the sun to keep track of their days. In this lesson, you learned about sunrises and sunsets. You learned that their colors are created by the angle of the sun, which happens when Earth rotates, making the sun appear to rise and set. This also helps us mark time, as you learned with this sundial activity.

NATURE JOURNAL ENTRY

Now that you've seen how time can be tracked as Earth rotates, turning us toward and away from the sun, reflect on all you've learned. Answer these questions in your journal.

1. *Can you think of other ways ancient people used the sun to mark time?*

2. *How important do you think the marking of time was to ancient people?*

3. *Why do you think many cultures built stone circles, such as Stonehenge, which mark the solstices and equinoxes?*

THE PHASES OF THE MOON

The moon is a fascinating sphere that orbits around Earth, taking 27.3 days to make a complete orbit. Unlike Earth, the moon does not spin as it orbits, which means we always see the same view of the moon's surface from here on Earth. Although the moon can look very bright, it does not give off its own light. Instead, the moon's surface reflects the light of the sun, which makes it appear to glow. Although the moon is much smaller than the sun, it appears to be the same size as the sun because it is much closer to us than the sun is.

The moon orbits Earth counterclockwise, but because the moon does not rotate, the sun always hits the same side of the moon. However, we can't always see the lit side of the moon here on Earth, which makes it look like the moon's shape is changing. During a complete orbit around Earth, the moon can be seen in eight different phases. Let's take a closer look at them.

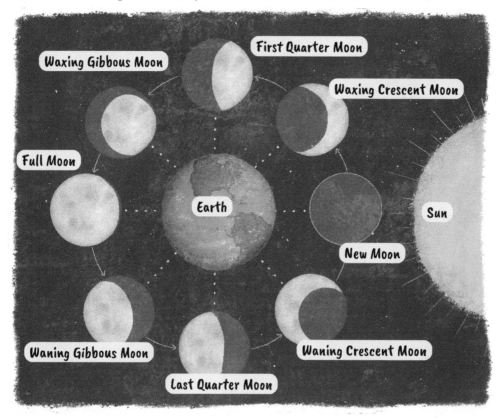

New moon. The beginning moon phase is known as a new moon. During this time, the moon isn't visible because it is between the sun and Earth. A solar eclipse can only happen during a new moon.

Waxing crescent moon. As the moon orbits around Earth, the sun catches it at an angle, giving us a waxing crescent moon. Because of the position of the sun and moon, this sliver looks like a backward "C."

First quarter moon. About seven days into the moon's cycle, the first quarter moon appears. During this phase, the moon is side by side with Earth, and we see its illuminated right half.

Waxing gibbous moon. When the moon is three-quarters full, it is known as a waxing gibbous moon.

Full moon. Fourteen and a half days into its cycle, the moon becomes a full moon as Earth is fully between the sun and moon. A lunar eclipse can occur only during a full moon.

Waning gibbous moon. As the moon continues to orbit Earth, the bottom fourth vanishes. This phase is known as the waning gibbous moon.

Last quarter moon. When the moon is side by side with Earth again (this time on the opposite side), it is again half lit by the sun. We call this phase the last quarter moon.

Waning crescent moon. The final phase of the moon is the waning crescent, and, again, only a sliver of the moon is illuminated—this time, in the shape of a normal letter "C."

Fun Fact

DID YOU KNOW THAT PEOPLE ONCE THOUGHT THE MOON HAD SEAS ON ITS SURFACE?

So they named the dark spots we see *lunar maria*, which means "moon seas" in Latin. Later, these dark spots were discovered to be remnants from volcanic eruptions that happened within the past three billion years (with some as recent as 10 million years ago)!

THE MOON CYCLE

TIME:
A FEW MINUTES EVERY NIGHT
FOR 30 DAYS

CATEGORY:
OBSERVATION, OUTDOOR

MATERIALS
PENCIL

QUARTER

YELLOW AND GRAY MARKERS,
COLORED PENCILS, OR
CRAYONS (OPTIONAL)

TIP

➡ Try starting this activity with the new moon, so you can see the progression of the moon every night.

Have you ever gazed up at the moon and wondered what phase it was in? Or why it keeps getting bigger and smaller each month? Just how long does it take the moon to complete a cycle? In this activity, you will observe and chart the shape of the moon every night for an entire cycle.

PREP WORK

1. In your journal, use the pencil to trace the quarter 30 times over the course of the page. This will help you keep track of the moon phases. You may want to create two columns of 15 circles each or three columns of 10 circles each. Make sure to leave enough room to the right of each circle to make a note of the phase.

INSTRUCTIONS

1. Beginning at any time during the moon's cycle, observe the moon at night. Use the pencil or markers (if using) to fill in the first circle in your journal with the shape of the moon. Next to the shape, write down the date (month and day), time, and the phase of the moon.

2. After your first night of observing the moon, do you think the moon will continue to increase or decrease in size? Where do you think the sun is located in conjunction with Earth and the moon?

3. Continue filling in the circles each night, starting at the top of the first column and working your way down, then continuing with the next column, until all 30 circles are filled.

4. Keep trying to estimate how the moon will continue to change, and record any thoughts you have on your observations, as well as how correct you were.

TIP

➥ If a night is cloudy and you can't see the moon, leave the circle blank and make a note of it. The next night, after you've filled in the moon's shape, compare that shape with the shape from two nights ago. Fill in the missing night with a shape between the two.

NATURE JOURNAL ENTRY

This lesson taught you all about the phases of the moon. Reflect on this lesson and activity as you answer the following questions in your journal.

1. *Did the moon appear at the same time every night?*

2. *Was the moon the same size every night? If not, why do you think the size also changed?*

3. *What was your favorite phase of the moon and why?*

CONCLUSION:

This activity helped you prove that as Earth orbits around the sun and the moon orbits around Earth, the moon appears to change shape every day. Over the course of a month, the moon waxes (or more of it becomes visible) until it is a complete circle. After the full moon, the moon wanes (or less of it becomes visible) until it is completely gone from the night sky. The pattern on your paper should mimic the sun's reflection on the moon.

LOOK UP AT THE STARS

Take a walk outside during a new moon—away from the light pollution of the city if you live in one—and you'll see billions of tiny lights dancing across the sky: stars!

Stars, like our sun, are made up of gases (hydrogen and helium) that form a hot ball with a core of nuclear fusion. Some stars live to be trillions of years old, until they burn up all their hydrogen fuel.

Ancient people did not know this about stars but held them in high regard. Navigators used stars to help them travel at night, staying on course by using the North Star as their guide. People connected the dots of star groupings, called constellations, and imagined them to be various creatures such as Cetus, the sea monster, or mythological people and creatures such as Orion.

Because people did not have televisions, cell phones, or even books to entertain themselves, stories were a popular past time. Ancient cultures and civilizations created stories about groups of stars—stories passed along through generations. Today, the International Astronomical Union recognizes 88 constellations, 12 of which are the signs of the zodiac, most of which reflect names and lore from Greek mythology.

Because of Earth's rotation and orbit, we see different constellations at different times of the year. For instance, in the Northern Hemisphere, Orion can be seen only in the fall and winter.

Can you think of any stories about constellations? Have you ever looked up at the sky and noticed the stars forming a shape? What story emerged from that image?

Fun Fact

DID YOU KNOW THAT PEOPLE IN THE NORTHERN HEMISPHERE SEE DIFFERENT CONSTELLATIONS THAN PEOPLE IN THE SOUTHERN HEMISPHERE SEE?

These constellations remain constant, never rising or setting, and they are referred to as circumpolar constellations.

CREATE A CONSTELLATION

TIME:
30 TO 60 MINUTES

CATEGORY:
CREATIVE WRITING, INDOOR/
OUTDOOR, OBSERVATION

MATERIALS
HEADLAMP OR FLASHLIGHT

PENCIL

Ursa Minor

The Little Dipper

TIP

➡ **You may wish to use a stargazing app to help you locate and chart your patterns, but don't let the app dictate the patterns you see. Create a constellation that fits your world view.**

Do you ever look up at night and watch the stars? Do you know any of the constellations in the sky? Have you ever wondered how they were created or who created them? Have you ever made up your own constellations by observing patterns of stars? In this activity, you'll look at the stars in the sky, find a pattern, and sketch it, then make up a name for your new constellation and a story to go with it.

PREP WORK

1. Go outside on a clear night, preferably when the moon is new, so the moon's light won't block your sight.

2. Look up at the stars and observe any patterns you see appearing. Don't try to find existing constellations that you know. Instead, use your imagination to see if new patterns emerge. With the billions of stars in the sky, you'll start to see patterns easily.

3. Imagine how ancient civilizations must have viewed the sky. Ask yourself what they might have seen and what they might have thought about all the stars they saw in the sky.

INSTRUCTIONS

1. After observing the sky for a while, does a particular pattern keep jumping out at you? Can you use your imagination to create a shape from the pattern you see?

2. Turn on the headlamp and use the pencil to sketch the pattern in your journal, noting any particularly large stars in the pattern.

3. Note the location of your pattern in the sky—is it in the south? West? North? East? Use any landmarks to help you remember the location, such as "right above the oak tree in our backyard" or "to the right of the building next door."

4. Go inside and connect your star dots to create your shape if you haven't already. Create a name for your constellation—perhaps it reminds you of your dog? Or maybe your favorite action figure or superhero?

5. Write a story that explains the name of your constellation.

NATURE JOURNAL ENTRY

In this lesson, you learned how the constellations came to be created by ancient people from all cultures around the world. Reflect on the lesson and activity as you answer these questions in your journal.

1. *Why do you think stargazing was so popular in ancient civilizations?*

2. *What are some of your favorite existing constellations and why?*

3. *How do the constellations in the Southern Hemisphere differ from the ones in the Northern Hemisphere?*

CONCLUSION:

This activity helped you experience how the constellations were created. Ancient people all around the world saw patterns in the stars and named them as reminders of the events, people, animals, or myths in their everyday lives. Though these are official constellations now, we shouldn't stop observing and adjusting these ideas to fit our modern world. The constellations that we know today were named hundreds of years ago (or longer) to share ideas and events of the time.

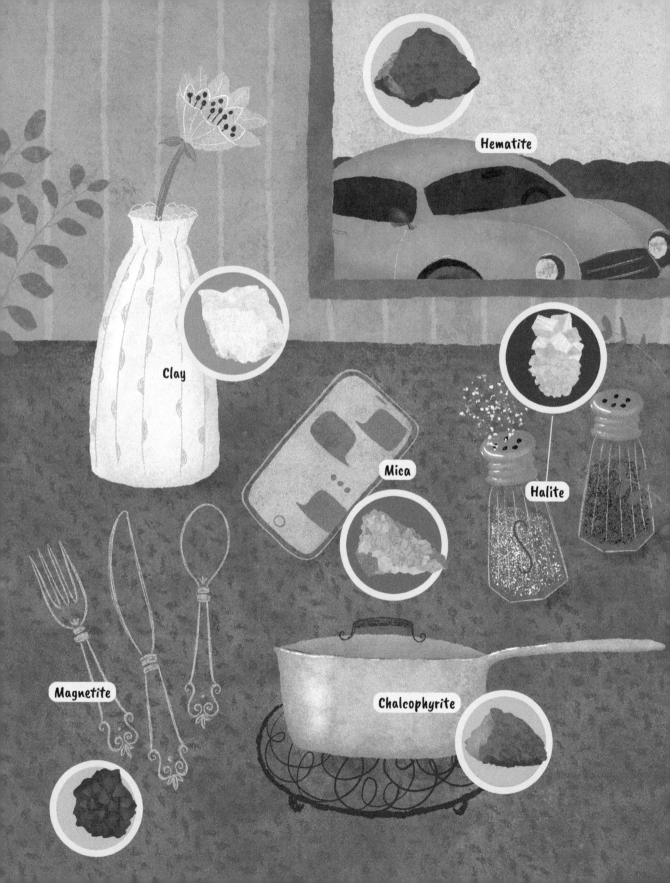

THE GROUND
BENEATH US

2

I n chapter 1, we explored the atmosphere and beyond. Now, let's come down to Earth and investigate what our great planet is made of and how it ticks.

We'll start by exploring the difference between rotation and revolution and how they affect our sunlight and weather. Then we'll go deeper into the core of Earth to find out what it's made of. Next, we'll explore the crust, or top layer of Earth, and all the rocks and minerals found there. Some of these really old rocks form fossils, and we'll study how they are made and what they can tell us about the past. Finally, we'll explore the different types of landscapes that make up our beautiful Earth and break them down into different types of landforms.

HOW THE WORLD SPINS

Earth is always spinning—or rotating—around its own axis in a counterclockwise motion. The axis is an invisible line that goes through the center of Earth, through the north and south poles. If you were to observe the spin of Earth, you would notice that Earth's axis is not straight up and down but tilted, which is known as the axial tilt.

Billions of years ago, Earth did spin around on an axis that was straight up and down; however, another planet collided with Earth and left a dent in it. That planet fell into orbit around Earth and became our moon. The old axis line is called the obliquity line and it runs perpendicular to the orbital, or equator line. See the illustration on page 27.

As you learned in chapter 1, Earth takes 24 hours to complete one rotation on its axis. One rotation equals one day. We can't feel Earth move because it is such a large object compared with us, but in reality, it is rotating at almost 67,000 miles per hour! That's about 120 times faster than the average commercial jet flies.

In addition to rotating around on its own axis, Earth also revolves around the sun. Some people refer to the Earth's movement around the sun as a *rotation*, but it is actually a *revolution*, which means "to go around an object." It takes Earth 365.25 days to make one complete revolution around the sun. The location of Earth in its revolution around the sun creates our equinoxes and solstices (see page 6).

Fun Fact

DID YOU EVER WONDER WHERE LEAP YEAR COMES FROM?

Because it takes one-quarter of a day to complete our annual revolution around the sun, every four years we use the equivalent of an entire extra day to revolve around the sun. To account for it, we add that day—February 29—to our calendar once every four years and call it a "leap year."

THE DIFFERENCE BETWEEN NIGHT AND DAY

TIME:
15 TO 20 MINUTES

CATEGORY:
EXPERIMENT,
INDOOR, OBSERVATION

MATERIALS
GLOBE

DARKENED ROOM

FLASHLIGHT

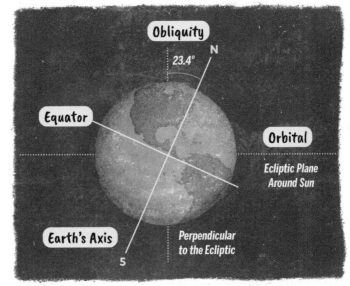

TIP

➡ You might find it helpful to have someone hold the flashlight and spin the globe for you, so you can more fully observe the day and night reflections from the flashlight on the globe.

Have you ever wondered how night and day happens? Or why we experience day while people living on the other side of Earth experience night? Or why there are different time zones all around the world? In this activity, you'll create a model of Earth spinning to understand how night and day are created and why only half of Earth experiences day at one time.

PREP WORK

1. Set the globe on a table or other flat surface, so you can easily spin it with one hand while holding the flashlight with the other.

2. Close the blinds or curtains, and turn off any lights to darken the room, so you can better observe where the light falls.

ACTIVITY

INSTRUCTIONS

1. Think about Earth's rotation and observe the globe. Why does the sun first appear in the east and set in the west? What do you think will happen when you shine the flashlight on the globe?

2. Imagine the flashlight as the sun, shining onto Earth from one side. Turn on the flashlight, and hold it off to the side, pointing it at the center of Earth. At the same time, start spinning Earth in a counterclockwise direction.

3. What's happening with the light from the flashlight? Is the entire globe lighting up or only a portion of it? Though you are spinning your globe much faster than the actual Earth appears to spin, remember that one entire spin equals one day.

CONCLUSION:

You just proved that the sun can only shine on one side of Earth at a time. As Earth spins on its axis, the sun lights half of Earth, creating day, while the other half of Earth faces away from the sun, creating night. People created different time zones, so the sun appears to rise and set at about the same time no matter where you are on Earth. This way, everyone has a regularly scheduled day and night.

NATURE JOURNAL ENTRY

Now that you've learned about Earth's rotation on its axis and how day and night are created, as well as the seasons and the length of a year, reflect on what you've learned. Answer these questions in your journal.

1. Describe what happened in this activity and add a sketch to show how the sun lights only part of Earth at a time.

2. In the morning, which part of your country does the sun appear in first?

3. What would happen if we didn't add an extra day to our calendar every four years?

EARTH'S LAYERS

On Earth's surface, we can easily observe soil, but is the entire planet made of soil—all the way to its center? Actually, soil is only part of one of Earth's four main layers, which include the inner core, outer core, mantle, and crust. Let's take a closer look at Earth's layers, starting at the center of our planet and working outward.

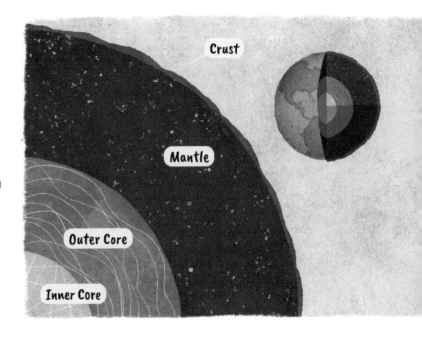

Inner core. The inner core, located in the very center of the earth, is a solid sphere made up of iron, nickel, gold, silver, platinum, palladium, and tungsten. The core is 1,500 miles across, which is roughly the size of half of the United States. Because of the pressure on the inner core, it remains solid even though its temperature can be 10,000 degrees Fahrenheit (more than 10 times hotter than lava) or higher.

Outer core. The outer core is about as thick as the inner core it wraps around. The outer core layer is liquid iron, reaching a temperature of 10,345 degrees Fahrenheit. Being liquid, the outer core spins much faster than Earth spins, which creates Earth's magnetic field.

Mantle. The mantle is split into two parts, the upper and lower. The lower mantle is closest to the outer core and is mostly solid and less dense than the upper mantle. The lower mantle ranges in thickness from 400 to 1,800 miles, and can be up to 7,000 degrees Fahrenheit. The upper mantle is 200 to 250 miles thick, is semi-molten to solid, and has a temperature range of

900 to 1,600 degrees Fahrenheit. The upper mantle contains more iron and magnesium and less silicon than the crust.

Crust. The crust is the thin outer layer of Earth. It ranges from 3.1 to 43.5 miles thick and is mostly made up of silica and aluminum. There are two different types of crust: the continental crust and the oceanic crust. The oceanic crust is found where the oceans are and includes dense rocks made of igneous materials from volcanoes and magnesium. The continental crust creates our continents and is thicker, made from rocks that are full of aluminum, oxygen, and silicon. The oceanic crust covers 60 percent of Earth, and the continental crust covers 40 percent.

The crust and the upper mantle are made up of different pieces, which we call tectonic plates. These plates fit together like puzzle pieces but are all slowly moving at different speeds and in different directions—away from one another, past one another, and sometimes into one another. When they collide, the plates can become locked together, creating what we call a fault line.

Eventually, they build up so much energy from moving that a shock, or seismic, wave occurs. In the ocean, a seismic wave creates a tsunami, a giant tidal wave that can crash onto a continent and cause a lot of destruction. If a seismic wave happens on a continent instead of in the ocean, an earthquake occurs. Movement from the tectonic plates can also cause explosions, volcanos, and landslides.

Tectonic movements are responsible for the formation of mountains, the expansion of the seafloor, and the regulation of temperature.

Fun Fact

DID YOU KNOW THAT THOUSANDS OF EARTHQUAKES OCCUR AROUND THE WORLD EVERY DAY?

Though most of them are so small that only special machines can detect them, these shifts in our tectonic plates are continually reshaping the continents and oceans.

CREATE A 3D EARTH MODEL

TIME:
30 TO 60 MINUTES

CATEGORY:
CRAFTS, INDOOR

MATERIALS
PIECE OF WAX OR
PARCHMENT PAPER

WORK SURFACE

SIX DIFFERENT COLORS OF CLAY:
RED, ORANGE, YELLOW, BROWN,
BLUE, AND GREEN

ROLLING PIN

BUTTER KNIFE

TIP

➤ If you want to hang your model, screw a small eye hook into the top before drying it (for self-hardening clay) or baking it. After your model is dried, you may want to paint it with a clear sealant, such as Mod Podge, to make it shiny.

Scientists observe the layers of Earth using seismic waves. From these observations, scientists have been able to create a model of Earth's layers. You can use your skills of observation to recreate a three-dimensional model of Earth using clay and the information from the lesson.

Safety First: *Be careful when using the knife to cut into your model Earth.*

PREP WORK
1. Gather your supplies and lay the wax paper on top of your work surface.

INSTRUCTIONS
1. Look at the diagram of the layers of Earth on page 29. You will create your model from this illustration.

2. Ask yourself which layers appear to be the thickest and which appear to be the thinnest.

3. Using the orange clay, roll out a ball about 1 inch in diameter. This ball will represent the inner core.

4. Using the rolling pin, roll out the red clay until it's about ½ inch thick. Carefully wrap this layer around the inner core, smoothing it out until the inner core is completely covered. This layer represents the molten layer of the outer core.

5. Next, roll out the yellow clay to a ¼- to ½-inch thickness. This layer represents the lower mantle, which varies in thickness. Wrap this layer over the outer core

and carefully smooth it in place, being careful not to squish the emerging Earth you are creating.

6. Roll out the brown clay until it's about ¼ inch thick. This layer represents the upper mantle. Apply it as you did the lower mantle.

7. You are almost finished! Roll out a thin layer of blue, just enough to cover the entire upper mantle. Once you've applied this layer to your Earth, roll out some green pieces, and use your imagination to create the continents on Earth.

8. Once you've created your Earth, it's time to cut into it, so you can see all the layers! Carefully use the butter knife to slice from top to bottom, halfway into Earth.

9. To reveal Earth's layers, repeat this cut a few inches to the right to cut about one-quarter of your Earth.

CONCLUSION:

You demonstrated that Earth is made up of four layers. These layers can be solid or liquid depending on the temperature and presence of pressure. Scientists learned about these layers using seismic waves to record the types of materials each area of Earth contained. By using this information, you were able recreate your own model of the layers of Earth.

NATURE JOURNAL ENTRY

You just learned all about the layers of Earth and the seismic activity in Earth's crust and upper mantle. Now it's time to reflect on what you've learned. Answer these questions in your journal.

1. *Why do you think it's impossible to dig through all the layers of Earth?*

2. *Although explorers have been able to map out most of the continents by physically exploring the continental crust, the greatest depths of the oceanic crust have not been so easy to explore. How do you think scientists are helping explorers to learn about the shape of the oceanic crust?*

Igneous

Sedimentary

Metamorphic

ROCKS AND MINERALS

Earth's crust contains many types of rocks and minerals. Rocks and minerals are *inorganic*, which means they don't come from plants or animals. They are also *natural objects*, which means they come from Earth and are not man-made.

Do you know the names of some of these rocks and minerals? Take a moment to think of all the ones you can name and write them down in your journal.

Minerals are made of the same chemicals and have the same structure the whole way through. Minerals can be found in all kinds of materials, including inside of our own bodies. One familiar example of a mineral is salt. There are four different classes of minerals: carbonates, oxides, silicates, and sulfides. Let's take a closer look.

Carbonates. Carbonates make up a small percentage of Earth's crust and are composed of a combination of calcium and carbon, called calcite. Carbonates are found in all three types of rocks.

Oxides. Oxides make up a small percentage of Earth's crust and are created with oxygen and another chemical element. Oxygen and iron combine to make magnetite, which can be found in 3 percent of Earth's crust.

Silicates. Silicates make up the largest percentage of Earth's crust and contain a combination of silicon with other chemical elements. The two most common types of silicate minerals are quartz, which contains silicon and oxygen and makes up 12 percent of the crust, and feldspar, which contains minerals such as aluminum, calcium, sodium, and silicon, and makes up about 51 percent of Earth's crust.

Sulfides. Usually metallic in appearance, sulfides make up a small percentage of Earth's crust and contain many valuable minerals such as silver, zinc, lead, copper, and iron.

Minerals and rocks are similar and can be hard to tell apart. The main difference is that rocks are made from two or more minerals clumped together. Rocks can be all kinds of textures, from hard to soft. Three types of rocks that are found in Earth's crust: igneous, metamorphic, and sedimentary. Let's take a closer look.

Igneous. Igneous rocks are created when the magma from an erupted volcano solidifies. When the magma cools, rocks and minerals form. Most igneous rocks contain silicate minerals and some sulfide minerals. Granite is an example of a common igneous rock.

Metamorphic. Extreme conditions, including high temperatures and lots of pressure over time, can transform igneous and sedimentary rocks into metamorphic rocks. Some common metamorphic rocks are marble, quartzite, and slate.

Sedimentary. When igneous rocks are weathered over time by water, pressure, wind, and heat, their chemical composition changes, and sedimentary rocks form. As igneous rocks are weathered down into smaller particles, they are carried away by water sources, such as glaciers and rivers, or by the wind until they settle and build up. As these small particles of rock become compacted, they harden and become sedimentary rock over long periods. Common sedimentary rocks include limestone, coal, and sandstone.

Fun Fact

DID YOU KNOW THAT ROCKS AND MINERALS ARE PART OF YOUR EVERYDAY LIFE?

You will most likely use more than three million pounds of rocks and minerals in your lifetime!

Both rocks and minerals have been mined for use in everything from building materials, pavers, watches, computers, and cell phones to dietary supplements, sandpaper, paint, and matches. Can you think of any materials in your home that are made from rocks and minerals?

MAKING PAINT FROM ROCKS AND CLAY

TIME:
1 TO 2 HOURS

CATEGORY:
CRAFTS, INDOOR/OUTDOOR

MATERIALS
SOFT ROCKS IN A VARIETY OF COLORS (AS MANY AS YOU'D LIKE)

OLD PILLOWCASE

HAMMER

SAFETY GOGGLES

SOIL AND CLAY IN DIFFERENT COLORS (AS MANY AS YOU'D LIKE)

STONE MORTAR AND PESTLE

SMALL METAL MESH STRAINER

JARS OR OTHER CONTAINERS (ENOUGH TO MIX PIGMENTS AND STORE DRIED PIGMENTS)

POWDERED GUM ARABIC

WARM WATER

Many of our paints today, including water and oil paints, are made with natural pigments from the earth. You can create your own palette of natural pigment paints from the rocks and soil that are all around you. If you have access to a natural stream, you will most likely find clay and soft rocks along its banks. You can use both to make paint.

Safety First: Be careful when smashing rocks with a hammer as the fragments tend to fly all around. Wear safety glasses and have an adult help.

PREP WORK

1. You will need to conduct two tests with your rocks to make sure they are suited for making into paints. The first test is to use your rocks to draw on the sidewalk or on another larger rock. If your rock leaves a mark, it will likely make a great paint.

2. Next, you want to test out your rocks to make sure they are soft enough to use. Place them one at a time in the pillowcase, and using your hammer and wearing your safety goggles, carefully give them a good whack. If they break, they are good for making pigments. If they do not break, they are most likely too hard to grind down.

3. If you've collected soil or clay, it most likely has water in it. Set it outside in the sun to dry out.

4. Sort your rocks and soils by color. If you have more than one of the same color, keep those together.

Ask yourself what colors you think they'll make. Imagine what each paint color could be used for.

5. Wearing your safety goggles, place a rock in the stone mortar, and use the pestle to start grinding your rocks into a fine powder. The finer the powder, the smoother your pigments will be. If you have more than one rock of the same color, only grind one at a time.

6. Place the mesh strainer over one of the jars and pour your powder into the strainer. Shake the powder through the strainer and return the larger particles to the mortar and pestle.

7. Continue to grind the larger particles into a powder, then strain it into the jar.

8. Repeat this process until you have ground down all the rocks, soil, and clay that you'd like. Be sure to pour each new color into a new jar.

9. Label each jar with the rock, soil, or clay you used. In your journal, make a list of the materials you used, where you found them, and the color they produced. To keep an even better record, you may find it helpful to add drawings or photographs of your materials.

INSTRUCTIONS

1. To make paint, you will need a bit of your pigment and a binder, something you add to the pigment to help it stick together. It will also help your paint stick to the surface of the thing you're painting. Many ingredients, including egg whites, honey, and oil or animal fat can make great binders. For this activity, you will use gum Arabic, which is made from the sap of a tree.

TIPS

→ You might want to leave one rock intact to place in each jar to help you better identify each color.

→ Paint a dab of color onto the jar label of your paint and your powdered pigment, so you will know which color each pigment makes when used.

2. Place ¼ teaspoon of gum Arabic into a clean jar. Add ¾ teaspoon of warm water to the powder and stir to dissolve.

3. Add ¼ teaspoon of your chosen pigment to the jar and stir to combine. You may need to add more pigment; play around with the texture until it's thick enough.

4. Paint a swatch of the color in your journal, making a note of the type of binder you used.

5. Repeat this step with any other pigments you want to use, all in separate jars. Your paints are ready to use! What will you paint with them?

6. Store your paints in sealed jars.

CONCLUSION:
Many rocks and minerals exist on Earth, and many of them are used in your everyday life, often in ways you don't realize. In this activity, you learned that paint is one of these uses. By grinding down rocks into a powder, you were able to create pigments that could be added to a binder to make paint.

NATURE JOURNAL ENTRY

You've gotten a glimpse at how much we incorporate rocks and minerals into our everyday lives. Now it's time to reflect on what you've learned. Answer these questions in your journal.

1. What are some items in your home that you didn't realize were made from minerals?

2. What are some items you did realize were made from minerals?

3. When you made your paint pigments, were there any colors that surprised you once you made your paints? If so, why?

FOSSILS

Do you know what a fossil is and why they are so important? Have you ever found a fossil when exploring outdoors? Fossils are the remnants of plants and animals from long ago that became trapped in the earth. When these remnants are trapped under layers of sediment, fossils are made. Over long periods, the sediments harden and create an imprint of the plant or animal that was there. After millions of years, as sediments settle and shift, these fossils may become exposed.

Often explorers, called archeologists, dig them up when they explore a location. Fossils are similar to the nature journal you are keeping—they are records, documenting life that lived millions of years before we did. Fossils can tell us many things, including the age of the stone in which the plant or animal was trapped, the evolution of a species, and the climate that existed when the plant or animal lived.

Fun Fact

DID YOU KNOW THAT ONLY
THE HARD TISSUE OF
PLANTS AND ANIMALS CAN
BECOME FOSSILIZED?

The soft parts rot away
long before the process
takes place.

MAKE YOUR OWN FOSSIL

TIME:
1 TO 2 HOURS

CATEGORY:
CRAFTS, INDOOR

MATERIALS
SILICONE CUPCAKE LINERS AND PLASTIC WRAP OR ALUMINUM FOIL

PLAY-DOH OR OTHER SOFT MODELING CLAY

VARIETY OF NATURAL OBJECTS (AS MANY AS YOU'D LIKE)

PLASTER OF PARIS

PLASTIC CONTAINER, SUCH AS AN OLD YOGURT CONTAINER

SPOON

TIPS

→ Use the spoon to smooth the plaster of Paris you poured into the molds. Your fossils will sit on a surface once removed.

→ You can also press plastic versions of insects or other creatures into the Play-Doh to create your fossils.

A real fossil cannot be made in a single afternoon, but you can make a replica of a fossil to get an idea of how they are formed and to see what they look like. In part one of this activity, you'll make a simple mold, and in part two, you'll use it to create a fossil. You'll want to gather a variety of objects to create your fossils. Some things that would make great fossils include pinecones, acorns, shells, leaves, flowers such as echinacea or daisies, bones, nutshells, seeds, and sticks.

Safety First: *Have an adult help you mix the plaster of Paris and be careful not to breathe in the powder.*

PREP WORK

1. If you're using silicone cupcake liners, line each cup with plastic wrap. If you're using aluminum foil, tear off a square for each object you're fossilizing and form the square into a circular dish. These will be your fossil containers.

2. Line the bottom of the prepared containers with a piece of Play-Doh that's about ½ inch thick.

INSTRUCTIONS

1. Observe your natural objects. Where did each one come from? List the objects you are using and where they came from in your journal. Imagine what kind of fossils your objects will make.

2. Press one object into the Play-Doh in each container, making sure the most textured side of the object is pressed into the Play-Doh.

3. Carefully remove all the objects, and set the containers aside.

4. Mindfully mix the plaster of Paris in the plastic container according to the instructions on the package.

5. Using the spoon, transfer the plaster of Paris into each container, being sure to get into all the cracks and crevices of the Play-Doh molds without damaging the impressions.

6. Let the plaster sit until it is completely dried, about 1 hour. While the plaster's drying, make a sketch of each object you are fossilizing.

7. Once the plaster is dried, carefully pull away the containers and Play-Doh from the plaster of Paris. You should have detailed fossils of your objects!

CONCLUSION:

Millions of years ago, plants and animals became fossilized when they died and their remains were buried by sediment. Their soft tissue rotted away, but their hard tissue didn't and was replaced by minerals in the sediment over time. In this activity, plaster of Paris mimicked sediment in a sped-up version of fossilization, helping you get a glimpse of how fossils are made.

NATURE JOURNAL ENTRY

Fossils teach scientists about the history of the world. You just made your own fossils that you can study just like a scientist. Now it's time to reflect on what you've learned. Answer these questions in your journal.

1. *Would you like to be an archeologist and go on digs to explore and discover fossils? Why or why not?*

2. *Why do you think it's important that scientists study fossils?*

LANDFORMS AND LANDSCAPES

The crust of our Earth is made up of many peaks and valleys, which we call landforms. Landforms are key features of our landscapes, and they can be found on continents and in the ocean. They are formed by natural forces, such as tectonic movement and erosion. Let's take a closer look at some common landforms.

Some landforms create various kinds of peaks, including the following:

Cliffs, the faces of rock that are sheer, overhanging, or vertical

Hills, rolling in appearance and smaller in height than mountains

Mid-ocean ridges, undersea mountain ranges

Mountains, areas of land that are elevated, often abruptly

Plateaus, high, flat surfaces

Ridges, the steep edges of hills or mountains that are continuous, long, and narrow

Volcanoes, openings in Earth's crust that can expel steam, gas, ashes, and even lava

Some landforms create various kinds of valleys, including the following:

Basins, areas of land that are lower than the surrounding land

Box canyons with walls on three sides

Canyons, deep cracks into earth with walls rising up on both sides

Gullies, eroded landforms caused by running water

Ocean basins that are under seawater

Ravines, narrow canyons created by bank erosion

Valleys, also known as dales, low spots between two higher land masses

Landscape is a word we use to describe all the visible features of the land that surrounds us, including features, landforms, and plants. A desert is a type of natural landscape, whereas a city skyline is a type of a man-made landscape.

Over time, both landforms and landscapes can change. Weather such as ice, rain, and wind can cause changes, as can changes in trees and plants, and the building or destruction of man-made features. Many changes to landforms are gradual, becoming noticeable only after several years to several thousands years.

Fun Fact

DID YOU KNOW THAT ANTARCTICA IS A DESERT?

A desert is any area that receives very little precipitation, so even though Antarctica has a lot of snow, ice, and oceanwater, it receives little rain, making it a "cold desert."

CREATE YOUR OWN MINI LANDSCAPE

TIME:
1 OR MORE HOURS

CATEGORY:
CRAFTS, OUTDOOR

MATERIALS

COLLECTION OF NATURAL MATERIALS, SUCH AS STICKS, MOSS, CLAY OR OTHER SOIL, ROCKS, SHELLS, ACORNS, ETC.

AREA TO BUILD YOUR LANDSCAPE

GARDEN HAND TOOLS, SUCH AS A TROWEL

BUCKET, FOR MIXING

WATER

TIP

➡ Try creating a landscape in a large shallow flowerpot on a balcony or tabletop. The same principles apply, just scale them down to fit the area you have to work in. Gather materials from a friend's house, nearby park, conservation area, or other wild space. Be sure to get permission first!

Are you drawn to a particular landscape? If you live on the plains, perhaps you wish you could see the mountains occasionally. Or maybe you live in the mountains and like how the desert looks, complete with sand and cacti. In this activity, create your dream landscape in a cozy spot in your backyard (or the yard of a friend or family member) using natural materials you can find outside along with easy-to-find materials like sand and gravel.

PREP WORK

1. Scout out an area that would make a great backdrop for your landscape scene. Roots of a tree often create little pockets that are perfect for building mountains with waterfalls. Fallen tree logs work well, too.

2. Decide what kind of landscape you want to build. Observe the shape of the location and the materials you have gathered.

3. Ask yourself what type of landscape you could create with the materials you have on hand. Do you need any additional materials, such as sand or gravel?

INSTRUCTIONS

1. Using the garden hand tools, scrape away any debris that will not fit into your landscape.

2. If you want to build up some mountains, hills, or plateaus, add some soil and water to your bucket. Add enough water to make a moldable mud.

3. Place the mud where you want it and begin sculpting it with the garden tools.

4. Continue building your landscape, adding small branches for trees, moss for grass, bits of dried grass, and more to create the landscape you've imagined.

5. Can you build a log house or a fence out of sticks? Vines can often be twisted together to make an archway. Flat rocks make great pavers and pathways.

6. Dig out a stream or lake, or create a canyon in your landscape if you'd like. Continue building your landscape until you're happy with it.

7. When you're finished, document your landscape in your journal: Describe what it looks like, draw a sketch, or paste in a photo. Do any combination of things to detail the landscape in your journal.

CONCLUSION:
You imagined a landscape you wanted to create and explored different ways of creating that landscape. Just as the possibilities are endless in our world's landscapes, so are the possibilities in creating your own version.

NATURE JOURNAL ENTRY

You learned about landforms and how they help form landscapes. Summarize how you created your landscape, and think about what you've learned in this lesson. Answer the following questions in your journal.

1. *Look around where you live. Can you describe the landforms that appear in your own landscape?*

2. *What changes have you noticed in your landscape since you've lived there?*

3. *What landscape did you choose to make for your miniature landscape and why?*

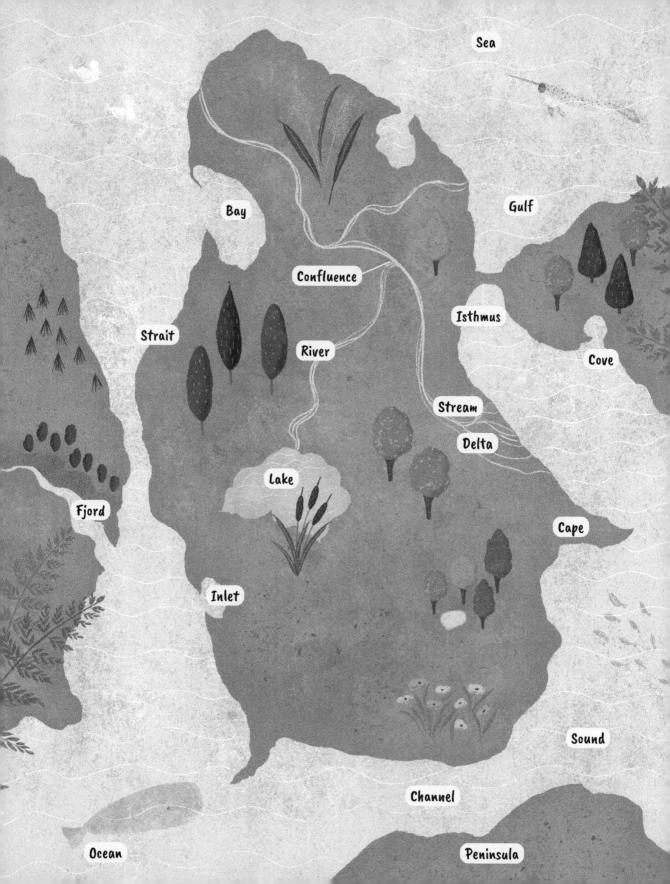

THE WATER THAT SURROUNDS US

When you think of water, what comes to mind? Perhaps a babbling brook that meanders through a nearby park, inviting you to jump in and catch tadpoles. Or the ocean, with its waves breaking on the shore, washing up seashells and seaweed on occasion. Or maybe you picture a serene lake you've boated on with your grandfather, the two of you fishing over the boat's edge.

The following lessons focus on the water that surrounds us on Earth. These four lessons will teach you about the differences between fresh and salt water and about the ecosystems that thrive in both environments. Many of your questions about water will be answered as you work through the lessons and activities.

BODIES OF WATER

When you think of all the bodies of water that exist in the world, you may start to realize that there are many kinds. How many can you think of?

Some bodies of water are fresh water and some are salt water. They can take many forms, including the following:

Bays, coastal bodies of water that are recessed into land and connect to a larger body of water

Bogs, spongey, cold-climate wetlands containing peat and moss

Cataracts, large or high waterfalls

Creeks, small bodies of natural running water that are bigger than streams but smaller than rivers

Lakes, either man-made or natural bodies of water that often fill a basin or other land depression

Marshes, freshwater or saltwater wetlands that support small plants, such as grasses, rushes, and sedges

Oceans, bodies of saltwater that cover much of Earth

Ponds, man-made or natural bodies of water that are smaller than lakes

Rivers, natural bodies of flowing water that run into another river, a lake, or an ocean

Seas, partially or fully landlocked places where the ocean and land meet

Sounds, inlets of seawater that are diverted and protected from the sea by land

Streams, the smallest bodies of natural running water

Swamps, wetlands that can support woody plants, like trees and shrubs

Waterfalls, bodies of water that fall over cliffs to create cascades of water

Explorers used large bodies of water to travel all around the world, so they could explore new lands. Many people who live near the ocean rely on it for their livelihood and main source of food. Water from lakes, seas, and other bodies is continually evaporating into the air, which then becomes rainfall to water the plants on Earth. Our own bodies, which are mostly water, need constant replenishing as well, so water goes toward keeping us, and all other animals on this planet, hydrated.

Bodies of water also create natural borders for landscapes; they frame continents, countries, states, and even cities with their edges. Think about the body of water closest to your home. Does it create a natural border? Perhaps you live next to a river that separates two states or provinces. Or maybe you live near a large lake that creates a border between two countries. Or perhaps you live close to an ocean that separates two continents. Take a moment to describe this body of water in your journal.

Fun Fact

DID YOU KNOW THAT THE MAJORITY OF OUR PLANET IS COVERED IN WATER?

In chapter 2, you learned that oceans cover 60 percent of Earth. When you add in all the other bodies of water, more than 71 percent of Earth is covered in water. That's a lot of water!

BODIES OF WATER OBSERVATION

TIME:
A FEW MINUTES OVER A
COUPLE WEEKS

CATEGORY:
OBSERVATION, OUTDOOR

MATERIALS
LOCAL BODIES OF WATER

TIPS

→ This activity can be an ongoing project for you as you and your family venture around your community. You may want to extend this project six months or a year, picking it back up as you visit new bodies of water.

→ Check Google Maps to view the bodies of water in your community and how they connect to one another for an even better visualization of the waterways in your area.

Do you notice the bodies of water all around you? From mud puddles in your neighborhood to the river you might cross over to get to the next town, bodies of water are everywhere. Think about the sources of these bodies (for example, rainfall creates puddles or a river feeds into a local lake) and how sustainable they are. For instance, will the mud puddle always remain in your neighborhood, or is it seasonal and dependent on regular rainfall? Does the puddle dry up for extended periods? This activity helps you think like a scientist, collect data, and compare the results.

PREP WORK

1. In your journal, make a list of all the bodies of water in your area within a short distance. Have an adult help you brainstorm if you're having trouble remembering them.

2. Make a list in your journal with six columns. Column 1 should be labeled "Body of Water"; column 2, "Location"; column 3, "Source of Water"; column 4, "Sustainability (Year-Round, Seasonal, Precipitation Dependent)"; column 5, "Type of Water (Fresh or Salt)"; and column 6, "Miscellaneous Notes."

INSTRUCTIONS

1. Over the next couple weeks, start charting bodies of water that exist in your area as you visit them.

2. As you visit each one, observe them closely. Ask yourself questions about how they got there (natural or man-made), what the source of their water is (precipitation, overflow, ocean), if they contain water year-round or seasonally, and if they are fresh or salt water.

3. After you've compiled your list, take some time to look it over. Imagine you are in a helicopter flying overhead, can you see how any of these bodies of water are connected? How do they relate to one another (if they do)?

4. How does your community use these bodies of water? Take a few moments to think about the things these bodies of water provide for your community.

CONCLUSION:
You just explored the bodies of water that exist in your landscape and how they are used in your community. Your exploration should have given you an idea of the wide range of bodies of water not only in your landscape but also on Earth. This activity encouraged you to think scientifically about the bodies of water in your area.

NATURE JOURNAL ENTRY

Take a moment to write down what you learned exploring the different bodies of water. Consider the roles of these bodies of water on Earth. Once you've reflected on the activity, answer the following questions in your journal.

1. *Can you think of other ways water is important to us and our Earth?*

2. *How are the bodies of water in your area important to your community?*

3. *What would happen if the water source was removed for one of these bodies?*

4. *Would the other water sources be able to compensate for the missing source?*

FRESH WATER AND SALT WATER

Now that you've explored different bodies of water, let's zoom in a bit closer to learn about the two types of water: fresh water and salt water. Fresh water refers to lakes, rivers, streams, ponds, and rainwater, whereas salt water refers to the oceans and seas. So, how are they different from each other?

There's a clue in their names: Fresh water indicates that the water is fresh, whereas salt water indicates the water has salt. Though both waters do contain salt, there's not enough salt in fresh water to make it salty. You can drink fresh water without any problem, but if you tried to drink salt water, you would become dehydrated.

Where does this salt come from? Scientists believe that some of the salt comes from the fresh water rivers that pour into the ocean and some seeps out from the ocean floor.

Fresh water and salt water also differ in density. Density refers to the weight of the water. It might surprise you, but salt water is heavier than fresh water. If you were to weigh a cup of fresh water and a cup of salt water, the difference in weight would be noticeable.

The amount of salt in water also affects its ability to freeze. Fresh water freezes at 32 degrees Fahrenheit, but salt water must drop to 28.4 degrees Fahrenheit before it will freeze.

There is one more type of water, a mixture of fresh and salt water, called brackish water. Brackish water is found where fresh water meets salt water, such as a river flowing into an ocean. Can you think of any places where brackish water might occur?

Fun Fact

DID YOU KNOW THAT YOU CAN USE SALT WATER TO PRESERVE FOOD?

Although you can't drink salt water, a traditional method of preserving food is by using a brine, or saltwater solution. The salt water is mixed with vegetables such as cucumbers or cabbages to make pickles and sauerkraut.

FRESH WATER VERSUS SALT WATER

TIME:
30 MINUTES

CATEGORY:
EXPERIMENT, INDOOR

MATERIALS
CLEAR GLASSES (2)

WATER (16 OUNCES)

TABLE SALT (5 TABLESPOONS)

EGGS (2)

Have you ever tried to float in a swimming pool but just couldn't, only to go to the ocean and float without a problem? This is because salt water is denser than fresh water, making you more buoyant. In this activity, you will prove that salt water is denser than fresh water using simple household items found in your kitchen.

TIPS

➡ If you have access to ocean water, you can collect it to use in this activity instead of making your own salt water.

➡ If you'd like, you can compare the weight of each glass to determine the difference in weight between the fresh water and the salt water. Which one weighed more?

PREP WORK

1. Set out the glasses and add 8 ounces of water to each glass.

2. In one of the glasses, add the salt and stir until completely dissolved.

ACTIVITY

INSTRUCTIONS

1. What do you think will happen when you add an egg to each glass of water? Will it sink or float? Write down your hypothesis, or guess, for each glass in your journal.

2. Carefully place one egg into the freshwater glass. What happens?

3. Now, place the second egg into the saltwater glass. What happens?

4. Observe the two glasses of water with the eggs. Did the results end up being as you imagined they would?

NATURE JOURNAL ENTRY

You can't drink salt water, but you can float in it. Take some time to reflect on what you've learned, and answer any of the outstanding questions from the lesson and activity in your journal. When you're done, tackle these questions on the differences between fresh water and salt water in your journal.

1. *What happens to salt when it is stirred into a glass of fresh water?*

2. *Why is salt water denser than fresh water?*

3. *Why would an egg in brackish water not float to the top of the glass?*

CONCLUSION:

By adding salt to a glass of fresh water to create salt water, you proved that salt water is denser than fresh water. Just as you learned in the lesson, objects tend to float in water that is denser.

TIP

➡ You can expand this experiment to include brackish water. Fill a third glass with 4 ounces of water and add 2½ tablespoons of table salt, stirring to dissolve. Add an egg; it should float. If it does not, add another ½ tablespoon of salt and stir to dissolve. Once the egg is floating, add 4 ounces of fresh water to the glass. The egg should hover in the middle of the glass.

WATER ECOSYSTEMS

Bodies of both fresh and marine (salt) water contain ecosystems, a community in which living organisms interact with nonliving factors to create an environment that supports life. In most water ecosystems, there are plants, animals, bacteria, and fungi, as well as soil and water. Every organism within the ecosystem has a role in the community, which helps the system to survive and thrive.

Many types of freshwater ecosystems exist, including ponds, lakes, rivers, and streams. Most freshwater ecosystems have three groups that keep them healthy: producers, consumers, and decomposers. Let's take a look at these groups in a freshwater pond.

Producers. A producer changes energy from the sun and nutrients from the environment into food that can be eaten by others in the ecosystem. Producers are the basic source of food that consumers eat. In a freshwater pond, plants (such as duckweed and others) are producers.

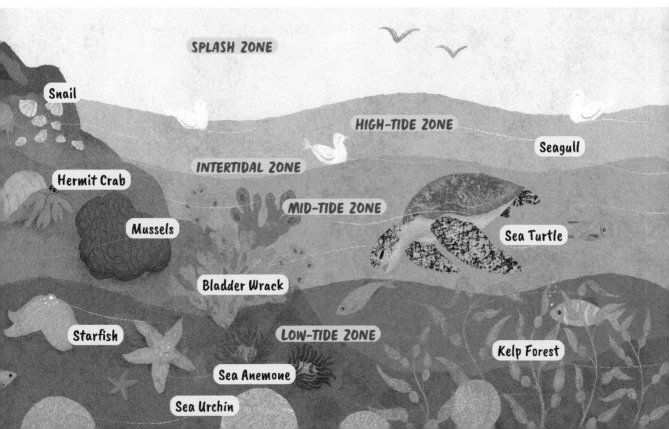

Consumers. A consumer is an animal that feeds on (consumes) smaller animals and plants in the ecosystem. Fish, frogs, and herons are all consumers.

Decomposers. Decomposers help break down (decompose) decaying plants and animals. They release nutrients back into the system for producers to use for energy. Bacteria and fungi are decomposers in a pond ecosystem.

Many types of marine ecosystems exist: marshes, coral reefs, the sea floor, tidal zones, and more. Tidal zone ecosystems exist in the space between low and high tides in the ocean. The three main zones are the splash zone, the intertidal zone (which contains both the high-tide and the mid-tide zones), and the low-tide zone. Let's take a closer look.

Splash zone. The splash zone is the area beyond the high tide. Water from high tide occasionally splashes into this zone, making the area salty, but otherwise the area remains dry. Crabs, snails, barnacles, oysters, green algae, cyanobacteria, and seagulls live in the splash zone.

Intertidal zone. This zone is between the high and low tide zones where the ocean and land meet. It can be a hard zone for organisms to survive in. Waves can disrupt organisms that are attached to rocks and other surfaces. The water temperature can range from extremely hot to extremely cold. Some organisms in this zone are barnacles, limpets, crabs, mussels, shrimp, bladder wrack, toothed wrack, and spiral wrack.

Low-tide zone. The low-tide zone is always submerged in water, unlike the other zones. This area is below the turbulent wave action, offering a refuge for the organisms, including kelp, anemone, sea stars, sponges, sea urchins, and sea cucumbers, that live in this zone.

Fun Fact

DID YOU KNOW THAT MORE THAN HALF OF ALL THE SPECIES ON EARTH ARE FOUND IN MARINE ECOSYSTEMS?

Some one million species live in these watery environments.

BUILD A MINIATURE ECOSYSTEM

TIME:
1 HOUR, PLUS WAITING TIME

CATEGORY:
EXPERIMENT, INDOOR/OUTDOOR

MATERIALS
GLASS CONTAINER, SUCH AS A FISHBOWL OR A GALLON MASON JAR WITH A LID

POND WATER OR FILTERED WATER

MARKER

MUD FROM A LOCAL POND OR A SUBSTRATE FROM AN AQUATIC STORE

SAND

GRAVEL

LEAFY UNDERWATER PLANTS FROM A POND OR STORE (3 TO 4)

LARGE ROCKS (2 TO 3, OPTIONAL)

SNAILS FROM A POND OR AQUATIC STORE (2 TO 3)

CHEESECLOTH, IF USING A FISHBOWL

RUBBER BAND THAT FITS AROUND THE OPENING OF THE FISHBOWL, IF USING A FISHBOWL

TIP

→ Collect materials from only one pond or stream.

Create a water ecosystem that will be self-sustaining for years with some maintenance. Collect your materials from a pond or stream, so you have a ready source of bacteria, though you can start from scratch. If you are starting without a pond or stream source, pay attention to the ecosystem until it can balance itself.

PREP WORK

1. Collect all your materials. Think about the layers in a pond and observe the pond you are collecting your materials from. Write down any details in your journal.

2. Wash the container with soap and water. Let it dry.

3. If you're using filtered water, let it sit out for 2 to 3 days before using, so the chlorine evaporates.

INSTRUCTIONS

1. Use the marker to mark one-quarter of the way up from the bottom of your container to give yourself a guideline for filling.

2. Add the mud or substrate first, filling the area about halfway to your mark.

3. Add a thin layer of sand to cover the mud. The sand will help keep your ecosystem a bit cleaner.

4. Add the gravel to fill the container to your mark.

5. Use your finger to carefully poke holes into the bottom layer and place plants in the holes.

6. Divide the remaining space into three parts. Mark the first part from the top down. This is your water fill line.

7. Carefully pour the water into the container.

8. Once your water reaches the fill line, add your snails! Gently place them at the bottom.

9. If you'd like, add a few larger rocks for decoration.

10. If you're using a fishbowl, secure the cheesecloth over the top of your ecosystem with the rubber band. Otherwise, put the lid on your container.

11. Set your ecosystem in a bright location out of direct sunlight.

12. Monitor your ecosystem. If the plants look unhealthy or the water starts to cloud, move it closer to sunlight. If you start getting algae, you have too much sunlight, so move it away from the light source. Algae can also mean that you need to add more snails.

CONCLUSION:

By creating and maintaining an ecosystem, you observed how an environment needs to maintain a delicate balance to thrive. You proved that a freshwater ecosystem needs producers, consumers, and decomposers to create a healthy system.

TIP

➡ You can combine pond or stream materials with items from an aquatic store. Just be sure to acclimate the animals to your ecosystem.

NATURE JOURNAL ENTRY

Write down your experiences doing this activity in your journal. Even if your ecosystem didn't thrive, valuable lessons can be learned. Answer the following questions to think a bit deeper about water ecosystems.

1. *Was maintaining an ecosystem easier or harder than you thought it would be? Why?*

2. *If you were to create a marine ecosystem, do you think it would be easier or harder to maintain than a freshwater system? Why?*

BIG AND SMALL WATER CREATURES

et's learn about the creatures that live in both freshwater and marine ecosystems.

Among the species that live in freshwater ecosystems are many types of fish, water bugs, and frogs. To live in freshwater, creatures need to spend a lot—or all!—of their time underwater. For fish, that means being able to breathe and move underwater. Instead of lungs, fish have gills that filter water and collect the oxygen before sending the water back into the ecosystem. Fish also have a variety of fins to propel them, keep them upright, and keep them below the surface of the water. Freshwater fish include largemouth bass, bluegill, yellow perch, lake trout, green sunfish, and channel catfish.

Water bugs often skim the surface of the water, but they sometimes live below the surface. Many water bugs have legs. Examples of water bugs include water striders, damselflies, dragonflies, water boatman bugs, mosquito larvae, diving beetles, may fly larvae, and whirligigs.

Frogs are common in freshwater ecosystems. They start their life inside eggs and hatch as fish-like creatures called tadpoles, complete with a fin-like tail and gills. As tadpoles mature through a process called metamorphosis, they lose their tail and develop lungs, so they can live on land. Because they can also breathe through their skin, they can stay underwater for a long time!

Many species of fish, including parrot fish, pipe fish, puffer fish, seahorses, sharks, tuna, and swordfish, live in marine ecosystems. Marine fish are adapted to live in salt water. Most saltwater fish cannot live in fresh water and vice versa.

On the coastline, many species, including crabs, mussels, oysters, limpets, barnacles, and snails live in and out of the water. Like fish, their bodies have adapted to life on water and sand. They have legs for quick movement and shells to protect them from predators. Most of them also have gills, requiring them to spend part of their life in water.

Fun Fact

Jellyfish are not really fish. They have no brain, heart, eyes, or bones, and they shoot a stream of water for propulsion.

RAISE A TADPOLE

TIME:
30 MINUTES, PLUS 3 TO 6 WEEKS
FOR LIFE CYCLE COMPLETION

CATEGORY:
EXPERIMENT, INDOOR

MATERIALS
GLASS CONTAINER, SUCH AS
A FISHBOWL OR A GALLON
MASON JAR

POND WATER OR FILTERED WATER

MARKER

MUD FROM A LOCAL POND OR
A SUBSTRATE

SAND

GRAVEL

LEAFY UNDERWATER PLANTS
FROM A POND OR AQUATIC
STORE (3 TO 4)

CHEESECLOTH (OPTIONAL)

ROCK BIG ENOUGH TO STICK OUT
OF THE WATER

TADPOLES OR FROG OR TOAD
EGGS FROM A POND

MAGNIFYING GLASS

TADPOLE FOOD OR
BOILED SPINACH

Frogs and toads begin their life in the water as tadpoles. As they become adults, they can move onto land, though some prefer to remain in the water. In this activity, you'll raise tadpoles to adulthood.

PREP WORK

1. Set up your habitat in the same manner as the Build a Miniature Ecosystem activity (see page 57), then add the large rock so it sticks out of the water. Don't cover your container with a lid, but if you'd like to keep other creatures out, use the cheesecloth to cover the top. The snails and tadpoles can live together, but you don't need the snails if you don't have them already!

2. Collect the tadpoles from the same source as the water and mud and add them to your habitat.

INSTRUCTIONS

1. Be sure to store your habitat out of direct sunlight.

2. Once your tadpoles are settled in, take time to observe them. Use the magnifying glass to look at them up close. Sketch what they look like in your journal.

3. Add a sketch to your journal of what you imagine they'll look like when they're grown up.

4. Every day, note any changes, and add a new sketch. Try to guess and imagine what type of growth will happen next, then compare your notes with the next stage of development. You might also find it fun to guess when the next stage will happen. Will it be a few days? A few weeks?

Early Stage Tadpoles

Eggs

Late Stage Tadpoles

Adult Frog

5. Be sure to feed your tadpoles with either tadpole food or a few pinches of boiled spinach.

6. Change your water weekly by removing two-thirds of the water and replacing it with either more pond water or filtered water that has been sitting for 2 to 3 days.

7. Once your frogs or toads have matured, release them back into the environment you collected them from.

NATURE JOURNAL ENTRY

You've learned about some of the many creatures that live in freshwater and marine ecosystems. You watched a frog or toad grow from a tadpole into a mature amphibian. Write your thoughts about this experience in your journal. Use these questions to help you think about your experience.

1. *What was the biggest surprise about raising your tadpoles?*

2. *What is your favorite freshwater creature and why?*

3. *What is your favorite marine creature and why?*

CONCLUSION:

Frogs and toads make up a good part of freshwater ecosystems. By raising tadpoles to frogs or toads, you observed their life cycle and watched them grow from a fish-like creature with gills into a mature frog or toad with lungs.

TIPS

➡ Make sure the tadpoles, water, and mud all come from the same pond.

➡ If your water is getting dirty really fast, cut back on the amount of food you're feeding your tadpoles.

➡ If you don't have access to tadpoles or frog or toad eggs, look online for a tadpole kit (see Resources, page 95).

The Anatomy of a
TREE

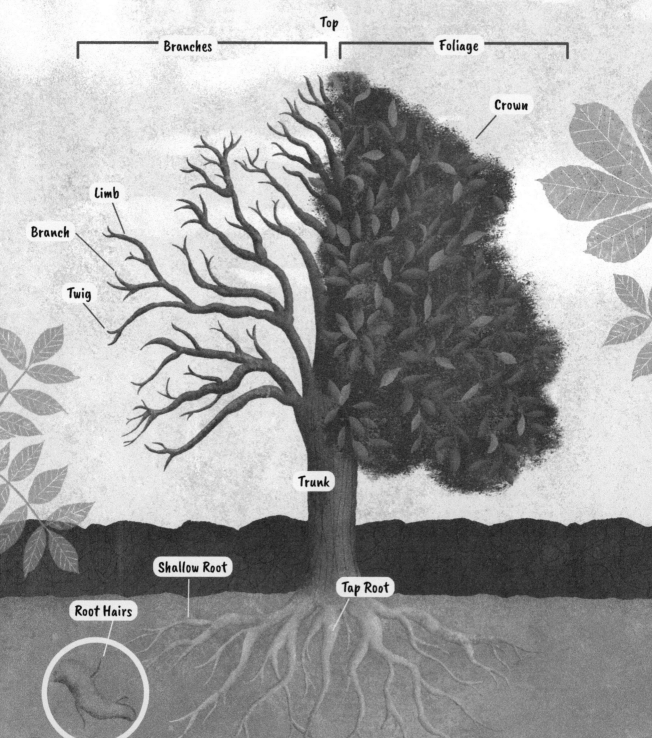

THE PLANTS
IN BETWEEN

Go outside and look around at the plants that grow in your neighborhood. What do you see? When you look up, do you see the tops of trees? At eye level, are there a variety of bushes? What grows down around your feet? At first glance, you may see a lot of green, but when you look closely, you'll notice leaf patterns, color variations, and different textures. Trees, shrubs, flowers, mosses, and even mushrooms dot the landscape around you.

This chapter focuses on the plants that fill the landscapes of our world. You'll learn about the plants that grow on Earth and inspire your inner botanist through a variety of lessons and activities.

4

White Ash Leaves

Horse Chestnut Leaves

White Oak Leaf

TREES AND LEAVES

Can you think of anything better than sitting under a tree, leaning against the trunk, and feeling the bark against your back? When you look up, all you see is a canopy of branches covered in leaves. Trees are the gentle giants of the plant world, providing shelter, lumber, food, medicine, textiles, and erosion control.

Think about the shape of trees. What keeps them standing when they grow so tall and their crowns grow so wide? Let's take a closer look at the anatomy of a tree.

Roots. Underground, a massive root system exists. Roots start out as large taproots, sinking deep into the earth, often as far down as the tree is tall. To support the tree, shallower side roots grow outward to the width of the tree's branches. Tiny root hairs emerge from the tips of the roots, which absorb water and nutrients from the soil.

Trunk. From a tree's roots grows a strong trunk that supports the tree. The trunk is covered with protective bark. The sap, a tree's blood, flows from the roots, up the trunk, and to the branches, bringing nutrients to and from the roots and leaves.

Limbs, branches, and twigs. Limbs emerge from the trunk, which give way to smaller branches that fork out into twigs.

Foliage. Foliage, the leaves of a tree, grows on branches and twigs.

Crown. The top of the tree is called the crown.

There are two main categories of trees: deciduous (often called broadleaf) and conifer (often called evergreen).

Deciduous trees lose their leaves at the end of their growing season (usually in the fall), then resprout them at the beginning of their next growing season (usually in the spring). Leaves are used to collect sunlight, rainwater, and air to help the tree make food.

When temperatures start dropping, trees actively shed their leaves to prepare themselves for cold weather, sealing off their branches from the cold temperatures and dry air. Because winters are generally drier, trees can't get enough water to replace what they lose through their leaves, so they shed their leaves to protect themselves from water loss. This occurs during a drought, too. Deciduous trees include maple, oak, cottonwood, walnut, apple, hawthorn, birch, ash, chesnut, gingko, elm, and aspen.

The word *conifer* means "to bear cones." Unlike deciduous trees, conifers keep their foliage year-round. Instead of broadleaves, conifers have needle-like or scale-like leaves that are designed to prevent water loss, so conifers don't have to shed all their needles in the winter. Conifers do shed some of their leaves, though this process often takes place in the spring.

About 200 species of conifers grow in North America and more than 500 grow worldwide. Some common conifers are juniper, cedar, arborvitae, pine, spruce, fir, cypress, hemlock, larch, and redwood.

Eastern Pine Needles

Douglas Fir Needles

Cottonwood Leaf

You can quickly determine if a tree is a deciduous or conifer by looking at their leaves or needles, but you can also examine the shape and arrangement of their leaves. Conifer trees have a variety of needles that can be round, triangular, or flat, which helps you determine the type of tree. The number of needles in a "bundle," or grouping, can also determine species.

Broadleaf trees have a variety of leaf shapes. If you examine the shape of a tree's leaves, along with its fruits and bark, you can determine different trees easily, though some species can be a bit harder to identify.

The age of a tree is determined by the number of rings that radiate out from the center of the trunk. Unfortunately, a tree has to be cut down to count the number of rings. Each ring on a tree marks a year's worth of growth and reveals its history. Some years, the rings are thicker than others, which provides evidence of droughts, floods, and other weather occurrences in the tree's history.

Ginko Leaf

Elm Leaf

Maple Leaf

Fun Fact

DID YOU KNOW THAT THE BERRIES OF A JUNIPER TREE ARE ACTUALLY TINY CONES?

The scales are fused together, giving the cone a berry-like appearance.

BROADLEAVES VERSUS EVERGREENS

TIME:
ABOUT 30 MINUTES

CATEGORY:
OBSERVATION, OUTDOOR

MATERIALS
AREA THAT HAS A
VARIETY OF TREES

CRAYON

PIECE OF STRING (60 INCHES)

TAPE MEASURE OR RULER

What kinds of trees grow in your backyard or neighborhood? Do you have both deciduous (broadleaf) and conifer (evergreen) trees growing? Why do you think each type is planted? Which kind of habitat does each tree offer to the wildlife in your area? Take a walk around your backyard or neighborhood to see how many of each type of tree grows near you. This activity will help you note the differences between the two types of trees and observe their growing patterns.

PREP WORK

1. Decide the area in which you will observe your trees.

2. Take a look around and estimate which type of tree—evergreen or broadleaf—you see more of based on their leaves.

3. Guess the total number of trees in the area.

INSTRUCTIONS

1. Count how many broadleaf and evergreen trees you can find, keeping a tally of each in your journal.

TIP

➤ If you don't have a lot of trees growing in your neighborhood, look for a local park.

2. Choose three to four broadleaf trees that have different leaf shapes, and use the crayon to do a leaf rubbing in your journal. Place a leaf, bottom-side up, under a sheet of paper, and use the side of the crayon to color over the leaf, leaving the imprint of the leaf on the page.

3. Do the same with some of the needles from the evergreen trees.

4. Compare a sapling (baby tree) to a full-grown tree of the same species. Consider how much the trunk of a tree grows each year, and compare that with the size of each trunk. With the baby sapling, you can probably wrap one hand or both hands around the trunk. With the grown tree, can you touch your hands together when hugging it?

5. After wrapping your hands around a sapling, recreate that same distance by clasping your hands together without the tree between them. Use the string to measure the distance across your hands, then use the tape measure to measure the diameter.

6. Repeat this step with the full-grown tree in mind, measuring the diameter of your arms that surrounded the tree. Compare the size difference.

7. How close were you at guessing which type of trees were more prominent in your area? How about your guess as to how many trees overall are in your area?

CONCLUSION:

Trees come in all shapes and sizes. They create habitats for birds, squirrels, raccoons, insects, and many other creatures. Some trees, such as evergreens, are secure homes for both seasonal and year-round creatures, whereas deciduous trees are better suited for summertime homes. Trees can often be identified by their leaves; however, to determine some trees, you need to examine their twigs, bark, fruits, or seeds.

NATURE JOURNAL ENTRY

You learned about the two classifications of trees, how to determine the age of trees, and why trees are so important to the environment. Reflect on the activity as you answer these questions in your journal.

1. *Did you observe any habitats in the trees?*

2. *What kinds of animals do you think live (or did you see living) in the trees?*

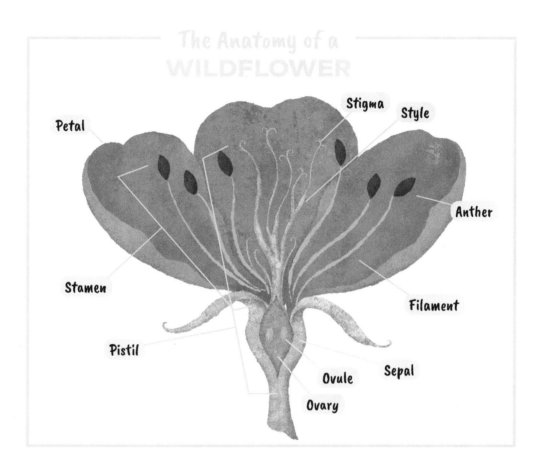

The Anatomy of a
WILDFLOWER

Petal

Stigma Style

Anther

Stamen

Filament

Pistil

Ovule Sepal

Ovary

WILDFLOWERS

The variety of shapes and colors in a field of wildflowers creates a spectacular view. Wildflowers are generally native flowers, meaning they have always grown on the land on which they are found, and they were not introduced to an area from another location, country, or continent.

Wildflowers can vary greatly depending on the location. Wildflowers that grow on prairies, such as Echinacea, chicory, New England aster, goldenrod, ox-eye daisy, and butterfly weed, may not be found in higher altitude alpine meadows. In those locations, you might see lupines, sticky monkey

Sticky Monkey Flower

Lupine

Echinacea

flowers, Indian paintbrush, and arnica. Wood-lands host violets, trillium, jack-in-the-pulpit, and Virginia bluebells.

Most wildflowers have very similar parts. A bisexual flower has both male and female reproductive parts. Some flowers may only have male or female reproductive parts and are known as unisexual. Let's break down those parts further.

Petals. Not all flowers have petals, but most do. The flower's petals are often a vibrant color, which attracts pollinators.

Sepals. Found directly under the petals, sepals may be green or the same color as the flower petals. Sepals often protect flower buds and support the flower when it blooms.

Female reproductive parts (pistil). The female reproductive parts, known collectively as the pistil, are located in the center of the flower. At the base is the ovary, in which the ovule is located. It becomes the fruit. The ovary is attached to a long tube known as a style. There may be one style and ovary or several on a plant. The tip of the style is known as the stigma.

Male reproductive parts (stamen). The male parts generally circle the female parts on a bisexual flower. The stamen is broken into two parts: the filament, which is the stem of the stamen, and the anther, which is found at the top of the filament. The anther holds the pollen.

So why do flowers come in all shapes, sizes, and colors? Botanists, scientists who study plants, have found many reasons for these differences. Some flowers are capable of pollinating by the wind, so they generally do not have showy flowers, because they don't need to attract a pollinator.

Other flowers rely on insects and birds for pollination. As the insects drink the nectar, some of the pollen sticks to their legs. When they walk to another flower, the pollen may fall off, effectively pollinating the flower.

Some plants are tubular, which attracts hummingbirds. Other plants are very small, so only tiny insects can pollinate them. Bees, wasps, flies, ants, butterflies, and moths are some types of pollinators. Can you think of others?

Butterfly Weed

Fun Fact

DID YOU KNOW THAT SOME FLOWERS ONLY POLLINATE WHEN THEY ARE BUZZED BY BEES?

If you've ever heard a bee buzzing on a flower, you've witnessed buzz pollination! The pollen on the anthers of these flowers are only released through the vibration of a bee's buzz.

Violet

Chicory

FLOWER WATERCOLORS

TIME:
10 MINUTES,
PLUS 1 HOUR TO STEEP

CATEGORY:
CRAFTS, INDOOR, OBSERVATION

MATERIALS
VARIETY OF COLORFUL FLOWERS,
SUCH AS PURPLE, RED, ORANGE,
AND YELLOW

CONTAINERS, SUCH AS 4-OUNCE
JELLY JARS (3 FOR EACH FLOWER)

HOT WATER

LEMON JUICE

BAKING SODA

POPSICLE STICKS

WATERCOLOR PAPER

PAINTBRUSH

Vibrant wildflowers are pretty to look at and good to attract insects, but they also make great plant dyes! In this activity, you will collect flowers to turn into watercolor paints, which you'll use to paint a picture.

Safety First: *Be careful when pouring the boiling water.*

PREP WORK

1. Remove the petals from the flowers.

2. Split each type of flower petal into three jars, adding at least 1 tablespoon of petals to each jar.

3. Heat your water on the stove until it's boiling.

INSTRUCTIONS

1. When the water is ready, carefully pour just enough hot water on the flowers to cover them. Let them steep for about 1 hour.

2. While the petals are steeping, use your scientist skills to observe the color changes in the water. Describe the colors in your journal.

3. Now, you can start adding lemon juice (an acid) and baking soda (an alkaline) to some of the paints. What do you think will happen when they are added? Do you think they will change colors or stay the same?

4. Leave the first jar untouched. In the second jar, add a few drops of lemon juice. In the third jar, add a sprinkle of baking soda. Use a Popsicle stick to stir the contents in each jar. What happened? Write your observations in your journal.

5. Now, you can start painting with your colors. First, you'll want to create a test strip for each color. Cut out a small piece of watercolor paper that will fit into your journal. Then dip a paintbrush in each color, one at a time, and paint a small line on the paper. Rinse your brush off between jars. Once you have all the colors painted, note the flower you used and which paints had the lemon juice and baking soda added to them. Add the test paper to your journal for future reference.

6. Finally, you're ready to paint! Use the test strip as a guide to choose your colors when painting your picture. Rinse the paintbrush with water between jars to keep your colors from getting mixed.

NATURE JOURNAL ENTRY

After you've finished recording your watercolor experiences, reflect on the lesson and activity while answering these questions.

1. *When you were steeping the flower petals, did some of the colors surprise you? If so, why?*

2. *Why do you think some flowers attract specific insects while others seem to attract all kinds of insects?*

CONCLUSION:

Wildflowers come in a variety of colors to attract pollinators. Some petals create quite vivid colors, whereas some petals make colors that are more muted.

TIPS

→ If you don't have access to a flower garden, try collecting flowers from a wild spot. Be sure to check your local rules on plant collecting.

→ If you purchase flowers from a florist for this activity, make sure they haven't been dyed. Sometimes florists dye flowers to make them more vibrant.

MORE UNIQUE PLANTS

The Anatomy of a Fern

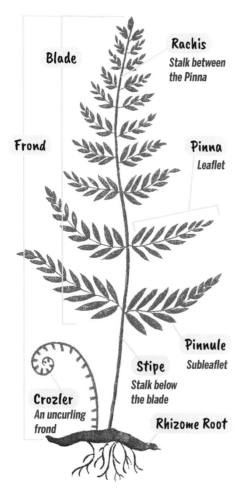

Blade

Rachis
Stalk between the Pinna

Frond

Pinna
Leaflet

Pinnule
Subleaflet

Stipe
Stalk below the blade

Crozier
An uncurling frond

Rhizome Root

Plants like lichens and mushrooms are not actually plants but organisms that are classified in other kingdoms. Before this lesson explores those kingdoms, let's take a look at two plants that are unique but still in the plant kingdom: ferns and mosses.

Ferns. While ferns have stems, roots, leaves, and vascular systems, unlike many plants, ferns reproduce via spores, which are similar to seeds. Ferns prefer moist habitats and lots of shade. They come in all different sizes, from barely an inch high up to 45 feet.

Mosses. Mosses range from about ½ to 20 inches in height. They evolved from algae and lack roots, stems, flowers, and vascular tissue. They can only grow where the air quality is good, and they produce their energy through photosynthesis and reproduce through spores. Mosses need moisture to survive and go dormant during drought. They are often found in shady areas on the ground, in trees, or on rocks.

Now let's take a look at mushrooms and lichens. Though you might hear people refer to them as plants, mushrooms and lichens are really organisms from other kingdoms.

Mushrooms. Mushrooms are in the fungi kingdom. Fungi cell walls are composed of chitin instead of cellulose (as plants are) and lack chlorophyll, so they cannot

Anthocerote Moss

Musci Moss

Hepaticae Moss

Portobello Mushroom

Portobello Mushroom Gills

photosynthesize as plants do. Other fungi include yeast, mold, mildew, and rust. Mushrooms reproduce by spores and grow from mycelium, which is the body of the mushroom. The part of the mushroom you see above ground is the fruit. In nature, mushrooms help decompose dead plant materials and are often found growing on deadfall in the woods. Though some mushrooms are highly toxic, several types of mushrooms are edible and medicinal.

Lichens. Lichens are a symbiosis, or partnership, of a fungus from the Fungi kingdom and an alga from the Protista kingdom, or sometimes a cyanobacterium from the Bacteria kingdom. The three types of lichens are crustose, foliose, and fruticose. To this day, scientists have never seen lichen reproducing! Lichens are used as antibiotics and antibacterials, dyes for clothing, nesting material for birds, and food for animals. They also break down rocky surfaces to prepare the area for trees and grasses to grow, help fertilize soil, and recycle airborne chemicals into the soil to help clean the air. Lichens usually grow on trees, stones, or the ground.

Fun Fact

DID YOU KNOW THAT MORE THAN 120,000 SPECIES OF FUNGI HAVE BEEN IDENTIFIED?

But scientists estimate there may be close to four million species in total!

MUSHROOM SPORE PRINTS

Shiitake Mushroom

TIME:
1 TO 2 HOURS, PLUS TIME TO
ALLOW THE SPORE PRINTS
TO DEVELOP

CATEGORY:
EXPERIMENT, INDOOR/OUTDOOR

MATERIALS
MUSHROOMS (AS MANY AS
YOU WANT)

SHEET OF WAX PAPER

WHITE PAPER

BLACK OR DARK BLUE PAPER

COOKIE SHEETS (2)

HAIR SPRAY (OPTIONAL)

TISSUE PAPER (OPTIONAL)

There are many mushroom look-alikes in nature. Sometimes, the only way to identify a mushroom is through its spore print. In this activity, you will collect some mushrooms that grow around you and create spore prints to see if you can identify the mushrooms. You'll also use Mushroom-Appreciation.com, a website that teaches people how to identify mushrooms.

Safety First: *Never put a wild mushroom in your mouth or put your hands in your mouth after touching a mushroom from the wild, since many are toxic. If you do not feel comfortable handling wild mushrooms, simply buy fresh mushrooms from the grocery store.*

PREP WORK

1. Collect a variety of mushrooms from your yard, local woods, park, or grocery store. You will need two of each kind. Look for fresh species, ideally with gills that are visible under the cap. This indicates they are ready to release their spores. Pored mushrooms will work, too.

2. Place the mushrooms on the wax paper, and organize them by color.

3. Place a piece of white paper on one cookie sheet and a piece of dark blue or black paper on the other cookie sheet.

INSTRUCTIONS

1. Observe all the mushrooms you have gathered. Based on the color of the mushroom, can you guess which mushrooms will have which color spore prints? Spores can range in color from white to cream to gray, brown, or black. Imagine what color each mushroom's spores will be.

2. Do a quick sketch of each mushroom in your journal, and write your guess next to each sketch.

3. Now that you've made your hypotheses, you can test them. Remove the stems from your mushrooms, and place one of each mushroom on the white paper and one of each on the dark paper.

4. Wash your hands.

5. Let your mushrooms sit for a few hours.

6. Peek at your mushrooms. Look for any dark coloration on the white paper or light coloration on the dark paper coming from under the edges of the mushroom caps.

7. After several hours, carefully remove your mushrooms and compare the results with your notes. Note the differences.

8. Head over to the Mushroom Appreciation website (see the Resources section on page 95) to try to identify your mushroom using the physical features of the mushroom and your spore prints. Write down your findings in your journal.

TIPS

➡ Try your hand at growing your own mushrooms. Many mushroom kits are available for purchase online (see the Resources section on page 95).

➡ Color your mushroom sketches, so they look like the actual mushrooms.

Spores of a
Shiitake Mushroom

9. If you'd like to save your spore prints and add them to your journal, you can spray them with the hair spray, which will set them on the paper. For extra protection, lay a piece of tissue paper over the spore print after attaching the prints in your journal.

Chanterelle Mushroom

Spores of a Chanterelle Mushroom

CONCLUSION:

Some plants, like mushrooms, ferns, and mosses, reproduce by spores. You tested that theory by making spore prints of mushrooms. You can use spore prints to help you identify mushrooms.

NATURE JOURNAL ENTRY

Reflect on your activity as you answer these questions in your journal.

1. *In this activity, you had to place mushrooms on both light and dark paper to determine the color of the spores. Why do you think the spores are different colors?*

2. *Do you think spores are more effective or less effective (or the same) at reproduction than flowers, which use pollen to reproduce? Why?*

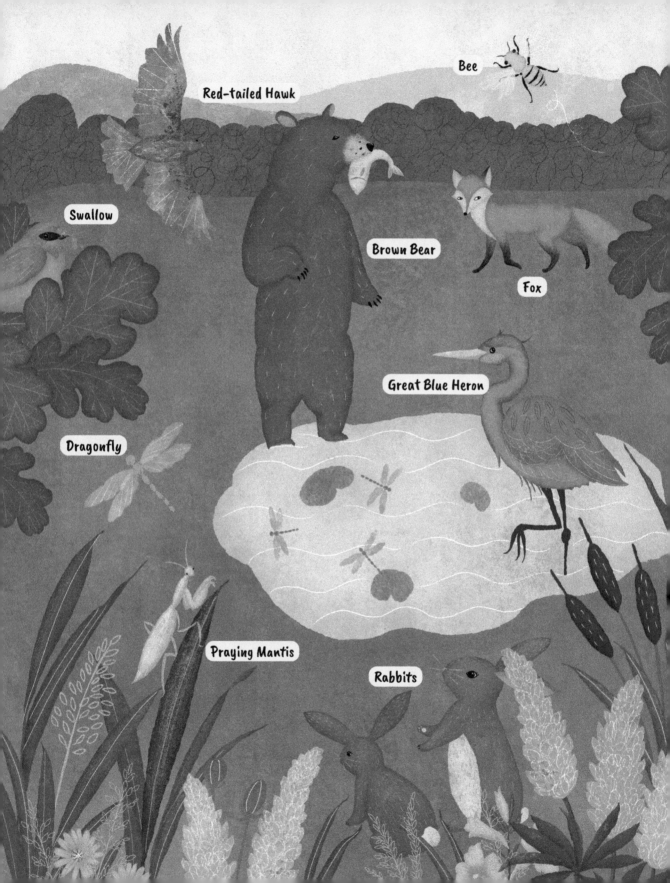

THE CREATURES IN BETWEEN

Some creatures crawl, others hop, and others fly. In both cities and the wilderness, the world is filled with creatures big and small—from the birds that chirp, honk, and chitter, to the insects that buzz, flutter, and crawl, to the creatures that scurry, lumber, or slink.

In this chapter, you will learn all about the organisms that live on land. If you're curious about birds, animals, and insects, this is the chapter for you! You'll learn about a variety of creatures and find answers to your questions about them as you make your way through the lessons and activities.

5

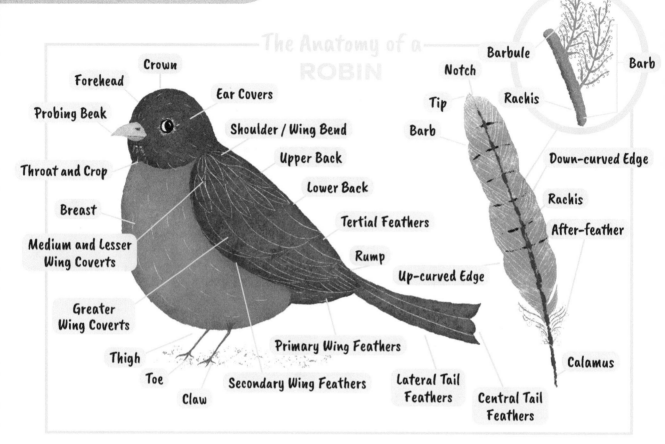

The Anatomy of a
ROBIN

Crown
Forehead
Probing Beak
Throat and Crop
Breast
Medium and Lesser
Wing Coverts
Greater
Wing Coverts
Thigh
Toe
Claw
Ear Covers
Shoulder / Wing Bend
Upper Back
Lower Back
Tertial Feathers
Rump
Primary Wing Feathers
Secondary Wing Feathers
Up-curved Edge
Lateral Tail
Feathers
Central Tail
Feathers

Barbule
Notch
Tip
Barb
Rachis
Barb
Down-curved Edge
Rachis
After-feather
Calamus

BIRDS

Have you ever woken up to the sound of birds singing outside your window? Or spent the afternoon watching birds at the bird feeder? Some are big, such as ostriches and emus, and some are tiny, such as hummingbirds, but all birds have similar characteristics. Let's take a closer look at key parts of their anatomy.

Feathers. Instead of fur, birds are covered with feathers, which help them take flight and remain in the air. Feathers are also designed to help birds shed water, so they stay dry in the rain. Birds have six different types of feathers: flight, contour, semiplume, filoplume, bristle, and down. Feathers can be all kinds of colors, which will help you identify the bird and whether it's a juvenile or male or female.

Wings. Birds have wings, and most species (though not all) use them to fly. After using their legs to thrust themselves into the air, birds flap their wings to lift them up into the sky. From there, the wings, which are cup-shaped, create airfoils that hold air under them to keep the bird suspended while they glide. Penguins, whose wings are better suited for helping them swim through the icy ocean, are one of the few birds that cannot fly. Ostriches, emus, and kiwis are some others that cannot fly. The wing's shape can help you identify the bird.

Hollow bones. Birds' bones are hollow, so they are lightweight. This quality gives birds an advantage when they fly.

Beaks. You can determine what a bird eats by the shape of its beak. Birds that tap into trees to catch insects have long thin beaks, whereas birds who eat seeds have shorter, thicker beaks. The shape of a bird's beak can help you identify them.

There are many types of birds. Let's look at a few groups of birds, and think about what each has in common.

Songbirds. Songbirds belong to the category of birds called Passeriformes, or perching birds. There are more than 5,000 species of songbirds! Birds in this group have developed a syrinx, or song box, which allows them to sing melodious songs. Songbirds include robins, nightingales, warblers, kinglets, sunbirds, skylarks, and sparrows. Even crows are considered songbirds, though most people wouldn't call their song melodious.

Insect-catching Beak
Swallow

Grain-eating Beak
Blue Tit

Nectar-feeding Beak
Ruby-throated Hummingbird

Chiseling Beak
Northern Flicker Woodpecker

Fruit-eating Beak
Toucan

Red-tailed Hawk

Birds of prey. Also called raptors, birds of prey hunt other animals, which are often fairly large in comparison with the bird's own size. Birds of prey have keen eyesight, allowing them to detect food from the sky during flight; they have large talons to grip and kill their prey; and they have curved beaks that easily cut and tear flesh. Not all birds of prey eat live animals. Some, such as vultures and condors, mainly eat dead animals, called carrion. Other birds of prey include hawks, eagles, falcons, ospreys, and kites.

Water birds. Water birds, or waterfowl, are birds that live on or around water. Freshwater birds include ducks, geese, swans, egrets, cranes, and storks. Saltwater birds include seagulls, penguins, pelicans, and puffins.

Great Blue Heron

Fun Fact

DID YOU KNOW THAT CHICKENS ARE CLOSELY RELATED TO TYRANNOSAURUS REX?

Remains of a T. rex found in 2003 provided enough DNA that scientists could determine that chickens, along with ostriches, are the closest related animal to the now extinct dinosaur.

BIRDWATCHING

TIME:
SHORT PERIODS OVER THE
COURSE OF SEVERAL DAYS
OR WEEKS

CATEGORY:
OBSERVATION, OUTDOOR

MATERIALS
BIRD IDENTIFICATION BOOK FOR
YOUR AREA

BINOCULARS

CELL PHONE OR ANOTHER
RECORDING DEVICE (OPTIONAL)

TIPS

➡ If you don't have one, set up a bird feeder in your backyard to attract birds. You can use a general bird feeder or add a few different types, such as a hummingbird feeder and a finch feeder.

➡ Offer a place for birds to bathe and drink water.

What kinds of birds live in your neighborhood? In this activity, you will observe the birds that live in your neighborhood and create a record of them in your journal. The goal of this activity is to try to identify 10 birds that are in your neighborhood.

PREP WORK

1. Set up a chart in your journal that has six columns. Label them "Date Seen," "Bird," "Description," "Location," "Male/Female," and "How Many."

2. Look through your bird identification book to see if any of the birds in the book look familiar to you.

3. Find a quiet spot to sit outdoors where you can observe the birds. You might find it easier to observe birds from your window during extremely hot or cold days, but try to get outside so you can hear their songs, too.

INSTRUCTIONS

1. Observe the birds in your area, and ask yourself if you recognize any of them. You might want to make a preliminary list of birds you expect to see.

2. As you start to observe the birds in your area, make notes on your chart. Can you tell if the bird you are looking at is male or female? A good rule of thumb is that male birds are more colorful than females, which are often drab in color.

3. Use your identification book to help you identify your birds. How many of each type of bird did you see?

4. Optionally, use a cell phone to record their songs, so you can compare the different birds with their songs.

5. Over the course of several days, or even a few weeks, observe the birds in your area and add them to your list. Try to discover at least 10 different types of birds. Can you find more?

Aerial-fishing Beak
Kingfisher

NATURE JOURNAL ENTRY

After learning about the different types of birds that live on this planet, you watched and discovered birds that live in your neighborhood. Think about the birds you observed, look back at your notes, then answer these questions in your journal.

1. *Why do you think male birds are often more colorful than female birds?*

2. *Do you see birds most often in pairs or random groups? Or both?*

3. *Do the bird groups change depending on the type of bird you're watching?*

CONCLUSION:
You observed many different birds. Depending on your neighborhood, you will have seen birds that fit into your location. For instance, in a city, you probably observed a lot of pigeons and sparrows, whereas in a more suburban setting, you probably saw a variety of songbirds. If you're near a body of water, you might have seen ducks, geese, or even swans. Just as you learned in the lesson, many types of birds live in our world.

INSECTS

S cientists estimate that between 2 million and 30 million types of insects are crawling, buzzing, and flying on Earth. Entomologists, scientists who study insects, say that more than 10 quintillion (10,000,000,000,000,000,000) insects roam Earth at any given time. That's a lot of bugs!

An insect has three bodyparts (a head, a thorax, and an abdomen), three sets of legs, and one or two pairs of wings. That description leaves out spiders, which are arachnids.

Let's take a closer look at the three body parts of insects.

Head. The first segment, the head, contains eyes (sometimes more than two), a brain, antennae, and mouthparts, which vary from insect to insect.

Thorax. The middle segment, the thorax, contains the wings and legs and attaches the head to the abdomen. The heart is located here.

Abdomen. The final segment is the abdomen. The genitalia, stomach, and rectum, are located here and often a stinger.

Which insects can be found in your neighborhood? Bees, butterflies, lightning bugs, grasshoppers, cicadas, crickets, flies, ladybugs, ants, praying mantises, mosquitos, and dragonflies are all insects. Though these insects all act differently, they share the same body characteristics.

Insects play many roles. Some help pollinate plants, as you learned in chapter 4 (page 71). Others help keep pest insects in check by eating them. Still others help clean up by feasting on decaying plants and animals.

Fun Fact

DID YOU KNOW THAT ANTS CAN CARRY OBJECTS 50 TIMES THEIR OWN WEIGHT WITH THEIR JAWS?

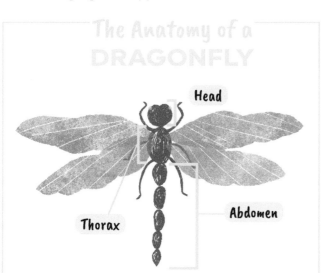

The Anatomy of a DRAGONFLY

Head

Thorax

Abdomen

ANT-TAC-TOE

TIME:
15 TO 30 MINUTES

CATEGORY:
CRAFTS, INDOOR

MATERIALS
RULER

BLACK MARKER

SQUARE OF CARDBOARD
(6-BY-6 INCHES)

NEWSPAPER

SMOOTH FLAT STONES, ABOUT THE
SIZE OF A QUARTER (12)

RED ACRYLIC PAINT

PAINTBRUSH

BLACK ACRYLIC PAINT

MOD PODGE

TIPS

⇒ Use a small canvas bag to store the playing pieces.

⇒ Want to make this game a buzz-tac-toe game? Paint one set of stones as a black bee, and the other set as a yellow honeybee.

Ant-tac-toe is a modified version of tic-tac-toe that helps you remember the body parts of an insect. This activity can be modified to use any insect, but is especially clever using ants, as there are both red and black ants in the world. Can you build an ant before your opponent?

PREP WORK

1. Using the ruler and marker, create a tic-tac-toe grid on the cardboard square. Set it aside.

2. Lay down a piece of newspaper, and divide your stones into two piles of six.

3. Squirt out a bit of red paint next to your first pile. Using the paintbrush, paint two ant heads on two stones, two ant thoraxes on two stones, and two ant abdomens on two stones. Set them aside to dry.

4. Meanwhile, rinse off your paintbrush.

5. Repeat step 3 using the black paint and the remaining six stones.

6. Rinse off the paintbrush.

7. Once the stones are dry, use your paintbrush to coat them in Mod Podge. This will seal the paint onto the stones. Let them dry.

INSTRUCTIONS

1. This game takes two people to play, so challenge someone to play with you!

2. The first player puts down a head on the board. Then it's the second player's turn. They also put down a head on the board.

3. The players continue to rotate, trying to build a complete red or black ant.

4. The player who makes a complete ant wins.

CONCLUSION:
The bodies of ants and other insects have three parts. This game helps you remember the order of the body parts: head, thorax, then abdomen.

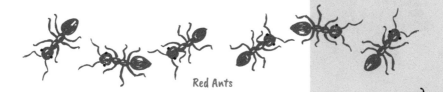

Red Ants

Black Ants

NATURE JOURNAL ENTRY

There's a lot to learn about insects. You learned they have three body parts, three sets of legs, and one or two sets of wings. You also learned they have many roles on Earth. Reflect back on the lesson as you answer these questions in your journal.

1. *Insects are beneficial, even if you think they're just pests. Can you think of any benefits that ants offer?*

2. *What would you do if you could lift objects that weighed 50 times as much as you?*

The Anatomy of a
SKUNK

Mostly black fur with white striping
from back of head to tip of tail

Black and White Bushy Tail

Ear

Eye

Nose

Sensory Whiskers

Each foot has five
toes and claws

Back Paw Print

Front Paw Print

CREATURES INSIDE (AND OUTSIDE) YOUR NEIGHBORHOOD

Not all animals live in wild places. Many animals, such as squirrels, raccoons, and rabbits, have learned to live where people live—in cities and neighborhoods. Perhaps you've seen a few!

Though outside animals are wild, unlike the domesticated animals we keep as pets, many have learned to tolerate people because they are exposed to them every day. Outside creatures often use the spaces that humans have made as their homes. For example, woodchucks often live near gardens for easy access to tasty vegetables. Skunks like to make their homes under porches, and bats often build their homes in chimneys. As natural habitats are destroyed to put up homes and businesses for people, more animals are learning to live with humans.

Many animals you've seen during the day, such as skunks, mice, opossums, raccoons, foxes, coyotes, and bats, are nocturnal—that is, they sleep through the day and are active at night. If you see one of these animals during the day, chances are it's hungry and still looking for a meal. Most of these animals eat smaller animals or eggs, whereas some, such as the bat, feast on insects or eat only plants.

As you venture farther away from urban areas, you may encounter even wilder animals. Depending on your location, there may be marmots, bears, wolves, cougars, elk, moose, deer, bison, antelope, mountain goats, or bighorn sheep. These animals all coexist. In the wild, herbivores (animals that eat plants) might become a meal for carnivores (animals that eat meat), but this creates a balanced habitat. Without this balance, the herbivores would overpopulate the area, eating all the vegetation and destroying the habitat. The herbivores would then get sick when no food is left for them.

Years ago, hunting wolves became illegal in the West. As the wolf population increased, the bison, antelope, and deer populations (which had overpopulated) started to shrink until balance was restored. Today, all these animals cohabitate well.

The same is true if you live in a warmer climate, such as Florida, where alligators, panthers, turtles, manatees, snakes, capybaras, and otters live. When these animals are left alone, they maintain a balanced habitat. Generally, when people get involved and try to control animal populations, wild animals either become destructive or endangered.

Brown Bear

Fox

Fun Fact

DID YOU KNOW THAT OPOSSUMS ARE THE ONLY MARSUPIAL ANIMAL IN NORTH AMERICA?

A marsupial has a pouch to carry its babies.

NEIGHBORHOOD WILDLIFE WATCH

TIME:
SHORT PERIODS OVER
THE COURSE OF SEVERAL
DAYS OR WEEKS

CATEGORY:
OBSERVATION, OUTDOOR

MATERIALS
BINOCULARS (OPTIONAL)

TIP

➡ If you live in a large city, you might be surprised at how many wild animals live in your neighborhood. Keep your eyes peeled and look for wild spaces, such as a local park or vacant lot.

Just how many wild animals live in urban and sub-urban locations may surprise you! Over the next few days or weeks, start tracking any animals you observe. Look for woodchucks hanging out by a busy roadway, or raccoons invading trash cans in the evening. Dusk is a great time to discover many nocturnal animals as they begin to wake up from their day's slumber.

PREP WORK

1. Create a chart in your journal. Make five columns and label them "Date Seen," "Animal," "Description," "Location," and "Notes."

2. Observe your neighborhood and look for wildlife hot spots.

INSTRUCTIONS

1. Start keeping a record of the animals you see. Ask yourself these questions:

- Do they travel alone, or do they travel in a group?

- Are they looking for food? If so, what do they eat?

- Am I seeing the same animal every day or different animals?

2. Over the course of the next several days or few weeks, see if you can notice 5 to 10 different wildlife animals in your neighborhood.

Deer

3. Once you've filled in your chart, think about the animals you saw. Were you surprised at the variety, or lack of, that you saw? Was one type of animal more prevalent than another? If so, why do you think that was?

Rabbit

CONCLUSION:

Many wild animals have learned to adapt to urban and suburban settings as their habitats shrink. By observing and noting the creatures in your neighborhood, you proved that many wildlife animals live in both urban and suburban areas.

TIP

➡ If you're not seeing any animals at dusk, try a different time of day. Dawn is another good time to see wildlife on the move.

NATURE JOURNAL ENTRY

You learned about the habitats of urban and wild animals and how the two groups overlap. You also learned the importance of balance in a habitat to keep it healthy. Think about the creatures that live in your neighborhood and answer these questions.

1. *Based on what you've learned about wild animals in their habitats, why might animals in urban environments still be hungry during the day?*

2. *Have you ever seen a nocturnal animal out during the day? If so, what kind of animal was it and what kind of food do you think it was looking for?*

RESOURCES

BOOKS

The following books are great resources to learn more about the topics in this book.

***Forest School Adventure: Outdoor Skills and Play for Children* (2018).** A great book written by Naomi Walmsley and Dan Westall to further explore the great outdoors with many ideas for crafts and activities.

***Nature Anatomy: The Curious Parts & Pieces of the Natural World* (2015) and *Ocean Anatomy: The Curious Parts & Pieces of the World Under the Sea* (2020).** Julia Rothman has written two great companion books that cover the topics in this book in more detail and include whimsical drawings.

***Play the Forest School Way: Woodland Games, Crafts, and Skills for Adventurous Kids* (2016) and *A Year of Forest School: Outdoor Play and Skill-building Fun for Every Season* (2018).** Written by Peter Houghton and Jane Worroll, these books include additional games and activities to encourage play outdoors.

***Shanleya's Quest: A Botany Adventure for Kids Ages 9 to 99* (2005) and *Shanleya's Quest 2: Botany Adventure at the Fallen Tree* (2020).** These books and card sets by Thomas J. Elpel are great for teaching botany through storytelling and games.

***The Bluest of Blues: Anna Atkins and the First Book of Photographs* (2019).** In this book by Fiona Robinson, learn more about Anna Atkins and her desire to capture the plants all around her. Anna explores and documents her findings while being educated scientifically by her father.

***The Kingfisher Science Encyclopedia* (2017).** Charles Taylor has written a great reference guide to dive deeper into science and natural subjects.

***The Organic Artist for Kids: A DIY Guide to Making Your Own Eco-Friendly Art Supplies from Nature* (2020).** This book by Nick Neddo provides more explorations, crafts, and activities for creating your own art supplies from nature.

***The Usborne Illustrated Dictionary of Science* (2012).** Written by Corinne Stockley, this book is a great reference.

JOURNALS

The following are a few of my favorite journals to use for sketching and writing. Use this list when you're looking for your nature journal.

Crafters Workshop Dylusions Dyan Reaveley's Creative Journal. This 5-by-8-inch journal is a great size for kids. Other sizes are available as well, including a square version. One disadvantage is that it doesn't have dot grids for writing guidance.

Dingbats Earth Dotted Medium A5+ Hardcover Journal. This is a standard journal that has smooth pages and is suitable for pen, colored pencils, and light markers.

Tekukor A5 Hardcover Dot Journal. This journal is great if you like to paint with watercolors. The pages are a bit thicker and can stand up to watercolor paint, marker, and colored pencil.

ONLINE

The following are a few online resources to learn more about the topics in this book and find more activities to do.

Grow-a-Frog. This is a great resource for tadpoles and activity kits. (GrowAFrog.com)

Herbal Roots zine. My website features more than 130 publications that teach children about the medicinal uses of herbs. In addition to downloadable ebooks, there are a variety of online classes that range from 30 days to one year that can be used to teach children about herbs, botany, and drawing. (HerbalRootszine.com)

Museum of Natural and Cultural History. This museum has a great webpage about the rocks and minerals on Earth. (MNCH.UOregon.edu /rocks-and-minerals-everyday-uses)

Mushroom Adventures. If you want to try your hand at growing mushrooms, lots of great kits are available on this website. Choose from portabella, cremini, white button, shiitake, and oyster mushrooms. (MushroomAdventures.com)

Mushroom Appreciation. This website is great to help you learn to identify a variety of mushrooms. Select the "Mushroom Identification" page from the "Categories" pull-down menu to get started. (Mushroom-Appreciation.com)

ACKNOWLEDGMENTS

I'd like to thank my partner, Greg, for agreeing that I stay at home and home-school our two youngest children, which gave me the opportunity to teach fun nature topics to all our children.

I'm also grateful to my parents for raising me on a farm so that nature was a part of my everyday life. Exploring the world around me was as natural as breathing the air and it instilled in me a desire to raise my own children in the same manner.

And I'd like to thank my children for being willing participants in learning about all things natural, while tolerating my geeking out over our many nature finds. A special thanks to my daughter Adelena, the creator of the Ant-Tac-Toe game, which I used with her permission.

ABOUT THE AUTHOR

Kristine Brown, RH (AHG), is a practicing traditional community herbalist who homeschooled two of her children for 11 years. She has taught classes for homeschooled children locally and coordinated numerous kids' camps on herbalism both locally and nationally. She also assists Leslie Alexander, PhD, RH (AHG), with the American Herbalist Guild Symposium's Herbal Activity Hub. Kristine is the writer and illustrator of the online children's publication *Herbal Roots zine*, which has been published since 2009, and the creator of several online courses that teach children about botany, drawing, and herbs. Teaching others about plants and sharing her knowledge with children—our future—is her passion. Kristine lives on a homestead with her partner, their two youngest children, and a variety of cats, dogs, chickens, goats, and a bearded dragon.

CPSIA information can be obtained
at www.ICGtesting.com
Printed in the USA
JSHW011747160821
17842JS00003B/7

OCEAN ANATOMY
ACTIVITIES FOR KIDS
Fun, Hands-On Learning

BY LAURA PETRUSIC
ILLUSTRATED BY KIM MALEK

ROCKRIDGE
PRESS

Copyright © 2021 by Rockridge Press, Emeryville, California

No part of this publication may be reproduced, stored in a retrieval system, or transmitted in any form or by any means, electronic, mechanical, photocopying, recording, scanning, or otherwise, except as permitted under Sections 107 or 108 of the 1976 United States Copyright Act, without the prior written permission of the Publisher. Requests to the Publisher for permission should be addressed to the Permissions Department, Rockridge Press, 6005 Shellmound Street, Suite 175, Emeryville, CA 94608.

Limit of Liability/Disclaimer of Warranty: The Publisher and the author make no representations or warranties with respect to the accuracy or completeness of the contents of this work and specifically disclaim all warranties, including without limitation warranties of fitness for a particular purpose. No warranty may be created or extended by sales or promotional materials. The advice and strategies contained herein may not be suitable for every situation. This work is sold with the understanding that the Publisher is not engaged in rendering medical, legal, or other professional advice or services. If professional assistance is required, the services of a competent professional person should be sought. Neither the Publisher nor the author shall be liable for damages arising herefrom. The fact that an individual, organization, or website is referred to in this work as a citation and/or potential source of further information does not mean that the author or the Publisher endorses the information the individual, organization, or website may provide or recommendations they/it may make. Further, readers should be aware that websites listed in this work may have changed or disappeared between when this work was written and when it is read.

For general information on our other products and services or to obtain technical support, please contact our Customer Care Department within the United States at (866) 744-2665, or outside the United States at (510) 253-0500.

Rockridge Press publishes its books in a variety of electronic and print formats. Some content that appears in print may not be available in electronic books, and vice versa.

TRADEMARKS: Rockridge Press and the Rockridge Press logo are trademarks or registered trademarks of Callisto Media Inc. and/or its affiliates, in the United States and other countries, and may not be used without written permission. All other trademarks are the property of their respective owners. Rockridge Press is not associated with any product or vendor mentioned in this book.

Series Designers: Jane Archer and Karmen Lizzul
Interior and Cover Designer: Jennifer Hsu
Art Producer: Tom Hood
Editor: Laura Apperson
Production Editor: Jenna Dutton
Production Manager: Riley Hoffman

Illustrations © Kim Malek 2021. Author photograph courtesy of Chella Photography.

ISBN: Print 978-1-64876-324-3 | eBook 978-1-64876-325-0
R0

FOR MY CHILDREN,
ADAM, MEGAN, AND BEN—
MY FAVORITE MARINE
SCIENCE EXPLORERS.

CONTENTS

DIVE INTO THE DEEP BLUE SEA

Welcome, future marine scientist! In this book, you will get to act like an explorer and think like a scientist as you learn about the anatomy of the ocean. Ocean explorers and marine scientists follow five basic steps to study the natural world around them. Following these steps provides validity and reliability to their discoveries. Let's explore how scientists have used these skills to learn more about the ocean.

The first step is to **observe**. Marine scientists, like Eugenie Clark, observe what they are studying. Clark was an American ichthyologist, or fish scientist, specializing in shark research. She and her colleagues noticed that sharks avoided a fish called the Moses sole. Her subsequent studies showed that this fish created an effective natural form of shark repellant.

The second step is to **ask** questions. For example, Sylvia Earle, an American oceanographer, wanted to answer the question *What diversity of marine life lies at the bottom of the ocean?* To answer this question, she founded Deep Ocean Engineering, a company that designed a state-of-the-art research submarine that allowed researchers to collect important data about the deep-sea environment.

The third step is to **imagine**. Charles Darwin, a naturalist and geologist famous for his theory of evolution, spent a lot of time documenting organisms in various habitats. His study of marine life focused on coral reef growth. He observed that coral reefs grew upward from deep reef structures around islands. He imagined the land surrounding the reef as slowly sinking over time while the reef continued to grow up toward the surface. This would explain how coral reef *atolls*, or reefs that surround a lagoon, formed from ancient sea volcanoes.

The fourth step is to **test**. Jacques-Yves Cousteau was a French naval officer, filmmaker, author, and researcher. Cousteau and Emile Gagnan, a French engineer, developed the first self-contained underwater breathing apparatus (*scuba*): the Aqua-Lung. Then, Hans Hass, an Austrian marine biologist, redesigned and tested different versions of the Aqua-Lung in order to create the advanced scuba equipment used by divers today.

The fifth step is to **reflect** on the results and ask how the information is important. For example, Rachel Carson, an American biologist, reviewed reports on fish populations for the US Fish and Wildlife Service. By reflecting on her research findings, she was able to write educational articles for the public on the health of the environment and its potential impact on humans.

In completing the lessons and activities in this book, you will build the same skills used by famous ocean explorers and marine scientists: **observing**, **asking**, **imagining**, **testing**, and **reflecting**. These five skills are useful to anyone who studies the natural world.

HOW TO USE THIS BOOK

This book is designed to be easy to navigate. Each of the six chapters explores a topic related to the world's oceans: anatomy of an ocean, fish and marine mammals, coasts and shorelines, coral reefs, the deep sea, and the polar regions. Each chapter contains three to four lessons along with an activity to inspire you to ask questions about the ocean and the life within it. You will be able to imagine the effects of natural ocean systems and test *hypotheses*, or ideas. Reflecting on these activities will help you better understand our ocean world. Let's dive in to see how each chapter is organized.

THE LESSON

There are 20 lessons divided among the six chapters. Each lesson gives you a learning *objective*, or goal. For example, in chapter 1, the lesson about ocean zones helps you understand how sunlight filtration changes with ocean depth. Each lesson asks you to imagine something in the natural world and consider the answers to thought-provoking questions. These questions prepare you for the activity, where you will test what you have learned and write down key observations in your journal, just like a scientist.

THE ACTIVITY

Activities come right after the lessons. Each activity begins with a summary of the learning objective, followed by a list of materials and prep work you'll need to do before starting the activity. Step-by-step instructions will guide you to create, model, simulate, or experiment. Some activities may require extra caution. Adult supervision for activities are indicated with a **Safety First!** warning. You'll also find a section that includes tips and ideas for even more activities.

OCEAN JOURNAL ENTRY

In addition to this book, you're going to need a blank journal where you can write down your ideas, questions, experiment methods, and observations. As you read the lessons and complete the activities, you might draw some data tables, make some drawings, write observations, or make hypotheses.

Most important, your journal is the place for you to reflect on what you've learned and answer the questions in each lesson. There will also be journal prompts after each activity—this is your place to write your thoughts.

What type of journal you use is completely up to you. Just pick out something you like and that inspires you. How you organize it is also your decision. You might want to divide your journal into 20 sections, one for each lesson and activity. Then, you can create subheadings such as "Questions," "Observations," "Hypotheses," and "Journal Prompts." You could also create entries in order with specific dates and headings, such as "Ocean Zones: Journal Prompts." Do what works for you.

Now that you've learned how to use this book, it's time to take the plunge and explore the anatomy of the ocean!

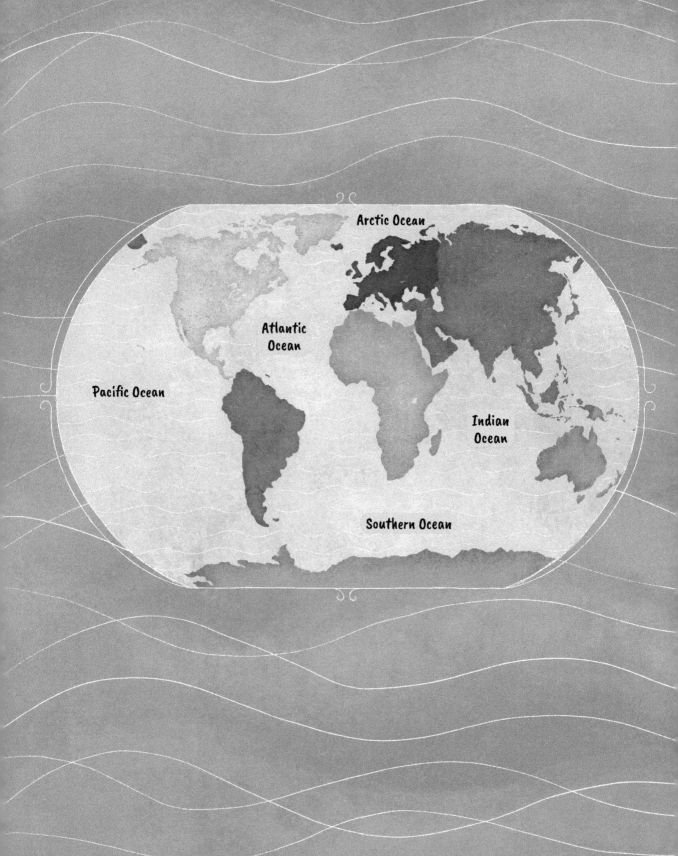

THE ANATOMY OF THE OCEAN

The enormous body of salt water we call the ocean covers 71 percent of the Earth's surface. While our world's oceans are connected, they are divided into five different basins: the Atlantic, the Pacific, the Indian, the Arctic, and the Southern Ocean (Antarctic).

Have you ever wondered what they are made of? Or how deep they are? Or what causes the waves that endlessly crash on the shore? In this chapter, you will dive into the deepest parts of the ocean to learn how it changes from top to bottom, observe how and what moves ocean waters, and explore why the ocean is salty.

OCEAN ZONES

The ocean has five *zones*, or layers: sunlight, or *epipelagic*; twilight, or *mesopelagic*; midnight, or *bathypelagic*; abyss, or *abyssalpelagic*; and the hadal zone, or *hadalpelagic*. Each layer begins at a specific depth below the ocean surface. Light at the surface is quickly filtered out. In fact, no sunlight reaches below 3,280 feet (1,000 m) in the ocean. This leaves most of the ocean cold and dark. Let's explore each layer in more detail.

Sunlight Zone: The sunlight zone, or epipelagic layer, starts at the surface of the ocean and goes down 656 feet (200 m). Most of the organisms of the ocean live in this zone because enough light can penetrate for photosynthesis to take place. *Photosynthesis* is the chemical process that *phytoplankton*, microscopic single-celled, plantlike organisms, use to make energy. There are 5,000 known species of phytoplankton alone, and scientists estimate they make 50 to 85 percent of the world's oxygen from their photosynthesis. The other type of plankton are *zooplankton*, animallike single-celled organisms that feed on phytoplankton. These species form the base of the food chain in most ocean ecosystems.

Twilight Zone: The twilight zone, or mesopelagic layer, begins at a depth of 656 feet (200 m) and goes down to 3,280 feet (1,000 m). The last bit of surface light reaches this layer, but not enough for photosynthesis. Without the sun's energy to warm these waters, temperatures drop quickly. The top of the twilight zone can have temperatures around 70 degrees Fahrenheit (21°C), but the deeper it gets, the temperature quickly drops to about 40 degrees Fahrenheit (4°C).

Midnight Zone: The third layer—the midnight zone, or bathylpelagic—begins just below the twilight zone and reaches a depth of just over 13,000 feet (4,000 m) below sea level, or below the surface of the ocean. The only light in this zone comes from *bioluminescence* created by the creatures living here, meaning they can glow from within. In the ocean, bioluminescence can be seen in animals such as the deep-sea angler fish, which looks like it has a fishing lure attached to its head that glows blue to attract prey (page 76).

Abyssal Zone: The fourth layer, also called the abyssalpelagic zone, reaches down past the midnight zone to almost 20,000 feet (6,000 m) below the surface. Only a few creatures can be found at these depths. One example is a sea pig. A sea pig is not really a pig, but a sea cucumber—an *invertebrate*, or organism without a skeleton, related to sea stars. Sea pigs use their branching tentacles to eat decaying material on the seafloor. Because their skin is poisonous, they have very few predators.

Hadal Zone: The last and deepest layer of the ocean goes down into deep trenches that extend below the seafloor. One of the most abundant organisms at these depths is the amphipod, a soft-shelled crustacean that looks like a flea. As scavengers, they search the trenches for decaying organisms for food.

Fun Fact

The lowest point on Earth is Challenger Deep in the Mariana Trench, at a depth of 35,827 feet (almost 7 miles). You would need to stack more than 1,020 school buses from front to back to reach the bottom!

Sunlight Zone

Twilight Zone

Midnight Zone

Abyssal Zone

Hadal Zone

LAYERS OF LIGHT

TIME:
20 TO 30 MINUTES

CATEGORY:
INDOOR, MODEL

MATERIALS
PENCIL AND STICKY NOTES
(OR PAPER) FOR LABELING

MEASURING CUPS

3 (8-OUNCE) CLEAR PLASTIC CUPS

WATER

RED, BLUE, AND GREEN
FOOD COLORING

SPOON, FOR MIXING

⅛ CUP OF WASHABLE
BLACK PAINT

FLASHLIGHT

TIP:

➡ Wash the spoon in between mixing each cup. This will avoid transferring materials from one "zone" to the next.

What would we be able to see at the bottom of the ocean? Would you need to use a flashlight? In this activity, you will create a model of how light filters through the five layers of the ocean.

PREP WORK

1. Gather all the materials into a place you don't mind getting wet.

2. Label 1 sticky note for each of the following: sunlight, twilight, deep-sea zones (grouping the midnight, abyssal, and hadal zones together).

3. Use the measuring cup to fill each plastic cup with ¾ cup of water.

STEP-BY-STEP INSTRUCTIONS

1. First, create the top layer, the sunlight zone. In one of the prepared plastic cups filled with water, add 1 drop of green food coloring. Gently stir with the spoon until the food coloring is completely mixed. Place the *sunlight* label directly under this cup, with the word facing up, covering the written part of the label completely.

2. Next, add 10 drops of blue food coloring into another prepared cup with water, stirring to mix. Place the *twilight* label under this cup, with the word facing up.

3. The last prepared cup will represent the darkest parts of the ocean, the deep sea. Pour the black paint in the water, stirring to mix completely. Add 5 drops of red food coloring and stir to mix completely. Place the *deep-sea zones* label under this cup, with the words facing up.

4. Observe your cups from the surface. How many labels are you able to read through the top of the water?

5. Place a flashlight on one side of each cup. Observe how much light shines through to the other side. Which zone allows the most light through the cup? Which zone(s) allow the least?

CONCLUSION:

Light is filtered from the layers of ocean water as you descend below the surface. In the deepest parts of the ocean, light can't get through. By observing how the flashlight filters through each cup, you were able to observe how each of these areas of the ocean filter light.

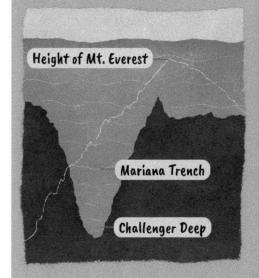

Height of Mt. Everest

Mariana Trench

Challenger Deep

OCEAN JOURNAL ENTRY

Now that you have explored how the ocean changes from top to bottom, let's reflect on how those changes affect life in the ocean. Write the answers to the following questions in your journal.

1. *Photosynthesis cannot occur past the sunlight zone. Where do you think animals in deep waters get their energy?*

2. *Since there is no light in the deepest parts of the ocean, how do animals living there know where they are and where they are going?*

WHY IS THE OCEAN SALTY?

The *salinity*, or how salty something is, of seawater is 35 parts per thousand. That means that if all the salt was taken out of 1,000 buckets of seawater, there would be 35 buckets filled with just salt! If you have ever gone swimming in the ocean, you may have noticed that as you dry off, a layer of salt remains on your skin and hair. When the saltwater from the ocean evaporates, the salt that was dissolved in the ocean water is left behind. It's too heavy to form a gas with the water, so it stays on your skin instead.

To understand where all the salt in the ocean comes from, it's important to learn about the minerals in Earth's *crust*, or the outside layer of the Earth. The crust of the Earth is made up of many different rocks and minerals. One of these minerals is salt. A combination of elements in the water—including sodium, chlorine, magnesium, calcium, potassium, and bromine—form different kinds of mineral salts. The most common salt in the ocean is made of the elements sodium and chlorine, which forms sodium chloride. This is also the same type of salt we use to season our food.

Fun Fact

Many animals that live in the ocean have adaptations to remove the salt from the water they consume. For example, sea turtles get rid of salt through their "tears!"

Thanks to the *water cycle*, the minerals found in the Earth's crust are redistributed into the oceans. Freshwater *precipitation*, like rain or snow, pours over the land and flows into rivers and streams. Along the way, it dissolves the salt in the ground. Eventually, these lakes and streams make their way into the ocean, taking the salt with it. As the ocean water evaporates, it creates clouds, and the salt from the Earth's crust is left behind in the ocean, making it salty. Many of these rain clouds travel to the land and repeat again the process of dissolving salt and bringing it to the ocean.

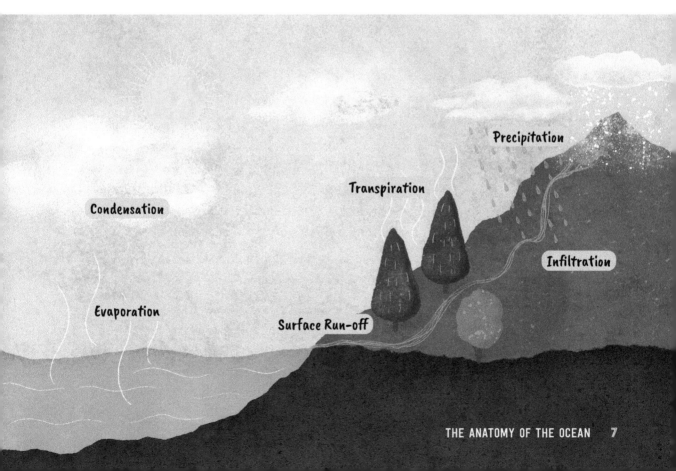

DISSOLVING THE EARTH'S CRUST

TIME:
15 TO 20 MINUTES

CATEGORY:
INDOOR, MODEL

MATERIALS
CLEAR OR WHITE SHALLOW DISH

ROOM TEMPERATURE WATER

SEVERAL ROUND,
RED-AND-WHITE-STRIPED
PEPPERMINT CANDIES

HOT TAP WATER

SPOON

Where does the ocean's salt come from? In this activity, you will model the process of salt dissolving from the Earth's crust, and you will explore the factors that affect the amount of salt that can dissolve in water.

PREP WORK

1. Gather your materials to work in an area you don't mind getting wet.

2. Fill the dish with ½ inch of room temperature water—just enough to cover the bottom of the dish.

> **Safety First!** Be very careful when working with hot water to avoid burns.

STEP-BY-STEP INSTRUCTIONS

1. Gently place one peppermint candy, flat-side down, in the dish. Imagine that the peppermint is the Earth's crust.

2. Allow your peppermint to sit in the water untouched for 1 minute. The peppermint is like a piece of the Earth's crust sitting under a lake or stream. What do you think will happen to the peppermint?

3. After the resting time is over, observe what happened to the peppermint. Record your observations in your journal.

4. Gently slide the peppermint across the bottom of the dish. What do you notice? What happened to the red coloring of the peppermint?

TIP:

➡ If you are having trouble seeing the red peppermint dye in a clear dish, try placing a white piece of paper under your dish.

5. Repeat the experiment using hot tap water. Use a spoon to move the peppermint in the water so you don't burn your hands. What happens to the peppermint? How is this the same or different from your first experiment? Record your observation in your journal.

CONCLUSION:

You have just observed the sugar of a solid peppermint candy dissolve in fresh water, similar to the way rainwater dissolves salt from the Earth's crust. Water seeping into the Earth's crust and flowing into rivers or streams dissolves the salt and eventually carries it to the ocean. Salt then builds up in the ocean as seawater evaporates to form clouds, beginning the process all over again.

OCEAN JOURNAL ENTRY

In this activity, you simulated the creation of salty seawater. Consider your observations from this activity to help you answer the following questions in your journal.

1. *What do you think would happen if you left the peppermint in the water for a few days?*

2. *Do you think there is a limit to how much salt the ocean can hold? Explain why or why not.*

OCEAN CURRENTS

The crashing of waves at the beach is one way we experience the constant motion of the ocean. In this lesson, we will learn where and how the ocean moves, as well as the forces that create this motion.

The movement of ocean water from one location to another is called a *current*. Surface currents are usually caused by wind, though the gravitational pull of the Sun and Moon also play a factor. The strength of wind-driven surface currents depends on the direction, speed, and duration (or time) the wind blows against the surface of the ocean. We experience these surface currents as waves. Waves are energy moving through water toward the shore. The longer, faster, and larger the *fetch*, or the ocean surface area affected, the greater the movement of the water.

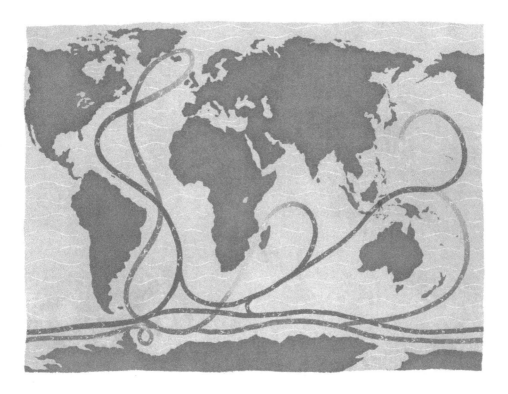

 COLD WATER   HOT WATER

Deep ocean currents are formed by a few more factors, which include the temperature and salinity of the water. Cold salty water tends to sink below warmer fresh water. This sinking creates a slow movement of water from high latitudes near the North and South poles toward the warmer waters near the equator.

The rotation of the Earth also affects the flow of currents. It moves the currents in a circular pattern called the *Coriolis effect*. Because of this effect, currents within each ocean basin move in a clockwise direction toward the North Pole in the northern hemisphere, and, in the southern hemisphere, a counterclockwise direction toward the South Pole. Ocean basins are large, bowl-shaped areas of the Earth that hold the major oceans. At the equator, these surface currents separate and draw cold water from deep currents coming from the poles, warming it at the surface. Surface and deepwater currents carry water all around the globe in a cycle called the *global ocean conveyor belt*. This conveyor belt continuously carries deep, cold water from the North and South poles to the equator and warm surface waters from the equator back to the poles.

Fun Fact

It takes approximately 1,000 years for one drop of water to circle the globe on the global ocean conveyor belt.

CREATING CURRENTS

TIME:
15 TO 20 MINUTES

CATEGORY:
INDOOR, EXPERIMENT

MATERIALS
ROCKS AND GRAVEL

9-BY-13-INCH SHALLOW
METAL PAN

ROOM TEMPERATURE WATER

GROUND BLACK PEPPER

DRINKING STRAW

In this activity, you will observe the effect *landforms* (or features of the Earth), wind direction, and wind duration have on floating materials on the surface of the ocean. You will create a model of an ocean basin and observe how changes made to this model affect how water moves through the basin.

PREP WORK

1. Gather your materials to work in a place you don't mind getting wet.

2. Arrange the rocks and gravel into piles at the edges of the pan, leaving space in the middle. These represent landforms.

3. Fill the pan with water, leaving the top of some of your "landforms" out of the water. This creates a model of an ocean basin.

STEP-BY-STEP INSTRUCTIONS

1. Shake a small amount of black pepper onto the surface of the water. Imagine that this is debris floating on the surface of the ocean.

TIP:

➡ If you can't tell which direction the black pepper is traveling, try adding more pepper, a little at a time, until you notice a pattern forming on the surface of the water.

2. Without touching the surface, blow gently through the straw from one side of the pan. This represents wind blowing over an ocean basin. What happens to the pepper on the surface?

3. Stop blowing through the straw and observe the location of the pepper. How did it change?

4. Begin blowing gently again through the straw in a different area over the pan. How does the position of the pepper change? How is it the same?

5. Repeat the experiment, changing the position and shape of the rocks and gravel. What changed? What stayed the same?

OCEAN JOURNAL ENTRY

In this lesson, you observed the effect that wind has in creating currents across the surface of the ocean. Use your experience from this activity to answer the following questions in your journal.

1. *What effect does wind have on debris gathering on the surface of the ocean?*

2. *If you were to blow over the pan without a straw, what factor would be changing: the speed, direction, area, or duration of wind blowing on the ocean surface?*

3. *Describe some ways you think currents affect marine life.*

CONCLUSION:

You have just created surface currents in a model of an ocean basin. How long, how fast, and from what direction the wind interacts with the surface of the ocean are major factors that determine these ocean currents. The longer you blow in a particular direction, the faster water in the model circles in the basin. The shape of the rocks and gravel, representing landforms, can also change the speed and directions of these currents.

TIDES

When we jump up in the air, the Earth's gravity brings us back down to the ground. *Gravity* is the invisible force created by the Earth that pulls objects toward its surface. The Earth's gravity is so strong that it keeps all of the ocean's water from flowing out into space. Like the Earth, the Moon and the Sun also have gravity. In fact, gravity keeps the Earth in orbit around the Sun, and the Moon in orbit around the Earth.

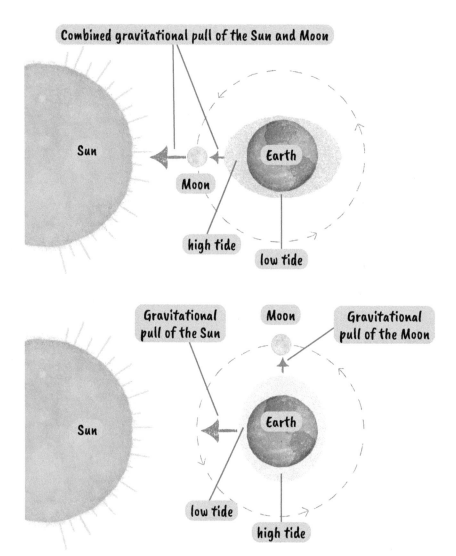

Combined gravitational pull of the Sun and Moon

Sun

Earth

Moon

high tide

low tide

Gravitational pull of the Sun

Moon

Gravitational pull of the Moon

Sun

Earth

low tide

high tide

The changing gravitational pull of the Sun and Moon can be observed in the ocean as *tides*, or the periodic rise and fall of sea level. The gravity from the Sun and Moon cause the sea level to bulge. That bulge follows the Moon and Sun around the globe. The positions of the Sun, Moon, and Earth change in daily, monthly, and yearly cycles. Because we can predict these positions in relationship to one another, we can also predict the position of tides as they change.

The daily rise and fall of the tides is called a *tidal cycle*. Some areas of the globe can experience as many as two high and low tides a day. When the sea level rises to its highest point, it's called *high tide*. When it falls to its lowest point, it's called *low tide*. The *tidal range* is the change in height of sea level from low and high tide. During a full moon and a new moon, tidal ranges are at their greatest, meaning that coastlines will experience the highest high tide and the lowest low tide during those times.

Fun Fact

The Bay of Fundy in Canada is considered to have the largest tidal range in the world. The sea level there can rise and fall up to 53 feet (16.15 m) in just one day!

MOVING WATER WITH THE MOON

TIME:
15 TO 20 MINUTES

CATEGORY:
INDOOR, SIMULATION

MATERIALS
20 PAPER CLIPS

EMPTY PLASTIC WATER BOTTLE

2 LARGE MAGNETS (AT LEAST
½ CM THICK AND 2 CM LONG)

How does the Moon's gravity affect the ocean's sea level? How and why do the tides move? In this activity, you will create a simulation of how the Moon's gravitational pull raises sea level and how it travels around the globe.

PREP WORK
Put the paper clips inside the plastic bottle and seal the bottle.

STEP-BY-STEP INSTRUCTIONS
1. Imagine that the paper clips in the bottle are the ocean's waters attached to the Earth and that the magnet is the Moon. Place one magnet up against the side of the water bottle near the top of the paper clip pile. What happens to the paper clips? How is this like the gravitational pull of the Moon on the waters of the Earth?

2. Move the magnet around the outside of the water bottle. This simulates the rotation of the Moon around the Earth. What happens to the paper clips? Record your observations in your journal.

3. Try placing the other magnet on the opposite side of the water bottle from the Moon. This represents the effect of the Sun's gravitational pull on the ocean. What do you notice? Record your observations in your journal.

TIPS:

➡ Hold your bottle upright when moving the magnet.

➡ Experiment with different-sized magnets to achieve a stronger hold on the paper clips within the bottle.

high tide

tidal zone

low tide

CONCLUSION:

The paper clips in this activity were attracted to the magnet similar to how the ocean waters are pulled by the gravity of the Sun and the Moon. Because the position of the Earth changes constantly in relationship to the Sun and the Moon, sea level rises and falls periodically throughout the day. Because we can predict the positions of the Sun, Moon, and Earth, we can predict the tides throughout the Earth.

OCEAN JOURNAL ENTRY

In this activity, you simulated the movement of tides around the globe due to the movement of the Moon and Sun in relationship to the Earth. Reflect on this activity to help you answer the following questions in your journal.

1. *Describe how the force of the magnet on the paper clips is like the gravitational pull of the Moon on the ocean.*

2. *Reflect on your observations when using two magnets to represent the Sun and the Moon. If both the Sun and the Moon have a gravitational pull on the Earth, do you think their forces can combine to create a larger tide? Why or why not?*

3. *Why might it be helpful to predict the change in tides in places like the Bay of Fundy?*

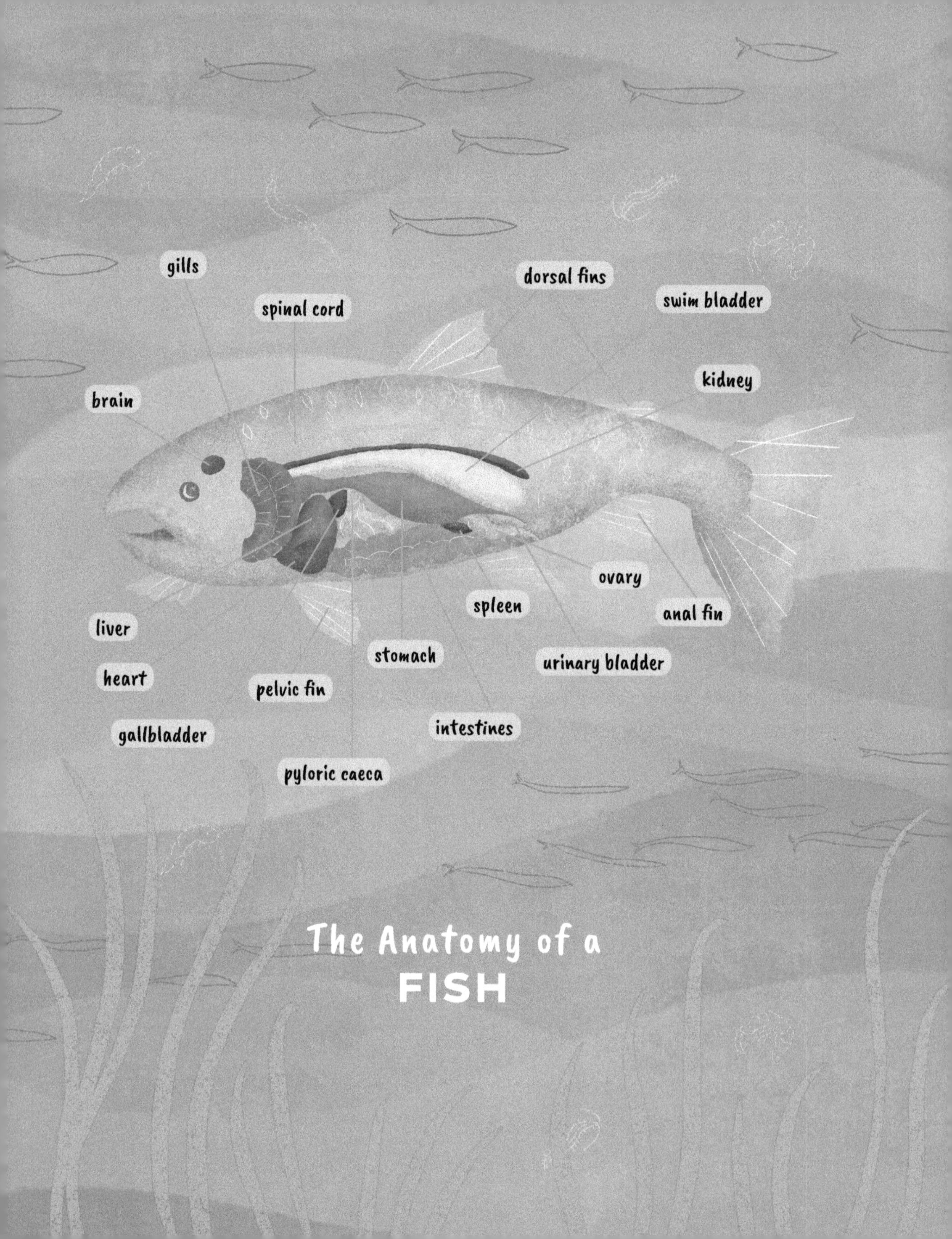

gills

spinal cord

dorsal fins

swim bladder

kidney

brain

liver

heart

gallbladder

pelvic fin

pyloric caeca

stomach

intestines

spleen

urinary bladder

ovary

anal fin

The Anatomy of a
FISH

FISH AND MARINE MAMMALS

2

The more than two million species of marine life are connected to each other through a *food web*, a series of interconnected food chains sustaining life. Food chains are a transfer of energy from one organism to another beginning with *producers*, or organisms that create their own food, such as phytoplankton. These producers provide a food source for *consumers* that eat them, such as animals like coral or crustaceans.

In this chapter, you will explore how animals find their way in the ocean, capture their prey, and swim with ease. This chapter is all about the diversity of marine life and the adaptations they have evolved for survival in their watery world.

ANATOMY OF A FISH

Fish are animals with unique adaptations for life in the ocean. Instead of using lungs to breathe like humans, fish use gills. When water is pumped over the gills, oxygen is collected and carbon dioxide is released. Some fish pump water over their gills with a bony plate called an *operculum*, or gill cover. Many fish swim in large groups called *schools*, which help keep them safe if a predator attacks. Most fish have fins to help them swim through the water.

Most fish species lay eggs and are *cold-blooded*, meaning they stay the same temperature as their surrounding environment. The fish species that do not lay eggs keep those eggs inside their bodies until they hatch. Male seahorses have a large pouch near their stomachs that holds their eggs until they are ready to hatch.

Most fish species are adapted to swimming upright, or vertically in the *water column*, the area between the seafloor and the surface in a specific spot. Some fish, like flounders, are flat-looking with mouths located under their bodies. This mouth position allows them to eat food on the seafloor as they swim over it. Flounders can also change their coloring to match the seafloor, disguising them from predators.

To understand more how fish are adapted to ocean life, let's explore why some objects float and some sink. *Buoyancy*, the upward force that water has on a submerged object, determines how well something floats. An object's buoyancy mostly depends on the object's density, not its size. Density is how much matter is in an object, or the *mass*, compared to how much space the object takes up, or the *volume*. For example, if you threw an orange and a penny into a swimming pool, the orange would float, but the penny would sink. Even though the orange is bigger than the penny, the penny is denser. It has more matter in a smaller space. If an object's density is lower than the density of water, like the orange, it will float. The penny's density is greater than water, so it sinks.

Fish are usually denser than ocean water is, which makes them sink. To prevent this, many fish have a *swim bladder*. Swim bladders are gas-filled organs inside the fish that can be emptied or filled to control the fish's buoyancy. The fish is able to control how much gas is in the swim bladder as needed. More gas in the swim bladder increases the volume of the fish, making it *positively buoyant*, allowing the fish to float up to the surface. Letting out the gas decreases the fish's volume, making it *negatively buoyant*, and lets the fish sink to a depth it wants. A fish that neither sinks nor floats is described as *neutrally buoyant*.

How is neutral buoyancy helpful to fish? Imagine constantly treading water in the deep end of a swimming pool to stay at the surface. Over time you could become extremely tired! If a fish does not have a swim bladder, it must continue to use energy to keep swimming.

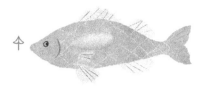

filled with oxygen

slightly deflated

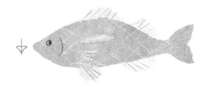

much less oxygen

Fun Fact

Sharks and stingrays don't have swim bladders. They control their buoyancy with oils in their liver. Oil is less dense than water, so it helps keep the shark from sinking.

FISH FLOATS

TIME:
10 TO 20 MINUTES

CATEGORY:
INDOOR, EXPERIMENT

MATERIALS
5-GALLON CLEAR
PLASTIC CONTAINER

SEVERAL ROCKS SMALL ENOUGH
TO FIT THROUGH THE OPENING OF
THE PLASTIC BOTTLE

EMPTY 12-OUNCE PLASTIC
WATER BOTTLE

TIP:

➡ Leave the bottle for a few minutes to determine its position in the bucket. This allows for any external air bubbles to settle that may interfere with your results.

How do fish stay afloat without sinking to the bottom of the ocean? In this activity, you will experiment with mass and volume to create neutral buoyancy, similar to the way fish create neutral buoyancy in their swim bladders.

PREP WORK

1. Gather your materials to work in an area you don't mind getting wet.

2. Fill the container with water up to 5 inches from the top.

STEP-BY-STEP INSTRUCTIONS

1. Imagine that the water bottle is a fish living in the middle of the water column—between the seafloor and the surface. The container is the fish's environment, or the ocean. The air space inside the bottle is the swim bladder of the fish. The stones are the mass of the fish.

2. Create a hypothesis by guessing how many stones you might need to add to your water bottle to make your fish neutrally buoyant, or so that the bottle doesn't sink completely to the bottom or float to the surface.

3. Test your hypothesis by adding stones to the bottle and placing the bottle into the water-filled container. Did it sink to the bottom? Float to the top? Describe your results in your journal.

4. Adjust the number of stones in the bottle to achieve neutral buoyancy. Add more stones if your bottle floats, and take out stones if it sinks to the bottom. How many stones did you need to keep the bottle neutrally buoyant?

CONCLUSION:

In this activity, you experimented to create neutral buoyancy in a plastic air-filled bottle. Fish create neutral buoyancy by maintaining the amount of gas within their swim bladders. By changing the rocks in your bottle, you adjusted the mass to create a model fish bladder that neither sinks nor floats. Fish achieve the same results by controlling the amount of gas in their swim bladders.

OCEAN JOURNAL ENTRY

This lesson taught you how a fish uses a swim bladder to maintain its position in the water column. Using what you have learned, answer the following questions in your journal.

1. *How many times did you need to adjust the number of stones in your bottle to achieve neutral buoyancy?*

2. *How long do you think it takes a fish to empty or fill their swim bladder?*

3. *If a fish lives on the bottom of the ocean, do you think it needs to have a swim bladder? Why or why not?*

ANATOMY OF A JELLYFISH

Jellyfish are not actually a type of fish. They are part of a group of organisms called *cnidarians*, invertebrates with tentacles that have stinging cells. They are more closely related to corals and anemone, and they are also considered a type of zooplankton because they are generally not strong swimmers and mostly drift on ocean currents. There are about 1,500 species of jellyfish, and they can be found in every ocean and at all depths.

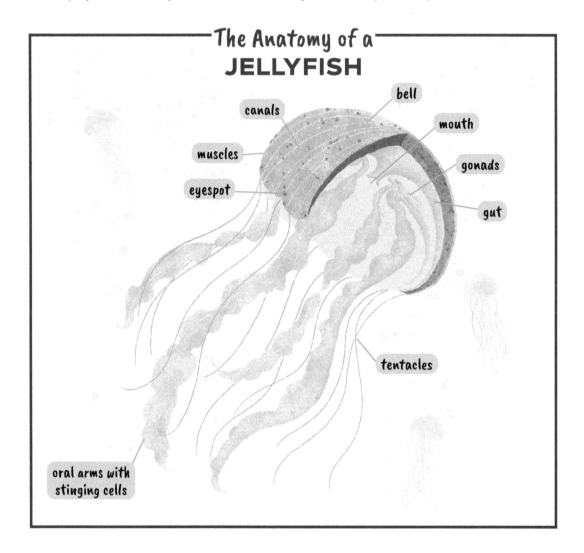

The Anatomy of a
JELLYFISH

bell
canals
mouth
muscles
gonads
eyespot
gut
tentacles
oral arms with
stinging cells

Jellies come in all shapes and sizes. The Australian box jellyfish, found in the warm waters of the Pacific, has one of the most deadly venoms on Earth and is considered the most venomous of all marine creatures. The lion's mane jellyfish is the largest-known species of jellyfish, with one specimen recorded at 8 feet (2.8 m) in diameter with tentacles up to 120 feet (36.5 m) long.

Jellyfish are remarkable animals with no heart, blood, or brains, and their bodies are made of approximately 95 percent water. Still, they can pump their *bell*, the bowl-shaped organ at the top of their bodies, to stay near the surface of the ocean. Most jellyfish even have eyespots located on their bell that can tell the difference between light and dark.

Jellyfish stomachs are located under their bell and they use tentacles to catch their food. Those tentacles contain millions of stinging cells, called *nematocysts*, that contain venom. The venom is released like a harpoon when the tentacles contact their prey. The venom paralyzes the prey. Jellyfish eat pretty much anything that gets caught in their tentacles, including some types of plankton, fish, or shrimp.

When jellyfish reproduce, they go through *metamorphosis*, like a butterfly. Baby jellyfish start as *polyps*, a stage of development in which the animal attaches upside down to the seafloor with tentacles extended upward. In later stages of its life cycle, a polyp releases a small juvenile jellyfish that will eventually grow into an adult.

Stinging Cells

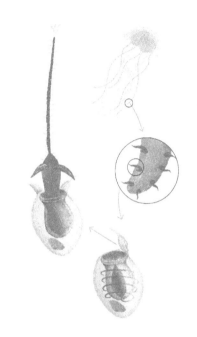

Fun Fact

A group of jellyfish can be called a *swarm*, a *bloom*, or a *smack* if found in large groups.

MAKING A STINGING CELL

TIME:
10 TO 20 MINUTES

CATEGORY:
INDOOR, SIMULATION

MATERIALS
1 (8-OUNCE) PLASTIC CUP

BALLOON, NOT BLOWN UP

5 FEET YARN OR STRING

1 (1-INCH) POMPOM

TAPE

How do jellyfish release their venom? In this activity, you will create your own version of a jellyfish stinging cell and practice launching it in a similar way that jellyfish do.

Safety First! *When launching your stinging cells be sure to work in an open area, avoiding other people.*

PREP WORK

1. Cut off the bottom of the plastic cup.

2. Cut the balloon in half crosswise. Save the bottom piece with the balloon's neck attached.

TIP:

➡ Be sure to hold the cup steady while releasing the tied end of the balloon.

STEP-BY-STEP INSTRUCTIONS

1. Slide the cut edge of the balloon over the bottomless half of the cup. Tie the neck of the balloon in a knot after it has been placed on the cup. This is going to be the outside of your stinging cell.

2. Tie one end of the string to the pompom. The pompom represents the venom inside the nematocyst.

3. Tape the other end of the string to the balloon from inside the cup. This will help illustrate the mechanism a nematocyst uses to inject venom in the jellyfish's prey.

4. Carefully wrap the string around the pompom and tuck it inside the cup.

5. Now comes the launch! Gently pull down on the tied end of the balloon while holding the cup. Imagine that a fish has just brushed up against a jellyfish tentacle. This is the signal to let go of the balloon and release the venom inside. What happens to the string and pompom? Record your observations in your journal.

CONCLUSION:

Jellyfish have some unique ways for obtaining food. Their stinging cells, nematocysts, inject venom into their prey, paralyzing it, so the jellyfish can have its meal. The model nematocyst that you created launched a pompom similar to the way that jellyfish use their nematocysts.

OCEAN JOURNAL ENTRY

You have just created your own version of a jellyfish stinging cell. Reflect on the activity as you answer the questions below.

1. *Since jellyfish don't have organs like sharp teeth or claws for catching prey, what is the advantage of having nematocysts?*

2. *Why do you think jellyfish have so many nematocysts in their tentacles?*

3. *Do you think a jellyfish can reload their nematocysts? If so, describe how you think they might do it.*

ANATOMY OF A SHARK

There are more than 500 different species of shark. The largest species, the whale shark, can reach up to 39 feet (11.9 m) in length. At the other end of the spectrum, the smallest shark is the dwarf lantern shark, and it measures in at about 7.9 inches (20 cm), just over the size of an average adult hand.

Sharks are a type of fish called *elasmobranchs*. Elasmobranchs are unique among fish because their skeleton is made of cartilage instead of bone. Our ears are an example of an organ made of cartilage. Cartilage provides a lightweight, flexible support structure for sharks and other elasmobranchs, including stingrays and manta rays. In addition, it allows for quick movements to help them hunt, and the lighter skeleton helps them maintain buoyancy, since they don't have swim bladders like other fish.

Sharks can have anywhere from five to seven gill slits on each side of their head that help them breathe and even eat. Some sharks are predators and some are filter feeders. Instead of biting and chewing prey, filter feeders collect small particles of food from the water. Usually they do this by using specialized structures on their gills.

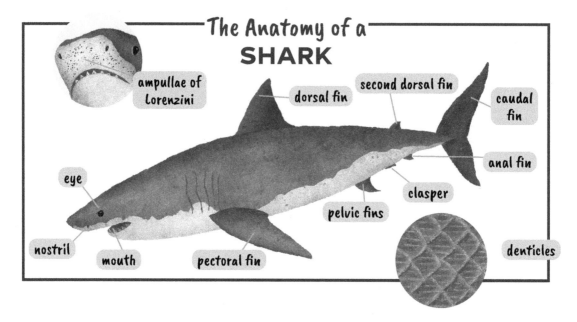

The Anatomy of a SHARK

- ampullae of Lorenzini
- dorsal fin
- second dorsal fin
- caudal fin
- anal fin
- eye
- clasper
- pelvic fins
- nostril
- mouth
- pectoral fin
- denticles

Unlike bony fish, sharks do not have gill covers. Water must continuously flow over their gills to extract oxygen so that they can breathe. A lot of sharks, like the great white and whale sharks, must keep swimming to keep water flowing over their gills to breathe, so they never stop moving. Other species, like the nurse shark, can pump water over their gills using their cheek muscles, or *buccal* muscles, and can be found resting on the seafloor sometimes.

Sharks that spend most of their time on the ocean floor are often called *carpet sharks*. These tend to have more flattened bodies with coloring that helps them camouflage. The tasselled wobbegong shark, found in the coral reefs of Australia and throughout the islands of Indonesia, has spotted coloring that blends in with the surrounding color. It even has special skin flaps that can cover its mouth and head, so the tasselled wobbegong can hide and attack when unsuspecting prey swim close by.

Some sharks, like the great white and mako shark, are built to be fierce ocean predators. These sharks' mouths contain rows of teeth that continuously replace themselves. If they lose one, there is another right behind it to take its place. They also usually have about eight fins, including large *dorsal fins* on top of their bodies, providing control and balance and making them fast in catching their prey. *Pectoral fins* on the sides of their body help them to make quick turns, and *caudal fins*, or tails, propel the shark through the water.

Aside from expertly crafted fins, sharks have other special features, like slim, torpedo-shaped bodies and *denticles* that help them increase their swimming speed. Denticles are super-tiny teeth-like scales with ridges and grooves that reduce the friction of water as it flows over the shark's skin. Together, the torpedo body shape and the denticles help the shark swim faster. Sharks with these body types tend to live in open ocean waters.

Fun Fact

Sharks have organs under their mouths called *ampullae of Lorenzini*. These organs can detect electrical currents given off by prey or items that might be hidden under sand or rocks.

SHARK SKIN

TIME:
15 TO 30 MINUTES

CATEGORY:
INDOOR, CRAFT

MATERIALS
DRAWING UTENSILS SUCH AS
COLORED PENCILS, CRAYONS,
OR MARKERS

2 OR 3 WHITE HARD-BOILED EGGS
IN THEIR SHELL

PAPER

CLEAR-DRYING GLUE

TIP:

➡ Instead of drawing on your eggs, you may dye or paint them to add your own artistic flair.

In this activity, you will use your imagination to design a shark to include dorsal, pectoral, and caudal fins. Using eggshells, you will add texture to your projects to represent denticles.

Safety First! *Be sure your hard-boiled eggs are completely cool before peeling them to avoid any burn injury.*

PREP WORK

1. Use markers to give the eggs some color. Choose colors you would like to have on a shark of your own design.

2. Peel the shell from the egg and crush it into small pieces.

STEP-BY-STEP INSTRUCTIONS

1. Consider the adaptations that sharks have that make them either excellent predators or filter feeders. Reflect on characteristics such as body shape as well as the number of fins, their size, and their shape. What will the shark's mouth look like?

2. On a sheet of paper, draw an outline of a shark, including details like the body shape, fin size and position, as well as the mouth. Color in your shark outline.

3. Once your drawing is complete, spread a thin layer of glue over your shark design, covering it completely.

4. Sprinkle the crushed eggshells over your shark. These will represent shark denticles.

5. While the glue dries, describe your shark's scales, fins, skeleton, and body shape in your journal. How do these adaptations help them in the ocean?

whale shark

great white shark

nurse shark

bonnethead shark

CONCLUSION:
You drew a shark that has a lightweight skeleton of cartilage and a streamlined body shape. The eggshells you added to your shark design represent denticles, very small plate-like scales on the shark's skin that reduce the friction of water flow over its body as it swims.

OCEAN JOURNAL ENTRY

After creating your picture of a shark, reflect on the activity as you answer the questions below.

1. *Describe where your shark lives. Does it sit on the seafloor or swim in the open ocean? How is its body adapted for its environment?*

2. *Describe how your shark eats. Is it a filter feeder like the whale shark, or is it a predator like a great white?*

ANATOMY OF A WHALE

D id you know whales are the largest animals on the planet? A blue whale can weigh as much as 400,000 pounds (181,437 kg) and can reach nearly 100 feet (30.5 m) long! Whales belong to a group of marine mammals called *cetaceans*. They have lungs and breathe air through blowholes on the tops of their bodies. Like other mammals, including humans, they give live birth and nurse their young. Many species inhabit arctic waters.

There are two kinds of whales: *toothed* and *baleen*. *Toothed whales* include dolphins, porpoises, and orcas. These whales have sharp teeth in their mouths for capturing their food. *Baleen whales*, like the blue whale and the

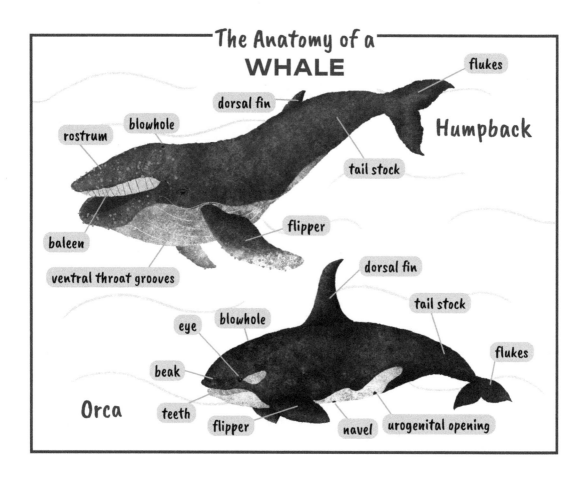

The Anatomy of a
WHALE

flukes

dorsal fin

Humpback

blowhole

rostrum

tail stock

baleen

flipper

ventral throat grooves

dorsal fin

tail stock

eye   blowhole

flukes

beak

Orca   teeth

flipper   navel   urogenital opening

humpback, have structures in their mouth called baleen. Each piece of baleen resembles the bristly end of a broom. Baleen whales use these structures to filter their food from large gulps of water.

All mammals have some form of hair. Whales have much less hair than other mammals or they only have hair during one stage of their life. Dolphins, for example, have whiskers when they are born that disappear as they age, usually within a week. So, instead of large amounts of hair to keep warm in the ocean, whales have a thick layer of *blubber*. Blubber is a type of fat that keeps whale bodies warm in near freezing temperatures.

Since much of the ocean is dark, toothed whales have a unique sense called *echolocation* to find food. Echolocation is a process that allows whales to navigate and find prey using sound. Dolphins and orcas push air through their blowholes to create clicks and whistles. An organ in the whale's head called a *melon* directs the outgoing sound. Traveling quickly through water, these sounds bounce off of prey and return to the whale, similar to your voice echoing off a cave wall. The sounds are received in the fat-filled cavities of the whale's lower jaw. This information gives the whale the location of prey in the water.

Fun Fact

Some whales can sing! Baleen whales, like the humpback, can create a wide range of clicks and whistles called *whale song*. These sounds aren't used for echolocation, though. Rather, researchers believe that humpbacks use their songs to communicate with one another.

WHALE SENSES GAME

TIME:
10 TO 20 MINUTES

CATEGORY:
OUTDOOR, GAME

MATERIALS
LARGE OPEN OUTDOOR AREA

2 TO 4 PLAYERS

BLINDFOLD

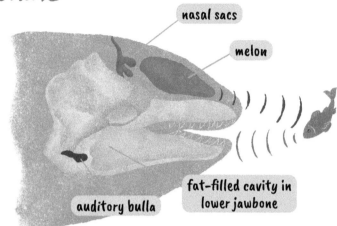

nasal sacs

melon

fat-filled cavity in lower jawbone

auditory bulla

In this activity, you will stretch your senses to experience what it is like for a whale to find their food using echolocation. You will need to rely on your sense of hearing to find your fellow players while blindfolded. The object of the game is for the whale player to use their sense of hearing to "tag" the fish players.

Safety First! *Choose an open play area that is safe from any dangerous objects or moving vehicles, such as your backyard or a playground.*

TIP:

➡ You can change the level of difficulty of the game by allowing fish players to move during the game and allowing the whale players unlimited calls.

PREP WORK

1. Clear the play area of unsafe obstacles that a blindfolded player may trip over.

2. Decide which player will be first as the blindfolded whale and which players will be fish.

STEP-BY-STEP INSTRUCTIONS

1. Begin by moving the whale player to the middle of the play area and blindfolding them.

2. Once the whale player is unable to see, the fish players will scatter out over the playing area representing fish within the ocean. Fish players may not move after they have picked a spot.

3. The whale player locates fish players by listening for their responses to his or her calls. When the whale player yells, "Echo!" all fish players must respond, "Location!"

4. Whale players may only call a total of 10 times in a game. If a fish player is caught, the game ends and the caught fish becomes the whale for the next round.

CONCLUSION:

You have just experienced how some whales use echolocation in the ocean. Relying on your sense of hearing to identify the location of fish players using a calling system is similar to the way the whale uses an echo to find food in the dark ocean.

OCEAN JOURNAL ENTRY

In this activity, you learned what it is like to find objects using echolocation. Reflect on your experience playing the game as you answer the questions below.

1. *What advantage does echolocation give whales when finding their prey?*

2. *Describe how our sense of hearing is similar to the echolocation of a whale. How is it different?*

The Anatomy of a
KELP FOREST

mackerel

sea otter

garibaldi fish

sea lion

sea urchin

sunflower sea star

abalone

red algae

COASTS AND SHORELINES

3

This chapter brings us to the place where ocean meets land: coastlines and shorelines. A *coastline* is the area of land from high tide toward land, and a *shoreline* is the area of ocean waters from high tide toward the ocean. Rocky cliffs and sandy beaches create diverse and dynamic habitats. Coastlines and shorelines constantly change with tide and wave action. Since sea level changes with the tides, the place between high and low tide is called the *intertidal zone*. This chapter explores the ways shorelines are created and changed while looking at some of the diverse habitats that can be found there.

ANATOMY OF A BEACH

A day at the beach often means feeling sand between your toes and listening to the sound of waves crashing on the shore. What creates these beautiful places we love to travel to? This lesson explores how beaches form, what they are made of, and the types of organisms that can be found there.

Beaches, the narrow strips of land found at the transition between the coastline and shoreline, are usually made of sand, or rocks broken down into incredibly small pieces. The rocks break down and form sand during a process called *weathering*, when waves crash onto a beach or rocks, wearing them down. *Erosion* occurs when these particles are moved from their place of origin. Waves erode beaches when they move sand along the shoreline though *longshore currents,* or currents that move parallel to the shoreline, which are formed as waves crash and then pull back out to sea along the shoreline.

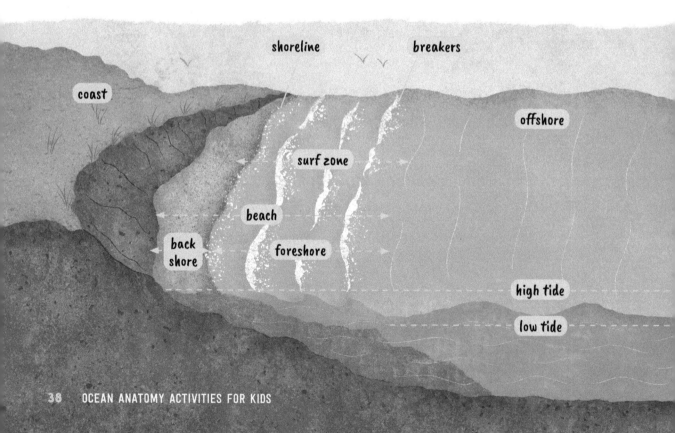

While there are many different types of sandy beaches, sand is not the only thing that can make up a beach. Beaches can be made of pebbles, rocks, boulders, and even seashells! The color of sand at a beach is determined by the type of *sediment* it is made from. Sediments are small particles of solid material moved by wind and water. For example, you can find many black sand beaches on the Hawaiian Islands because of the often-black lava that makes up the islands themselves. The whitest beach in the world, according to Guinness World Records, is Hyams Beach in Australia. The sand at this beach is made primarily of quartz.

Beaches provide a habitat for several different species of birds worldwide. Many will nest along the coastline and feed on the rich sea life on the shore. Some of the more common birds found on beaches include seagulls, pelicans, and sandpipers. Pelicans, using their large bill, gulp down surface seawater containing fish. The American white pelican's throat pouch can hold up to 3 gallons of water!

Ghost crabs, also known as sand crabs, are a common resident of many tropical and subtropical sandy beaches. They live in intricate burrows and usually tunnel through the sandy intertidal zone.

Fun Fact

Adult parrotfish can create up to 1,000 pounds (450 kg) of sand per year by chewing on coral with their beak-like jaw. Once in their gut, the coral is ground up even further and eliminated as sand!

CHANGING BEACHES

TIME:
10 TO 20 MINUTES

CATEGORY:
INDOOR, EXPERIMENT

MATERIALS
SHALLOW 9-BY-13-INCH METAL PAN

SAND, GRAVEL, AND STONES (TO ACT AS YOUR SEDIMENT)

12-OUNCE WATER BOTTLE FILLED WITH WATER AND CLOSED

SPRAY BOTTLE FILLED WITH WATER

WATER

path of sand particles

longshore current

How does rain and wave action affect beach formation? In this activity, you will experiment with different forms of water erosion to observe their effects on beach sediment.

PREP WORK

1. Gather materials to work in an area you don't mind getting wet.

2. Create a beach on one side of the pan by placing the sand in a pile reaching to the top of the pan. Your beach model should slope down toward the middle of the pan.

3. Once your beach has been created, fill the pan with water until it reaches halfway up the side of the pan.

STEP-BY-STEP INSTRUCTIONS

1. First, we will examine how rain affects the erosion of a beach. Begin by spraying the top of your beach with the spray bottle until you notice water gathering and running down the slope of your beach. Where does the water travel? How did it change the shape of your beach? Record your observations in your journal.

2. Next, we will explore how wave action affects the erosion of a beach. Lay the sealed water bottle on the water side of the pan parallel to the beach. Slowly roll the water bottle toward the beach along the bottom of the pan. This will simulate waves hitting the shoreline. What happens to the beach? Record your observations in your journal.

3. Roll the water bottle faster. What happened to the beach? How is this different than the first time you created waves with the water bottle? Record your observations in your journal.

4. Once you have completed each step, repeat the experiment again but change the position and type of materials used for the beach. What changed after conducting the experiment the second time? What stayed the same?

TIP:

➡ Allow the water to settle in your experiment before increasing your waves' speed.

OCEAN JOURNAL ENTRY

Reflect on the simulation of rain and waves on your beach model as you answer the questions below.

1. *Did you observe a relationship between the amount of rain an area receives and the amount of erosion? Explain why.*

2. *Did you observe a relationship between the strength of the waves hitting the beach and the amount of erosion? Explain why.*

3. *In what ways did changing the composition of your beach change your experiment's results?*

CONCLUSION:

This activity simulated some of the physical forces that create and keep shaping beaches. Beaches are created from the weathering and erosion of rocks and other materials, such as shells. Wind, rain, and waves are some of the forces behind this process. The spray bottle of water simulated rain's effects on beach erosion. By rolling the water bottle through the model you were able to observe how wave action affects erosion. Together, these forces make the beach a *dynamic* landform, meaning it's constantly changing.

TIDE POOLS

One unique place to observe marine life is in a *tide pool*. They contain organisms within a specific space, like a natural aquarium. On the Pacific Coast of the United States, tide pools can be quite colorful, harboring purple sea urchins, orange sea stars, and the giant green anemone. The giant green anemone is related to jellyfish and gets some of its green color from the relationship it has with the microalgae and *dinoflagellates*, also considered a type of algae, living inside of it.

limpets

sandpiper

pelican

barnacles

seagull

wrack

mussels

bull kelp

anemone

sea star

Tide pools are created by rocky depressions on shorelines in the intertidal zone, like miniature valleys. When the tide moves out to sea, this "valley" remains filled with water, making it an isolated pool. The seawater in tide pools is regularly refreshed when the tide rises. *Seaweed*, the common name of many species of large marine algae, covers rocks in green, red, and brown mats. These mats float like tangles of hair when the tide is in and seawater covers these pools.

Creatures that live in a tide pool are subject to dramatic physical changes throughout a tidal cycle. At low tide, tide pool organisms have an increased risk of becoming dinner for someone else, and some may even be exposed to the air! Crabs and wading birds search these exposed pools for food. Humans can also disrupt these small ecosystems, so it's important when visiting to not touch.

Also when the tide is low, organisms are cut off from a fresh seawater supply and temperatures in the pool can rise quickly from sun exposure. Oxygen levels can drop dramatically, and animals risk drying out. But animals that are permanently attached to the shoreline have adaptations to withstand their time on dry land. Barnacles, a type of crustacean related to crabs, stay permanently attached to their position in the tide pool. They can close up their shell tightly to keep from drying out when exposed to the air.

When the tide rises again to cover the tide pool and replenish the seawater, waves pound the rocks with incredible force, threatening to pull animals away from their habitat. To keep from being washed out to sea by wave action, tide pool organisms have the ability to produce a tight grip on intertidal rocks. Animals like sea stars and urchins hold onto rocks using thousands of tiny feet-like suction cups.

Fun Fact

Barnacles produce a cement-like material to help them stay put in a tide pool. Scientists consider it to be one of the most powerful natural glues in existence!

CREATE A TIDE POOL

WAIT TIME:
1 TO 2 DAYS

CATEGORY:
INDOOR, CRAFT

MATERIALS
NEWSPAPER TO COVER
A WORKSTATION

DISPOSABLE PAPER BOWL

ALUMINUM FOIL

ROLLING PIN

1 TO 2 POUNDS OF AIR-DRY CLAY

RULER

WASHABLE ACRYLIC PAINT
(SEVERAL COLORS)

PAINT BRUSHES

SCHOOL GLUE (LIKE ELMER'S)

In this activity, you will create a sculpture of a tide pool from clay. Using what you have learned about the tide pool habitat, add details to the tide pool, including the animals and seaweed that inhabit these waters.

PREP WORK

1. Cover your workstation with newspaper to keep it clean.

2. Place the paper bowl upside down on the newspaper and cover it with aluminum foil.

STEP-BY-STEP INSTRUCTIONS

1. Begin by rolling out your clay into a circle about ½ inch thick and approximately 2 inches wider than the diameter of the top of the bowl. You can measure this by laying your bowl upside down on top of the rolled-out clay. Cut the clay to the right size.

2. Once you have your clay piece cut, lay the clay circle on top of the aluminum foil on the upside-down bowl. Press the clay down to mold it to the shape of the bowl.

3. Using leftover clay, create three-dimensional sculptures of some of the creatures that live in tide pools, such as barnacles, anemone, and sea stars.

4. Allow the air-dry clay bowl and the animal sculptures to harden overnight.

5. Once all the clay sculptures are fully dry, carefully flip over the bowl and remove both the bowl and the

aluminum foil from the inside of the clay. This is the base of your tide pool.

6. It's time to bring your tide pool to life! Paint rocks and seaweed inside of your tide pool base. Paint the animal sculptures to give them color too. Allow these to dry for 1 to 2 hours.

7. Use glue to attach the animals to the inside of the tide pool base. Once the glue is dry, just like the tube feet of sea stars and the glue of barnacles, it will keep the animals in place.

OCEAN JOURNAL ENTRY

In this activity, you created a sculpture of a tide pool and added organisms to reflect the ecosystem that can be found there. Use your experience from the creation of your sculpture to help you answer the questions below.

1. *Describe some of the ways the environment of a tide pool changes drastically throughout the day.*

2. *Describe the adaptations that animals like barnacles and sea stars must have to help them stay put in the tide pool ecosystem.*

3. *How is your model of a tide pool similar to or different from the tide pools you might find along the coast?*

CONCLUSION:

In this activity, you created a sculpture of a tide pool. The clay bowl represents the depressions found along rocky coastlines that create the tide pool ecosystem. Gluing your animals to your sculpture represents the way that the animals found in tide pools can tightly stick to the tide pool's rock surfaces to avoid being swept out to sea with the tide.

TIPS:

➡ Applying an acrylic sealer will help preserve your sculpture after it has been painted.

➡ Store air-dry clay in a sealed container with a small amount of water to keep it from drying out.

ANATOMY OF A KELP FOREST

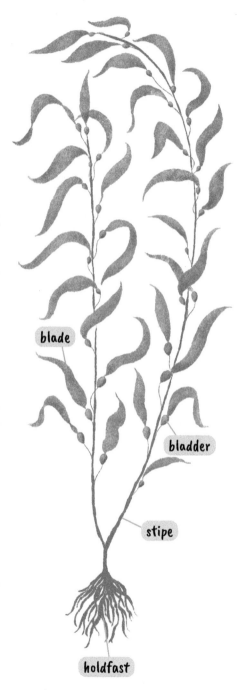

blade

bladder

stipe

holdfast

Imagine an underwater forest teeming with life. That's a *kelp forest*! Kelp forests can be found in cool waters around the world, but especially along the Pacific Coast of North America. The collection of kelp towers that make up these forests provides food and shelter for thousands of marine species. In this lesson, you will journey into a kelp forest to discover both what creates them and what animals call the kelp forest home.

Giant kelp is a species of large brown algae. There are more than 30 species of kelp that can be found in kelp forests, but giant kelp is the largest species of kelp—and algae—on the planet. It often reaches heights of 100 feet (30 m) and forms the towering structures that are characteristic of Pacific Coast kelp forests. In ideal conditions, giant kelp can grow up to 2 feet (0.6 m) in just one day! Like other algae, kelp can photosynthesize to create energy, so it needs to remain in the sunlight zone of the ocean.

Like forests on land, a kelp forest has a *canopy*, an *understory*, and a *forest floor*, but kelp forests face some unique challenges. The wave action that exists along the rocky shoreline can often threaten to wash the kelp out to sea. Giant kelp has four basic structures to help it survive in turbulent waters. *Holdfasts* at the bottom of the kelp attach to rocky earth, creating a cement-like hold. Stem-like structures called *stipes* help the kelp grow upward, and blades on the stipes, similar to leaves, help giant kelp absorb sunlight to keep growing. Finally, giant kelp uses floats, called *air bladders*, to keep itself upright.

Adorable sea otters can be found at the surface floating through the kelp canopy, anchoring themselves to the kelp while they sleep. They feast on invertebrates such as sea urchins, which in turn munch on the kelp itself. Large sea otters can eat up to 25 pounds (11.3 kg) of food a day! The sea otter's consumption of urchins keeps the sea urchin population balanced. Urchins can help clean up fallen kelp, but if they are left on their own, they can destroy a kelp forest.

Otters are not the only marine mammals found in these forests. Sea lions and seals feed on the fish here, and gray whales can be found filter feeding while they keep safe from predators like killer whales.

Fun Fact

There are more than 100 different species of rock fish near kelp forest habitats. They are one of the longest-living fish species.

KEEPING KELP AFLOAT

TIME:
20 TO 30 MINUTES

CATEGORY:
INDOOR, MODEL

MATERIALS
CRAYONS (GREEN AND BROWN)

12-BY-12-INCH SQUARE OF
WAX PAPER

RULER

SCISSORS

1 TO 3 MINI MARSHMALLOWS

STAPLER

ONE ROCK, ABOUT THE DIAMETER
OF A QUARTER

CLOTHESPIN

EMPTY 2-LITER BOTTLE WITH THE
TOP CUT OFF

WATER

In this activity, you will create a model that teaches you about the giant kelp's four basic structures—holdfast, stipe, blades, and air bladder.

PREP WORK

1. Gather materials to work in an area you don't mind getting wet.

2. Using crayons, draw and color a giant kelp on a piece of wax paper that is approximately 8 inches tall and no more than 3 inches wide. Make sure it includes a holdfast, stipe, and blades.

3. Label the structures on your diagram based on the illustration on page 46.

4. Cut out your kelp diagram from the wax paper.

5. Wrap the top of your kelp diagram around the mini marshmallow and staple it closed. Since marshmallows are filled with air, the marshmallow will act as an air bladder for your kelp model.

6. Wrap the holdfast at the bottom of the diagram around the rock and use the clothespin to secure it in place. The clothespin holds on to the rock and the wax paper diagram just like kelp holdfast holds on to the rocky seafloor. You now have a complete kelp model!

STEP-BY-STEP INSTRUCTIONS

1. Place your kelp model inside of the 2-liter bottle. Notice how it folds toward the bottom without water. Predict what will happen when it is submerged under water.

2. Slowly pour water into the container until the kelp is completely submerged. What happened to the kelp? Record your observations in your journal.

TIP:

➡ You may wrap more than one blade around the mini marshmallow if you are having trouble getting it to stay attached to the diagram.

OCEAN JOURNAL ENTRY

In this activity, you created a model of a giant kelp including its four basic structures—holdfast, stipe, blade, and air bladder. These structures are important for the kelp to create the habitat for so many organisms. Use your model as a reference to help you answer the following questions in your journal.

1. *What happened to the kelp once it was submerged underwater? Describe why you think this happened.*

2. *Describe the importance of the holdfast and the air bladder structures of kelp.*

3. *Describe how a kelp forest is similar to a forest that can be found on land.*

CONCLUSION:

In this lesson, you created a model of a giant kelp. Building these structures showed you how giant kelp are designed to grow in large, upright towers that withstand wave action and provide an essential habitat to so many species.

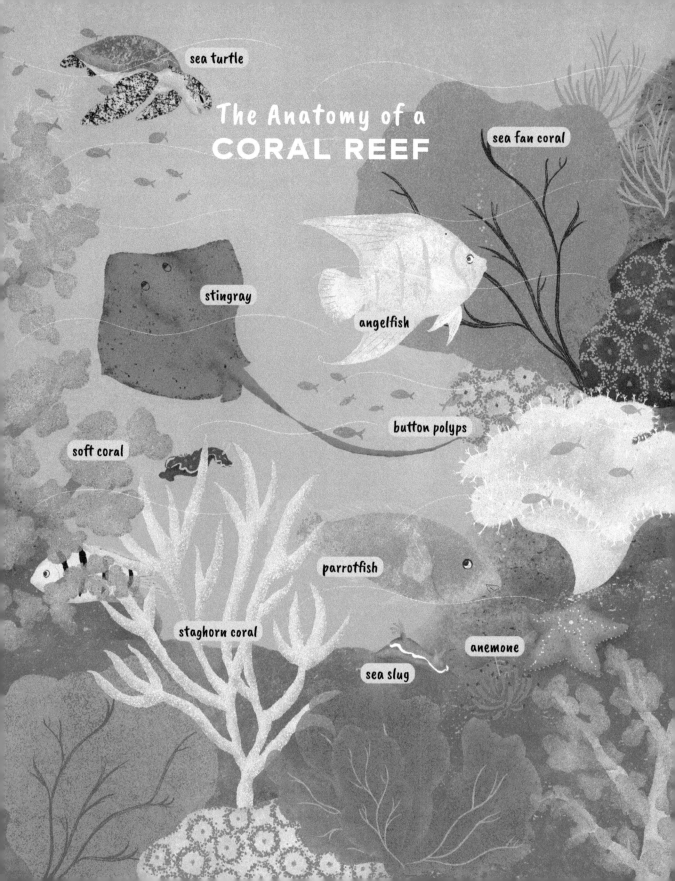

sea turtle

The Anatomy of a
CORAL REEF

sea fan coral

stingray

angelfish

button polyps

soft coral

parrotfish

staghorn coral

anemone

sea slug

CORAL REEFS

A coral reef is a submerged habitat that provides shelter for other organisms to eat and grow. The "tropical rainforests of the sea," they are the most diverse of all shallow-water marine ecosystems. They are estimated to contain nearly a quarter of all known species in the ocean! There are four different types: barrier reefs, patch reefs, fringing reefs, and atolls. *Barrier reefs* can be found offshore, near coastlines. They are separated from the shoreline by bodies of water called *lagoons* and often reach the ocean's surface. *Patch reefs* grow in shallow areas within lagoons. *Fringing reefs* begin closer to the shoreline and grow out toward the sea. Fringing reefs that keep growing around islands that are submerged in the ocean form a circular reef called an *atoll*.

ANATOMY OF A CORAL REEF

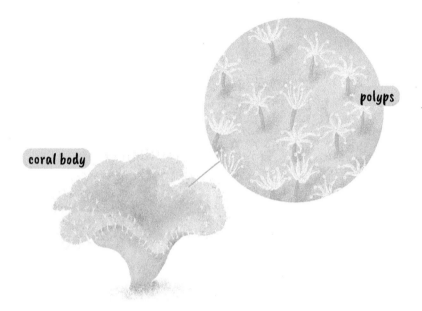

coral body

polyps

Coral reefs are created by tiny animals, related to jellyfish, called *coral polyps*. These polyps can live individually or in larger colonies that can take up a lot of space. Polyps have delicate bodies. They grow their skeleton on the outside of their bodies using calcium and carbonate ions from seawater. There are two types of corals: *soft coral* and *hard coral*. Soft corals form flexible skeletons that look more like plants. While they live in coral reefs, they are not considered reef builders. However, hard corals, also known as *stony corals*, continuously grow hard skeletons, gradually building up and out-ward. There are more than 3,000 species of stony corals, and they each form a different size and shape. When stony corals die, their hard skeletons remain intact. New corals can grow on top of these stony coral skeletons, gradually building up the reef. It may take hundreds or even thousands of years, but eventually this process makes the large coral reefs we see in oceans today.

Coral polyps usually have a clear body, but they can be quite colorful due to a photosynthetic algae living inside of them. These algae, called *zoo-xanthellae*, have a symbiotic relationship with the coral. A *mutualistic* or *symbiotic relationship* is one in which two different organisms benefit from each other. In the example of coral and zooxanthellae, the coral provides a home for the algae and the algae create essential energy for the coral. Some soft corals have the zooxanthellae, but stony corals require them to survive. Sometimes corals expel their zooxanthellae due to stress caused by a rise in ocean temperature. This is life-threatening for the coral: They lose their color, become white, and can eventually die if they don't recover. This is known as *coral bleaching*. Conservationists are working on combatting coral bleaching events from increased sea temperatures and other reef threats, including overfishing and water pollution, in order to protect these ecosystems. Many animals that live on a reef have evolved to mimic their colorful surroundings. For example, many pygmy seahorse species live exclusively on corals and hold a striking resemblance to their hosts—corals. These tiny seahorses grow no larger than an inch in length, and some are as small as a grain of rice. Because they are incredibly small and so well camouflaged, new species of pygmy seahorses have only recently been discovered.

Fun Fact

The Great Barrier Reef, the largest coral reef in the world, is located off the Australian coast. It is so large that it can be seen from space.

CORAL REEF ROCK CANDY

WAIT TIME:
1 TO 5 DAYS

SET UP TIME:
30 MINUTES

CATEGORY:
SIMULATION

MATERIALS
2 (3-CM) PIECES OF CIRCULAR-SHAPED HARD CANDY

2 TO 3 TABLESPOONS OF GRANULATED SUGAR ON A PLATE

3-QUART SAUCEPAN

1 CUP OF WATER

3 CUPS OF GRANULATED SUGAR

2 (16-OUNCE) MASON JARS

FUNNEL

FOOD COLORING

In this activity, you will simulate coral reef growth with the creation of rock candy! New corals can grow on top of established coral skeletons similar to the way that sugar crystals grow on established crystals in the formation of rock candy.

Safety First! *Use extreme caution when boiling water to avoid burns. Have an adult help you.*

PREP WORK

Wet the hard candy with water. While wet, roll the candy on the plate of granulated sugar, covering it completely. Set the candy aside to dry while you create the solution. Imagine that this sugar coating will become the first layer of a coral colony to settle on a reef.

STEP-BY-STEP INSTRUCTIONS

1. In a saucepan over medium heat, heat the water.

2. Once the water begins to simmer, add 1 cup of sugar at a time, stirring it until each cup dissolves completely before adding the next.

3. Heat until the solution begins to boil, constantly stirring the whole time.

4. Once the solution has reached a boil, remove it from the heat and allow it to cool for 20 minutes. Drop in a few drops of food coloring and stir to combine.

5. Arrange one hard candy at the bottom of each mason jar, leaving at least 2 inches of space between the candy and the sides of the jar. Imagine these are coral colonies growing on a reef.

6. After the solution has cooled, use the funnel to pour the solution into each jar. Imagine that this solution is seawater filled with the nutrients for stony corals to grow.

7. Now it's time to let your coral reef grow! Coral reefs take hundreds of years to mature, but your rock candy reef should form in about five days. Check on your reef once a day to observe any changes that have occurred. Write your observations in your journal.

OCEAN JOURNAL ENTRY

New sugar crystals growing on the existing crystals on the hard candy mimics the way that stony corals grow to form large reefs. Use your experience from this activity to answer the questions below.

1. *Hard corals build their skeletons out of a chemical called calcium carbonate found in sea water. The crystals of rock candy grew from the sugar dissolved in solution. How is their growth similar or different from each other?*

2. *Describe the symbiotic relationship between zooxanthellae and coral polyps. Why is this relationship important to corals?*

CONCLUSION:

This activity simulated the growth of a coral reef. Sugar crystals represented coral. Just as rock candy grew from the sugar crystals at the start of your reef, corals grow their structures on top of older coral skeletons. Over time stony corals build to form large reefs. Similarly, the sugar crystals in your rock candy reef grew to form larger pieces.

TIP:

➡ If you would like different colored corals, divide the sugar solution evenly, then add 2 to 4 drops of food coloring to each one. Separate the candies into different mason jars, adding the colored solution you choose for each one.

SEA STARS

In this lesson, we will examine the anatomy of one of the coral reef's inhabitants, the sea star. Sea stars, also known as starfish, are not actually fish, just like jellyfish aren't fish. Sea stars are part of a group of invertebrates called *echinoderms*, animals that have an *endoskeleton*. The endoskeleton is a hard internal structure made of calcium carbonate plates. Echinoderms have a thin layer of "skin" called the *epidermis* that covers the endoskeleton. The term "echinoderm" means *spiny skin*, which refers to the bumpy texture of these soft-bodied creatures.

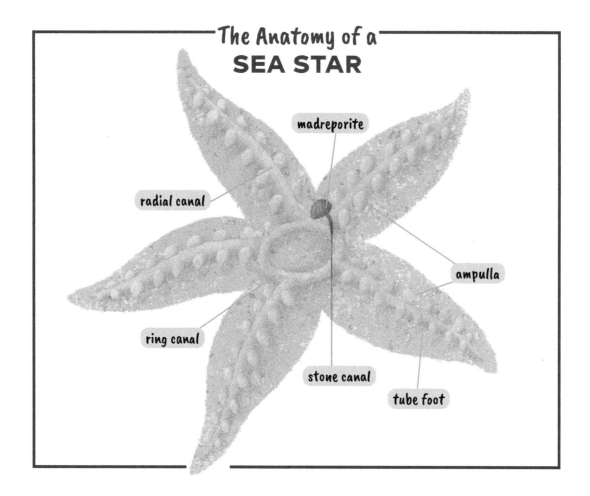

The Anatomy of a
SEA STAR

madreporite

radial canal

ampulla

ring canal

stone canal

tube foot

Sea stars have no brain, heart, or blood. Instead, they have an internal water vascular, or circulatory, system made of a series of water-filled tubes that the animals use to transport materials throughout their bodies. Muscle contractions cause pressure that moves water through these tubes to the hundreds of delicate tube feet on the underside of their bodies. These feet then are able to attach to surfaces like a suction cup, move, and capture prey. Sea stars also breathe by taking in oxygen through their tube feet.

A sea star pushes its stomach out of its body to consume its food. Most sea stars are predatory, seeking mollusks, like clams and oysters, to eat. The crown-of-thorns starfish eats coral. This sea star can eat more than 42 square feet (13 m²) of coral in one year. When the population of these sea stars gets out of control, they can cause serious damage to coral reefs. The most well-known predator of the crown-of-thorns starfish is the Pacific triton, a type of sea snail.

There are more than 2,000 species of sea stars, and most have five limbs—though not all. The cushion sea star's arms are reduced in size, which makes it appear round instead of star shaped. The largest sea star, the sunflower sea star, has anywhere from 15 to 24 limbs and can grow more than 3 feet (1 m) across. With this many limbs, it can move at a rate of more than 3 feet (1 m) per minute!

Fun Fact

Sea stars have the remarkable power to regrow portions of their body as adults. Some species can grow a whole new sea star from one lost limb.

SEA STAR FEET

TIME:
15 TO 30 MINUTES

ACTIVITY CATEGORY:
INDOOR, EXPERIMENT

MATERIALS
1 (8-OUNCE) CLEAR GLASS

WATER

1 PENNY

1 COTTON BALL

1 DRY BEAN OR PEANUT

1 TURKEY BASTER

TIMER OR A WATCH WITH A SECOND HAND

TIP:

➡ Try exploring how the turkey baster holds other submerged materials that you may have in your house. Record times for each new material in the data table in your journal. Do you notice any patterns?

Sea stars move using hundreds of tiny tube feet located on the underside of their bodies. These tube feet also enable the sea star to suction itself to surfaces. In this activity, you will use a turkey baster to model how a sea star's tube feet might grasp different surfaces. A single turkey baster represents one tube foot of the many hundred that each sea star has.

PREP WORK

1. Gather your materials to work in an area you don't mind getting wet.

2. Create a table in your journal with the following column headings: Penny, Bean, and Cotton Ball.

STEP-BY-STEP INSTRUCTIONS

1. Fill the glass two-thirds full of water.

2. Submerge the penny, cotton ball, and bean (or peanut) at the bottom of the glass of water.

3. Squeeze the rubber bulb of the turkey baster and hold it.

4. Submerge the end of the turkey baster into the glass of water.

5. Still squeezing the rubber bulb, place the tip of the turkey baster directly on top of the penny.

6. Release the rubber bulb and gently lift the turkey baster up from the bottom of the glass. What happened to the penny? Did it stick to the tip of the baster?

7. Try this process again. Time how long the penny sticks to the tip of the baster after you release the bulb. In the table in your journal, record how long the baster held on to the penny.

8. Repeat steps 3 through 7, except this time, place the tip of the turkey baster on the bean. How was it the same as or different from the penny?

9. Lastly, repeat steps 3 through 7 again, but place the tip of the turkey baster on the cotton ball. How did this experience compare with the bean and penny?

OCEAN JOURNAL ENTRY

This activity allowed you to explore the way sea stars use their tube feet. Reflect on your experience as you answer the following questions in your journal.

1. *In your own words, describe how sea stars use pressure changes to grab onto surfaces.*

2. *Does the type of surface affect the time an object can be held by the turkey baster? What might this mean for a sea star's ability to grab on to surfaces?*

3. *What are some advantages of having tube feet like the sea star?*

CONCLUSION:

You have just explored how pressure changes within a closed tube, like that of a sea star's feet, grab on to different surfaces. When you squeezed the bulb of the turkey baster, this reduced pressure inside the tube. Higher pressure outside the tube pushes objects onto the tip of the baster, causing it to grip. Sea stars contract muscles inside their bodies to reduce internal pressure around their tube feet. Higher pressure outside the feet allows those feet to form a grip on surfaces. Each sea star's tube foot is small compared to the whole animal. However, with hundreds or even thousands of these feet spread out under the animal, it can create a grip strong enough to move itself through the water.

SEA TURTLES

Sea turtles are air-breathing reptiles that spend their whole lives in the ocean and are one of the many *vertebrates*, or animals with a backbone, that rely on the coral reef habitat for food. There are seven different species of sea turtle: leatherback, loggerhead, green, hawksbill, flatback, olive ridley, and Kemp's ridley.

Just like freshwater turtles, most sea turtles, except for the leatherback, have a hard shell called a *carapace*. However, instead of legs and claws like freshwater turtles, they have flippers. You may have seen a freshwater turtle pull its head and legs inside of its shell for protection, but sea turtles do not have the space inside their shell to retract their heads or limbs.

Hawksbill sea turtles, a medium-size species of sea turtle famous for their golden-brown shell and beak-like mouth, are frequent visitors to coral reefs. Here they seek shelter and search for food. They love to munch on sea sponges. Sea sponges are invertebrates that can often be found tucked into cracks and crevices of the reef. The hawksbill uses its pointy mouth to reach the sponges. The hawksbill can consume more than 1,000 pounds (453.6 kg) of sponges a year. It keeps the sponge population in check and prevents them from overrunning important reef-building corals.

Sea turtles leave the ocean only to lay their eggs. Depending on the species, sea turtles lay eggs once every two to three years, or as often as once a year. During a nesting season, 65 to 180 eggs are laid two to six times, in two-week intervals. The eggs incubate in the nest for approximately two months.

Hatchlings usually leave the nest in a group during the night. The moon's reflection off the ocean guides sea turtle hatchlings toward the sea. Traveling across the beach into the shallow waters of the ocean in the cover of darkness helps them to avoid predators such as birds and large fish, but this tactic is not always successful. It's estimated that only 1 percent of hatchlings survive to adulthood.

Fun Fact

Female sea turtles return to the beach they were born on to lay their eggs. Researchers believe that they use the magnetic field of the Earth to find their way. This sense is called *magnetoreception*.

SURVIVAL OF SEA TURTLES

TIME:
10 TO 20 MINUTES

CATEGORY:
INDOOR, GAME

MATERIALS
2 (16-OUNCE) PAPER CUPS

CRAYONS OR MARKERS

20 MINI MARSHMALLOWS (OR JELLY BEANS)

1 (6-SIDED) DICE

Sea turtle hatchlings have many threats to their survival. They can become a meal for a hungry predator or get entangled in fishing gear. Sea turtles confuse plastic pollution for food and become sick after eating it. Human activity on beaches also disrupts their nesting grounds. In this activity, you will simulate the survival of sea turtle hatchlings after leaving the nest.

PREP WORK

1. Label one paper cup "1: Nesting Beach." Feel free to get creative and draw a sea turtle nest on the side of the cup.

2. Label the other cup "2: Threats." List or draw some of the threats to sea turtles, such as predators, entanglement, fishing, plastic ingestion, and beach erosion.

STEP-BY-STEP INSTRUCTIONS

1. Begin with all the mini marshmallows outside of the cups. Each marshmallow represents a hatchling about to leave the nest. Knowing each hatchling faces several threats, predict how many of the 20 will survive.

2. Select a hatchling and roll the dice to determine its fate. If you roll a **1**, the hatchling is placed in the nesting beach cup. These hatchlings survived to return to their home beach to nest. If you roll a number **2 through 6**, the hatchling is placed in the threats cup. These hatchlings do not survive.

TIP:

➡ Pretend that you have eliminated some threats to sea turtle survival by reducing plastic pollution. Repeat the experiment, this time changing the rules. Sea turtles for which you roll the numbers 1 and 2 will be placed in the survival cup.

3. Repeat this process for all 20 hatchlings. Compare the number of hatchlings in each cup. Write your observations in your journal.

4. Repeat the experiment after recording your results. How was this simulation the same as or different from the first?

OCEAN JOURNAL ENTRY:

This activity provided you with an opportunity to experience the probability of sea turtle survival. Use your experience from the activity to help you answer the questions below.

1. *How many of the hatchlings made it to their home beach? Is this greater than or less than the number that were captured by threats? How does it compare to your hypothesis?*

2. *Find the percentage of your sea turtles that survived by dividing the number that survived by 20 and multiplying your answer by 100. How does this percentage compare to the true survival rate of 1 percent?*

3. *Human activity that creates pollution and beach disruption is a threat to sea turtle survival. Write down some ways humans might be able help sea turtles.*

CONCLUSION:

Sea turtles hatch on sandy beaches, and then they return to their home beach to lay their eggs as adults. This activity explored the probability of hatchling survival. Due to many threats from human activity or natural predators, most do not survive to adulthood. In this simulation, using a 6-sided dice, the survival rate was less than 17 percent. In the wild, sea turtles are thought to have a much lower survival rate of 1 percent.

The Anatomy of the
OCEAN FLOOR

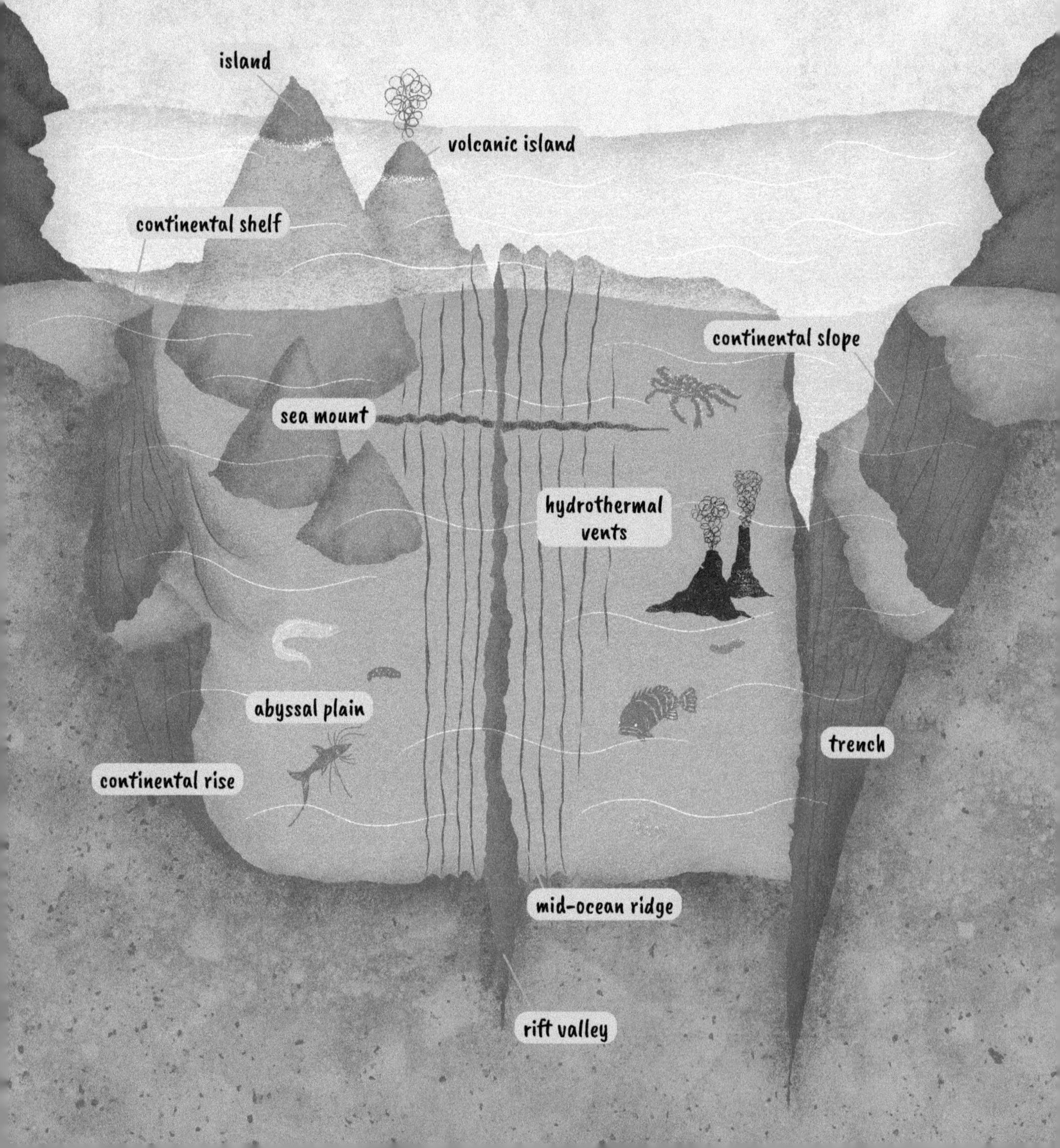

island

volcanic island

continental shelf

continental slope

sea mount

hydrothermal
vents

abyssal plain

continental rise

trench

mid-ocean ridge

rift valley

DEEP SEA

Imagine a very cold, completely dark place with miles of water overhead. This is the environment of the deep sea, located about 3,280 feet below the surface of the ocean. As you descend into the twilight zone, the light disappears quickly, and by the time you've reached the midnight zone, the average temperature of the water is about 39 degrees Fahrenheit (4°C). The pressure increases the deeper you go. At 3,280 feet below the surface, the pressure is about 100 times greater than that at the surface. Down in the Mariana Trench, the pressure is more than 1,000 times greater! That force is like an adult elephant placing all its weight on just one square inch of seafloor. In this chapter, you will explore other organisms that live here, too, and the ways they survive these intense conditions.

5

ANATOMY OF THE OCEAN FLOOR

The average depth of the ocean is 12,100 feet (3,688 m), more than two miles (3.2 km). Much of the seafloor consists of a layer of *detritus*, or decaying material and sediment. This layer, which in some places can be miles thick, provides a habitat for bottom-dwelling organisms. Food is scarce in these regions, so many organisms that live here scavenge for their food or wait patiently for food to pass by. The Johnson's sea cucumber, a relative of the starfish, slowly crawls through this detritus in search of its meals. Other invertebrates, such as cold-water corals, make their homes here, filterfeeding on particles brought to them by deep currents. The tripod fish has long projections from its fins—like stilts—that can sense food drifting in the currents and then direct the food toward its mouth.

Volcanoes can also be found on the seafloor. Many of these volcanoes are produced in areas where the seafloor is spreading apart. Like volcanoes on land, undersea volcanoes form when *magma*, or molten rock below the crust, pushes through cracks in the Earth's crust. This rock cools to form large undersea mountain ranges, like the Mid-Atlantic Ridge. Water sometimes seeps into these cracks and becomes superheated by the hot magma, sometimes reaching temperatures of 700 degrees Fahrenheit (371°C). Eventually, it bubbles back to the seafloor surface through chimney-like structures

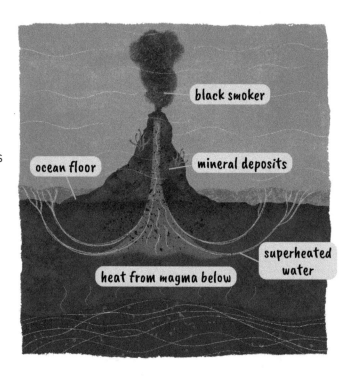

black smoker

ocean floor

mineral deposits

superheated water

heat from magma below

call *hydrothermal vents*, a type of hot spring. These vents carry dissolved chemicals from the magma below, such as hydrogen sulfide. Bacteria use hydrogen sulfide to grow using a process called *chemosynthesis*, similar to the way that algae at the surface use the Sun's energy with photosynthesis. This bacteria growth supports a whole ecosystem of other organisms that live near these steaming hot vents, such as vent mussels, a relative of clams and oysters. Pompeii worms, currently known as the most heat-tolerant animal in the world, attach themselves directly to the vent chimneys. They have been known to thrive in temperatures of up to 176 degrees Fahrenheit (80°C)!

Many animals have a symbiotic relationship with the hydrogen sulfide–eating bacteria. The giant tube worm, an invertebrate with no digestive system, grows these bacteria inside their bodies in exchange for the nutrients they create. The Yeti crab grows its own colony of bacteria on its hairy front legs and claws for food.

Fun Fact

Even though the water coming from hydrothermal vents is incredibly hot, it does not boil due to the extreme pressures found on the seafloor.

HYDROTHERMAL VENT MODEL

WAIT TIME:
1 DAY

ACTIVITY TIME:
10 TO 20 MINUTES

CATEGORY:
INDOOR, MODEL

MATERIALS
8-OUNCE EMPTY WATER BOTTLE

1 POUND OF AIR-DRY CLAY

9-BY-13-INCH SHALLOW
BAKING DISH

1 TABLESPOON OF BAKING SODA

SMALL DISH

BLUE FOOD COLORING

SMALL FUNNEL

¼ CUP OF VINEGAR

TIP:

➡ Be sure to quickly remove the funnel to allow you to observe the solution reemerge through the top of your model.

In this activity, you are headed to the site of an undersea volcano. You will model the way that hydrothermal vents create hot springs of chemical-rich water on the seafloor. Ocean water seeps through cracks in the seafloor, reaching hot magma. As the water is heated, it dissolves chemicals from the surroundings, carrying it back up with it through the vents.

PREP WORK

Let's begin by creating the hydrothermal vent. Starting from the bottom of the bottle, cover the bottle in air-dry clay. Leave the top of the bottle open. This creates the hydrothermal vent "chimney" that water is released through. Allow it to dry overnight.

STEP-BY-STEP INSTRUCTIONS

1. After your hydrothermal vent is dry and ready for use, place your vent model in a shallow 9-by-13 dish.

2. Put the baking soda in a small dish and add two drops of blue food coloring. The baking soda represents the chemicals found in the Earth's crust and the blue coloring will represent hydrogen sulfide below the vent.

3. Once fully mixed, put the blue baking soda into the hydrothermal vent model through the top opening.

4. Place the funnel through the opening in the top of your model. Pour the vinegar through the funnel. The vinegar represents ocean water seeping through the Earth's crust to reach the hot magma below. What happened? How did the vinegar change after entering the vent? Describe your observations in your journal.

OCEAN JOURNAL ENTRY

In this activity, you created a model of a hydrothermal vent. Reflect on your experience to help you answer the questions below.

1. *How is the growth of bacteria around the hydrothermal vent ecosystem similar to the growth of algae within the sunlit ecosystem? How are they different?*

2. *What are some ways in which marine organisms are adapted to living in a hydrothermal vent habitat?*

CONCLUSION:

Hydrothermal vents are hot springs of water with dissolved chemicals found at the bottom of the ocean. They consist of superheated ocean water bubbling up from under the seafloor, where it interacts with magma. You created a model of this process using the chemical reaction between baking soda and vinegar. Just as water seeps through the cracks of the seafloor and reacts with the hot magma, the vinegar in your model vent reacted with the baking soda stored below. Both reactions carry new chemicals from interactions below the surface, before they return up through the vents.

COUNTERSHADING SQUID

Squid belong to a group of mollusks called *cephalopods*, animals that have tentacles near their heads and swim with jet propulsion. Squid have elongated bodies with eight arms and two longer tentacles, each covered with suckers. The giant squid lives in the twilight zone of the ocean at depths between 1,000 and 2,000 feet. They have large eyes to help them find food in dark waters and can move up to 25 miles per hour (40 kph) when attacking prey. However, they are not at the top of the food chain in this environment. Sperm whales will dive deep in search of giant squid for a meal.

Most squid species live in the open ocean waters searching for fish and shrimp. Unlike some of their mollusk relatives, squid do not have a protective

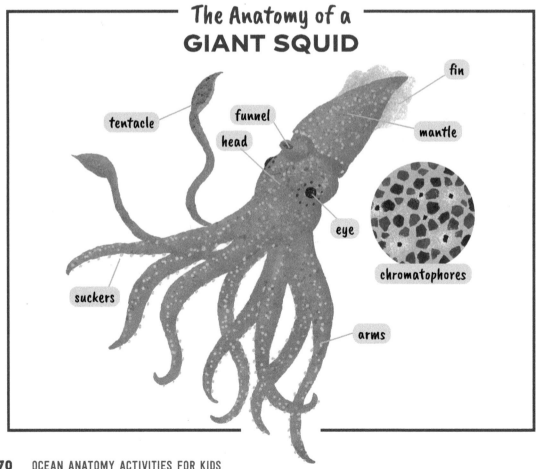

The Anatomy of a GIANT SQUID

tentacle

funnel

head

fin

mantle

eye

chromatophores

suckers

arms

shell. Instead, they use camouflage to protect themselves from predators. One form of camouflage used by squid is called *countershading*, in which an animal's coloring is darker on the upper side of their bodies and lighter on the underside. When a predator looks down in search of a squid from above, the darker coloring of the squid's topside blends in with the dark bottom of the ocean, helping it hide. When a predator is searching for a squid from below, the squid's lighter bottom half blends in with the brightly lit ocean surface.

Countershading is not the only camouflage trick used by squid. Their skin contains color-changing organs call *chromatophores*, sac-like organs containing pigments, a type of coloring, that can be black, brown, orange, red, or yellow. The squid can expand and contract these sacs with special muscles. By changing the size of these colored organs, the squid can change its overall coloring to match its surroundings within seconds.

Have you ever noticed how sunlight dances and sparkles in the water? Squid also can mimic the way light changes as it moves through water with special chromatophore organs called *iridophores*, which contain reflective plates that give the squid an iridescent appearance.

Fun Fact

The colossal squid is the heaviest invertebrate animal in the world, with some weighing in at more than 1,000 pounds (453.6 kg).

SQUID CAMOUFLAGE WINDSOCK

WAIT TIME:
30 MINUTES

ACTIVITY TIME:
10 TO 20 MINUTES

CATEGORY:
INDOOR, MODEL

MATERIALS
3 OR 4 SHEETS OF WHITE
8.5-BY-11 CARDSTOCK

MULTIPLE COLORS OF TISSUE
PAPER (BLUE, GREEN, YELLOW,
AND BROWN)

ALUMINUM FOIL

PAINTBRUSH

CLEAR-DRYING WASHABLE GLUE

STAPLER

MARKERS

SCISSORS

RULER

STRING OR YARN

TIP:

➜ If you do not
have a stapler, your
squid body can be
assembled using
clear tape.

In this activity, you will create a squid model that shows how it camouflages itself in the open ocean. When choosing colors for your squid model, imagine the squid's environment. Near the surface, ocean filters sparkling sunlight; however, below the squid, you'll find that the deep ocean presents a dark backdrop.

PREP WORK

1. Begin by creating the body of your squid. Squid have long torpedo-shaped bodies. Roll a sheet of the 8.5-by-11 cardstock into a tube and staple in place.

2. Cut eight 2-by-8-inch strips of any color tissue paper. These will represent the arms of the squid.

3. Cut two 2-by-10-inch strips of any color tissue paper. These will represent the tentacles of the squid, which are longer than its arms.

4. Tear small pieces of tissue paper of different colors and sizes to represent the chromatophores that squid use for camouflage. Tear small pieces of aluminum foil of different sizes to represent iridophores.

STEP-BY-STEP INSTRUCTIONS

1. Use the paintbrush to apply glue to the body of your squid. Place most of the small pieces of tissue paper and aluminum foil over the "top" of the squid body. Place only a few on the sides and almost none on the "bottom." Allow the glue to dry. How do the chromatophores of your squid model create countershading? Describe your observations in your journal.

2. Once the glue has dried, it's time to add more details. Staple the arms and tentacles around the bottom of the cylinder. Using markers, draw eyes on your squid body, near the tentacles.

3. Squid have triangular-shaped fins at the back of their bodies opposite their head and tentacles. Using scissors and a ruler, measure and cut a triangle with 8-inch sides from a piece of white cardstock. Staple or glue this to the top side of your squid, allowing the corners to reach out past the squid body.

4. Finally, make a small hole on each side of your squid model near the top, on the opposite end of the tentacles. Tie one end of the string to one of the holes and tie the other end to the other hold to create a loop. This will let you hang your squid outside in a light breeze.

5. Watch your squid capture the wind. Imagine it is swimming near the surface of the ocean. What do you notice about how the sunlight affects your squid's appearance? Record your observations in your journal.

CONCLUSION:

In this activity, you created a windsock model of a squid. When your model blows in the breeze, it simulates squid camouflage. When decorating your squid's body, you used tissue paper to represent chromatophores and aluminum foil to represent iridophores. Adding more of these organs to the top of your squid simulates the countershading effect seen in squid found in the open ocean. The movement of the windsock model through the breeze simulates the way iridophores reflect light from the surface of a squid's skin while swimming in the ocean.

OCEAN JOURNAL ENTRY

Answer the questions below in your journal.

1. *Describe how chromatophores and iridophores are used by squid to create camouflage.*

2. *In what ways is your squid model similar to or different from a squid in camouflage?*

BIOLUMINESCENCE

Many of the animal species that live in the deep ocean have adapted to living in constant darkness with the ability to create their own light, called *bioluminescence*. Bioluminescence is a chemical process that generates light within living organisms. If you have ever seen a firefly light up at dusk, then you have witnessed bioluminescence. Scientists estimate that 76 percent of known marine animals create bioluminescence!

Organisms that produce bioluminescence contain a chemical called *luciferin* within their bodies. When the animal combines luciferin with oxygen, light is created. This is similar to breaking a glow stick: Liquids mix within the tube to create a light-generating chemical reaction.

Marine organisms create light for several reasons. In many cases, bioluminescence helps predators attract prey. Deep-sea anglerfish have a bioluminescent lure attached to their head. It dangles the lure in front of its large mouth in hopes of drawing prey close enough for a quick bite. Some animals use bioluminescence to attract mates instead of prey. The female syllid fireworm, found on the seafloor, signals mates with bright flashes.

Some animals use bioluminescence to find their food. The stoplight loosejaw fish has the ability to produce two colors of light—both green and red. Red light is completely gone from the midnight zone these fish inhabit, so the stoplight loosejaw's prey is not adapted to seeing it. Using red light, the loosejaw can see its prey without the prey seeing it back.

Other animals use bioluminescence to startle or distract predators. Instead of squirting dark ink as a distraction, like the squid species living in the sunlight zones, the vampire squid found in the twilight zone lets out a substance filled with bioluminescent particles that can glow with twinkling light for up to 10 minutes, confusing the predator.

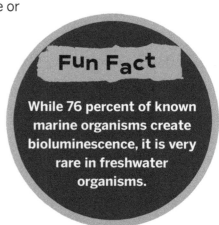

Fun Fact

While 76 percent of known marine organisms create bioluminescence, it is very rare in freshwater organisms.

FISHING LIKE AN ANGLERFISH

WAIT TIME:
1 HOUR

TIME:
20 TO 30 MINUTES

CATEGORY:
INDOOR, CRAFT

MATERIALS
NEWSPAPER

2 PAPER PLATES

WASHABLE PAINT (DARK BLUE, BLACK, OR RED)

2-INCH CIRCLE OF WHITE CARDSTOCK

GLOW-IN-THE-DARK PAINT

SCISSORS

TOOTHPICKS

STAPLER

GLUE OR TAPE

MARKERS

HOLE PUNCH

PIPE CLEANER

In this activity, you have a chance to simulate how organisms in the deep sea use light to lure prey in close. Using your imagination and creativity, you will create an anglerfish model, complete with a glow-in-the-dark lure. Once it's complete, observe how the lure works to attract prey.

Safety First! *Toothpicks can be very sharp, so handle them with care to avoid injury.*

PREP WORK

1. Lay down some newspaper or other covering to protect your workspace. Turn both paper plates upside down. Paint the entire bottom of both plates with dark paint. Most species of anglerfish are not brightly colored since most animals do not have to see well in deep ocean zones. Allow the plates to dry completely. These will become the body of your fish.

2. Paint one side of the cardstock circle with the glow-in-the-dark paint, allowing it to dry before painting the other side. This will create the bioluminescent lure for your fish.

3. Stack both painted paper plates one on top of the other. Using scissors, cut out a large triangular-shaped piece from the stack, like a piece of pie. You should end up with two triangle pieces that are about a quarter of the size of the original paper plates.

4. Cut one of the triangles in half. These will become the two pectoral fins on the side of the body of your anglerfish.

5. Fold the other triangle piece in half. This will become the tail fin of your anglerfish. The leftover paper plates will form the body.

STEP-BY-STEP INSTRUCTIONS

1. Species of anglerfish often have extremely large mouths with very long, sharp, pointy teeth. The toothpicks will represent these teeth. On the unpainted sides of both plates, tape the toothpicks around the opening you cut out the triangle from. These will be your anglerfish's mouth.

2. Now it's time to attach the tail. On one paper plate, on the opposite side of the mouth, glue half of the folded triangle to the unpainted side, allowing the rest to hang off the plate.

3. Once the teeth and tail have been attached, place the unpainted sides of the plates together, making sure to match up both sides of the mouth. Staple the plates together along the edge to create the final fish body.

4. Next, glue or tape the pectoral fins to the fish body, one on each side.

5. Using markers, draw small dark eyes near the top of the mouth. Anglerfish do not have large eyes or great eyesight.

6. It's time to add the anglerfish's lure. Using a hole punch, make a hole through the glow-in-the-dark circle. Attach one end of the pipe cleaner through the hole. Cut a hole in your fish body near the top of the mouth and attach the other end of the pipe cleaner. Many

TIP:

➡ If you would like to have a three-dimensional lure you can substitute the paper circle for a glow-in-the-dark bead.

anglerfish species dangle the glowing end of their lure next to their large mouths.

7. Place the lure under direct light for 5 minutes. This acts to "charge" the paint of the lure. Imagine this is like the mixing of chemicals inside the lure.

8. Enter a dark room and observe the light given off from the lure. Move the lure back and forth. What does it look like? Write your observations in your journal.

CONCLUSION:

In this lesson, you created your own version of an anglerfish. These fish use a bioluminescent lure attached to their head. They dangle it in front of their mouth to lure prey closer. You created an example of this behavior when you moved your crafted fish in a dark space.

OCEAN JOURNAL ENTRY

In this activity, you crafted a model of an anglerfish, complete with a bioluminescent lure used to attract prey. Use your experience to answer the following questions in your journal.

1. Describe at least two ways deep-sea marine life use bioluminescence.

2. To power the light from your anglerfish lure, you needed to expose it to light for some time. How does a real anglerfish create bioluminescence?

3. Imagine having your own built-in flashlight! In what ways would this be useful to you?

snowy owl

polar bear

arctic fox

arctic hare

walrus

narwhals

The Arctic Region

emperor penguin

orca

Adélie penguin

Weddell seal

The Antarctic Region

POLAR REGIONS

This chapter takes you on an expedition to the polar regions: the Arctic Ocean in the north and the continent of Antarctica in the south. These polar regions contain the coldest climates on the planet: The coldest temperature ever recorded was in Antarctica at -128.6 degrees Fahrenheit (-89.2°C) in 1983. Much of the land and sea at the poles is covered by snow and ice throughout the year, and winter lasts from March until October. The Arctic Ocean is the smallest ocean on Earth and covers about 3 percent of the Earth's surface. It is home to marine mammals like the polar bear, walrus, and narwhal. The continent of Antarctica holds almost 90 percent of all the world's ice and 70 percent of the world's freshwater—locked in ice. Here you will see animals such as the emperor penguin, Weddell seals, and orcas.

6

SEA ICE

The formation of *sea ice*, or frozen ocean water that forms in the polar regions, is incredibly important, not only to the polar ecosystems but also to the global climate. In the arctic, sea ice forms over the Arctic Ocean. In the Antarctic, sea ice forms around the continent of Antarctica. These polar ice sheets, which range in thickness from mere inches up to 15 feet (4.5 m), grow during cold winter months. They get smaller in the summer but do not completely disappear.

Sea ice can't hold much salt. When it forms, most of the salt is concentrated into the ocean water below the ice. This incredibly salty water is denser than the surrounding seawater and therefore sinks toward the seafloor. This sinking creates a current of cool water toward the equator, helping moderate the world's climate.

ice sheet

land

sea ice

sea

seafloor

While the formation of sea ice creates temperature-regulating currents, the amount of sea ice is important to maintaining global climate as well. You may have noticed on a warm sunny day that wearing dark-colored clothing can make you feel incredibly hot. The color of surfaces affects how much of the Sun's energy is reflected from it. Darker colors absorb more heat energy than lighter colored materials do.

While this phenomenon affects how much heat is absorbed by your clothing, it is also true for the surface of the Earth. Bright-white sea ice reflects sunlight and keeps the polar regions cool. Up to 80 percent of the sunlight hitting the surface of the ice is reflected into space. When the sunlight strikes the surface of the dark-colored ocean, 90 percent of the Sun's light is absorbed. Warming temperatures gradually melt sea ice over time, reducing the amount of reflective surface and increasing the amount of heat absorption. About 15 percent of the world's oceans are covered by sea ice during part of the year. A steady reduction of this coverage contributes to global warming.

Fun Fact

Polar bears are the largest land carnivores in the world, and they use sea ice to hunt for seals.

KEEPING COOL WITH SEA ICE

TIME:
10 TO 20 MINUTES

CATEGORY:
INDOOR OR
OUTDOOR, EXPERIMENT

MATERIALS
1 (8.5-BY-11) SHEET OF BLACK
CONSTRUCTION PAPER

STAPLER

1 (8.5-BY-11) SHEET OF WHITE
CONSTRUCTION PAPER

TWO THERMOMETERS

A WARM, SUNNY DAY

TIP:

➡ Try this inside
using a 60-watt
incandescent light
bulb or reptile heat
lamp. Hold the pock-
ets 8 inches away
from the lamp. Try
once using a lamp
and once using only
the outdoor sun-
shine. Do you notice
a difference between
each experiment?

Does the color of a surface really affect the absorption of the Sun's heat energy? The polar ice caps
are extremely bright compared to the color of the
dark ocean waters that they cover. How do they
affect the local climate? In this activity, you will
explore the answers to these questions.

Safety First!
- *Use caution when handling glass incandescent
  bulbs or reptile heat lamps to avoid breakage.*
- *Incandescent bulbs and reptile heat lamps can
  become extremely hot. Be sure not to touch the
  bulb after it has been lit.*

PREP WORK
Fold the black sheet of construction paper in half
lengthwise. Staple the folded sides together to create a
pocket with an opening on top. Do the same thing with
the white paper.

STEP-BY-STEP INSTRUCTIONS
1. Create a table with two columns in your journal. Label
one column "white" and the other column "black." On
the first row of each column record the starting temperature readings of both thermometers. The white
construction paper envelope represents the arctic ice
sheets over the poles. The black envelope represents
exposed ocean waters once the ice sheets recede.

2. Place one thermometer tip in each construction paper pocket. Put both pockets outside in a sunny spot. In your journal, write a hypothesis about how you think the temperature will change after both pockets are exposed to the light.

3. Record temperatures of each thermometer in your table every 2 minutes for 10 minutes. How did the temperatures change over time? How are the temperatures similar or different between the two different colored envelopes? Do your observations support your hypothesis?

OCEAN JOURNAL ENTRY

This activity studied the effects of surface color on heat absorption. Reflect on your observations as you answer the following questions in your journal.

1. *How do you think the loss of sea ice would affect temperature in the polar regions?*

2. *If sea ice formation was reduced, how might that affect deepwater currents traveling from the poles?*

CONCLUSION:

In this lesson, you headed to the poles to observe the sea ice and its effects on the global temperature. The formation of sea ice plays an important role in keeping the Earth cool. The white-colored surface of sea ice reflects a large amount of the Sun's heat energy. This can be observed by the change in temperatures in your experiment. A white-colored surface like the pocket in your experiment stays cooler than the dark-colored pocket. Light energy is reflected by the white paper and absorbed by the black paper.

GLACIERS AND ICEBERGS

G laciers and icebergs are different from sea ice because they are formed on land out of compressed freshwater rain and snow. Eventually this compression forces snow to re-form into large ice crystals. This process can take hundreds of years and form ice crystals as big as baseballs! In Antarctica, glaciers can be up to 3 miles (1.6 km) deep. Over millions of years, the large amounts of packed ice in glaciers create depressions and carve valleys in the land below. The Great Lakes in North America are believed to have formed during a period in the Earth's history when glaciers extended from the North Pole down to where the United States is today. Melted freshwater from glaciers collects in low areas to form shallow pools on the glacial surface called *lakes*. The narrow channels that carry this water through the glacier to its base are called *moulins*. As a glacier moves from growth or melting, large, deep cracks called *crevasses* can form in the ice.

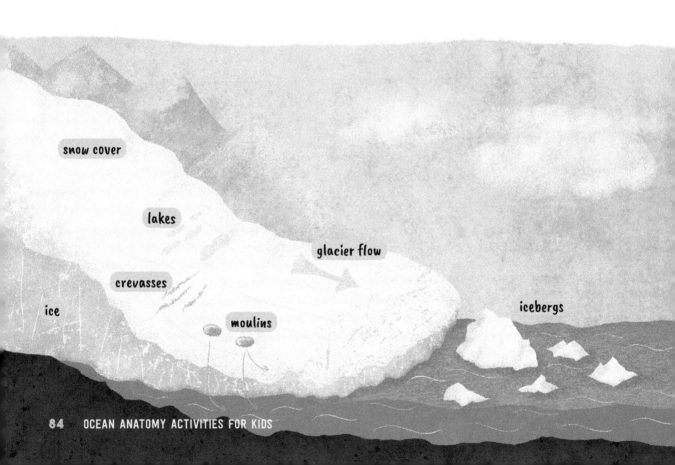

snow cover

lakes

glacier flow

crevasses

ice

moulins

icebergs

Icebergs are large chunks of glaciers that have broken off into the sea, a process known as calving. The world's largest recorded iceberg, B-15, broke off of the Ross Ice Shelf in Antarctica in March 2000. It measured more than 4,000 square miles (6,437 km²). Sometimes air is pushed out of the ice crystals when it is compressed as a glacier. Icebergs that break off from these glaciers have few to no air bubbles, making them appear crystalline and transparent.

Only 10 percent of an iceberg is seen above water, leaving the majority hidden below sea level. This phenomenon gave rise to the phrase "the tip of the iceberg," referring to the unknown factors of a circumstance. The hidden ice below the surface of an iceberg can pose a danger for ships traveling among them. Sharp, jagged ice can tear holes in the bottom of the vessel. This is what happened in 1912, when the *Titanic* struck an iceberg and sank. Following the tragedy, an international iceberg patrol was established to keep track of dangerous icebergs traveling in the path of ocean liners.

Fun Fact

Bergy seltzer is the term that mariners use to describe the fizzing sound icebergs make as they melt. The sound comes from the gradual release of air bubbles trapped within the ice.

MELTING ICEBERGS

TIME:
10 TO 20 MINUTES

CATEGORY:
INDOOR, MODEL

MATERIALS
2 SMALL BOWLS
½ CUP OF VEGETABLE OIL
BLUE FOOD COLORING
2 CUPS OF WATER
FUNNEL
EMPTY WATER BOTTLE WITH A CAP
SPOON FOR MIXING

TIP:

➡ Try freezing some of the oil mixture in an ice cube tray. Place a finished ice cube on top of the oil layer. Imagine that this is an iceberg. What do you notice about its position in the mixture? Write your observations in your journal.

What happens to the water of an iceberg after it melts? In this activity, you will examine how ocean water ends up layered due to the density differences between iceberg meltwater and salty ocean water.

PREP WORK

1. In a small bowl, mix together the vegetable oil and 1 drop of blue food coloring. This will represent meltwater from icebergs, created as they float into warmer waters.

2. In a separate bowl, mix together the water and 3 drops of blue food coloring.

STEP-BY-STEP INSTRUCTIONS

1. Imagine the darker blue water is cold, salty seawater found at the North and South poles. This water is denser than freshwater, so it sinks to the bottom of the ocean. Using a funnel, pour the blue water into the bottom of the plastic bottle.

2. Next, using the funnel, add the oil mixture to your bottle. This represents the freshwater that melts from icebergs. Just like sea ice, icebergs cannot hold salt and are therefore less dense than salty seawater. What happens to the solution in the bottle after this layer is added? Write your observations in your journal.

3. Put the cap tightly on the bottle. Gently shake the bottle. What happens to the mixture? Allow the bottle to sit undisturbed for 10 minutes. How does your mixture change over time? Record your observations in your journal.

CONCLUSION:

In this activity, you created a model of an ocean water column to demonstrate what happens as icebergs melt when they float into warmer waters. Cold, salty seawater has a greater density than the fresh meltwater of icebergs. Therefore, iceberg meltwater tends to float near the surface after it melts. You observed this phenomenon when the oil mixture floated above the water mixture in the bottle.

OCEAN JOURNAL ENTRY

This activity provided you with an opportunity to observe the density-dependent layering of ocean water that occurs when icebergs melt. Reflect on your experience as you answer the questions below in your journal.

1. *Describe how icebergs form. How do they disappear?*

2. *How is glacier formation different from sea ice formation? How is it the same?*

HOW ANIMALS KEEP WARM

If you are cold, you might choose to put on a sweater or coat. This extra clothing traps our body heat to keep us warm. Since humans are mammals, and all mammals are warm-blooded, we must maintain a specific internal body temperature to survive. In this lesson, we will learn how marine mammals of the polar regions, such as whales, seals, sea lions, and polar bears, have unique ways to keep warm in their extremely cold environment.

For many water-dwelling marine mammals, large amounts of fur can slow down their swimming, making it more difficult to catch fish. Instead, marine mammals have evolved an internal system of insulation in the form of a thick layer of *blubber*. Blubber is a type of fat beneath the skin that helps animals store energy, keep warm, and increase buoyancy, making it easier to float.

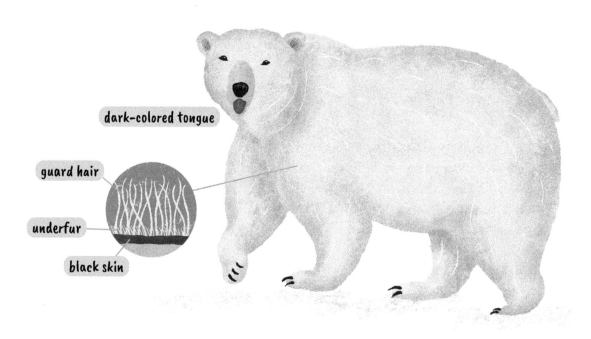

dark-colored tongue

guard hair

underfur

black skin

Sometimes called "unicorns of the sea," narwhals are a type of toothed whale that live in the Arctic Ocean. Males often have a large, straight horn coming from their heads. This horn is in fact a tusk, like that of a walrus or an elephant. In the narwhal, this tusk forms from the left front tooth of the whale. Narwhals spend their time fishing between sea ice sheets. To withstand the constant cold temperatures of their environment, a narwhal's body can be up to 40 percent blubber.

A polar bear's adaptations to staying warm combine both fur and blubber. In addition to a four-inch layer of blubber underneath their skin, a polar bear has two layers of fur. A short, dense underlayer is covered by a longer layer of protection called *guard hairs*. A polar bear's fur appears white but is actually transparent and hollow like a straw. The hollow structure of the fur reflects light, making it appear white. This white appearance has a bonus for the bear. It provides camouflage in the snow and ice, helping polar bears sneak up on their prey.

Fun Fact

Harp seals can weigh up to 300 pounds (136 kg) with all of their blubber, but before they get that big, they have long white fur to keep them warm.

MARINE MAMMAL INSULATION

TIME:
10 TO 15 MINUTES

CATEGORY:
INDOOR, EXPERIMENT

MATERIALS
1 CUP OF VEGETABLE SHORTENING

TWO RUBBER GLOVES

5-GALLON BUCKET OF ICE WATER

STOPWATCH

How do polar bears and other marine mammals manage to swim for long periods of time in icy arctic waters? In this activity, you will test the insulation abilities of vegetable shortening, a type of fat. How long will this type of insulation keep you feeling warm? Complete the activity below to find out.

PREP WORK

1. Gather your materials to work in an area that you don't mind getting wet.

2. Put the vegetable shortening inside one rubber glove.

STEP-BY-STEP INSTRUCTIONS

1. Put one hand inside the rubber glove with vegetable shortening. Be sure to spread shortening evenly throughout the inside of the glove. The shortening is a type of fat, like blubber. Imagine your hand is a narwhal equipped with a thick layer of blubber to insulate against the cold.

2. Fit the other glove over your other hand. This hand will represent a human without the thick layer of blubber that the narwhal has.

3. Place both glove-covered hands into the bucket of ice water. Do you notice a difference in the temperature you feel in each hand? Time how long you can hold each hand in the ice-water bucket. Which gloved hand stays warmer longer? Write your observations in your journal.

TIP:

➡ Have someone else try the experiment. Compare and contrast their results with your results. How are they the same or different?

4. Find other materials that you think might help to keep the uninsulated hand warm, such as cotton balls or shredded newspapers. Add these to the plain glove. Repeat the experiment. Did your results change? If so, how?

CONCLUSION:

Some animals, like the polar bear, use multiple layers of fur and a thick layer of blubber to insulate their bodies against the cold. In this experiment, vegetable shortening was used in place of blubber. By comparing the feeling of ice water on your hands, with and without the fatty insulation, you were able to experience how well blubber keeps polar animals warm.

OCEAN JOURNAL ENTRY

In this activity, you explored how blubber is used by marine mammals to stay warm. Reflect on your experience from the activity to help you answer the questions below.

1. *Which material seemed to insulate against the ice water the best? Why do you think this?*

2. *What advantage do polar bears have by having both fur and blubber? Why would having fur be a disadvantage for a narwhal?*

RESOURCES

Use these resources to expand your exploration of marine science topics. The videos and books provide detailed explanations on specific topics in marine science. The websites provide digital resources and curricula with additional learning activities that complement this book. The organizations provide easily navigable fact-based resources for additional learning.

BOOKS

Jacques Cousteau: The Ocean World by Jacques-Yves Cousteau

Oceanology: The Secrets of the Sea Revealed by Maya Plass

WEBSITES

SEA Curriculum from the University of Hawaii at Manoa: Manoa.Hawaii .edu/sealearning

Lawrence Hall of Science: Mare.LawrenceHallOfScience.org

Marine Science Explorers: MarineScienceExplorers.com/resources

ORGANIZATIONS

National Oceanographic and Atmospheric Administration: OceanService .NOAA.gov/kids

National Geographic Ocean Education: NationalGeographic.org/education

VIDEOS

"How Do Ocean Currents Work?" TEDEd by Jennifer Verduin: Ed.TED.com /lessons/how-do-ocean-currents-work-jennifer-verduin

ACKNOWLEDGMENTS

I'd like to thank my husband, Eric, for supporting all of my educational and professional endeavors. There is no better partner for sharing my love of exploring our ocean planet. I'd like to thank my parents for always encouraging me to pursue my dreams. And lastly, I'd like to devote a special thank-you to all of my previous science educators for instilling in me a lifelong passion for learning.

ABOUT THE AUTHOR

 **Laura Petrusic** is a professionally certified science teacher and marine science educator. She holds an undergraduate degree in marine science from the University of South Carolina and a master's degree in science education from the Florida Institute of Technology. Laura has designed and delivered marine science educational content to students of all ages, creating programs within the formal classroom, outdoor education, science centers, and homeschool groups.

She is the curriculum and content developer for Marine Science Explorers and offers a variety of online courses for K–12 students in marine science. Her philosophy of learning is inquiry based, integrated, and student centered, thus allowing students to make connections with the natural world in a way that is relative to their lives.

Laura currently lives in Lake Mary, Florida. When she is not teaching, she enjoys beachcombing and camping adventures with her husband and three children.

CPSIA information can be obtained
at www.ICGtesting.com
Printed in the USA
JSHW011453290921
19092JS00001B/3